FROM TINFOIL TO STEREO

FROM

University Press of Florida

Gainesville/Tallahassee/Tampa/Boca Raton
Pensacola/Orlando/Miami/Jacksonville

Walter L. Welch and
Leah Brodbeck Stenzel Burt

TINFOIL TO STEREO

The Acoustic Years of the Recording Industry

1877–1929

99 98 97 96 95 94 6 5 4 3 2 1

Library of Congress Cataloging in Publication Data
Welch, Walter L. (Walter Leslie), 1901–
   From tinfoil to stereo: the acoustic years of the recording
industry, 1877–1929 / by Walter L. Welch and Leah Brodbeck Stenzel
Burt.
   p.   cm.
Rev. ed. of : From tin foil to stereo / Oliver Read and Walter
Welch. 1976.
Includes bibliographical references and index.
ISBN 0-8130-1317-8
1. Phonograph—History. 2. Sound—recording and reproducing—
History. I. Burt, Leah Brodbeck Stenzel. II. Read, Oliver. From
tin foil to stereo. III. Title.
TS2301.P3W36   1994
621.389'3'09—dc20   94-4823

The University Press of Florida is the scholarly publishing agency
for the State University System of Florida, comprised of Florida A & M
University, Florida Atlantic University, Florida International University,
Florida State University, University of Central Florida, University of
Florida, University of North Florida, University of South Florida, and
University of West Florida.

University Press of Florida
15 Northwest 15th Street
Gainesville, FL 32611

CONTENTS ➴

ILLUSTRATIONS ⟶

following page 102

1. Original Edison tinfoil phonograph, 1877.
2. Edison talking doll, 1888–89.
3. Stock certificate for the Edison Toy Manufacturing Company.
4. Advertisement for the Universal Phonograph Company, 1897.
5. Advertisement for the Columbia Phonograph Company, 1897.
6. Advertisement for Lieutenant Bettini's Micro-Phonograph, 1897.
7. Advertisement for the Edison phonograph, National Phonograph Company, 1897.
8. Phonograph room at Edison Laboratory, Orange, New Jersey, 1897.
9. Plating room, Edison Berlin factory.
10. Inspecting room, Edison Paris factory.
11. Plating room, Edison Brussels factory.
12. Jean Wickli in the gold plating room, Edison Paris factory.
13. Copper plating, Edison Berlin factory.
14. Gold plating, Edison Berlin factory.
15. Machine shop, Edison Paris factory.
16. Line drawing of the Edison phonograph, 1888.
17. George Gouraud, left, supervising recording at Little Menlo, Beulah Hill, England, 1888–89.
18. Mary Helen Ferguson typing from dictation recorded on an Edison phonograph, 1888–89.
19. Unidentified man using an Edison phonograph for dictation.
20. Gouraud giving dictation into an Edison phonograph, Little Menlo, 1888–89.
21. Gouraud dictating while lying in bed, ca. 1888–89.
22. Gouraud dictating into an Edison phonograph, 1888–89.
23. Phonograph parlor at a Pennsylvania Railroad ferry juncture, 1891–92.

FOREWORD ➤

IT SEEMS unbelievable that the fundamental reference book of sound recording history should have been revised last in 1976 and become unavailable soon after. The first edition had appeared in 1959 and was the earliest profoundly researched account of all the technical and legal barriers that have had to be overcome to give us today's sound fidelity. Such was its popularity on publication that the shelves were soon emptied and used copies started to change hands at enhanced prices among researchers and machine owners.

Before 1959 those wishing to study sound recording history had to seek out technical papers of limited circulation or fall back on a handful of books relating a popular account of phonograph inventions, in several cases written by people apparently little connected with sound recording and retrieval; one, for instance, was a prolific chronicler of New Zealand topography and native history, another a U.S. animal psychologist and minister of religion. Such early accounts were entertaining, but each tended to follow its predecessors, reiterating incidents and anecdotes, some perhaps of dubious provenance; still, they were ventures of honest intention for a general market and satisfied a need of the time.

Roland Gelatt's *The Fabulous Phonograph* (1955) went to the next stage by exploring in medium depth the technical and political histories of talking machines; Gelatt included artists and repertoires and produced a well-regarded book of its type. Although its purpose was still to entertain the uncommitted reader, the book stirred the interest of many who began to realize what a fascinating story lay behind the phonograph's invention and implanted in some readers a wish to own some of these early machines, then readily available.

The first edition of *From Tinfoil to Stereo* was jointly authored by Walter L.

Welch and Oliver Read, both experts in sound engineering. Students and collectors were fortunate in having two such sympathetic compilers for this first account from primary sources because both were collectors of early instruments, and Professor Welch had several years' experience in the Syracuse University Audio Archives transferring musical performances from Edison cylinders and discs to tape for preservation and experiment. Dr. Read began collecting machines in 1939 and provided nearly one hundred machines as well as accessories from his collection for the illustrations.

This 1959 edition traced the capture of sound from Leon Scott's Phonautograph to the second year of stereophonic discs, when we had just turned from the novelty of steam trains and ping-pong in our living rooms to an appreciation for a fuller tone and clarity of depth in music. The second edition, which appeared in 1977, carried the story up to the German-invented video disc, today largely superseded by the video cassette. Edison's invention of dragging a stylus along a groove was one hundred years old for this edition, and groove recording continued for a further fifteen years. It is an irony that in September 1984 the first compact disc issued in the United States comprised Edison-recorded material.

In 1985 Walter Welch, the survivor of the original collaboration, felt that a third revised and updated edition should be made available. He invited Leah Burt to edit and correct the book chapters to 1929 under his supervision, and several cylinder and disc historians were also enlisted. Scientific progress treads on the heels of all whose task is to modernize.

A book like *From Tinfoil to Stereo* has to be reviewed periodically, the results of new research woven in every decade or two. Burt, whom we can thank for coordinating, correcting, contributing to, and editing this new edition, has spent much of her working life on archival work at the Edison National Historic Site in West Orange, New Jersey, helping to open the doors of knowledge to all from home and abroad who applied, and this is an opportunity to express the debt of gratitude Edison researchers and collectors everywhere owe to her. It is pleasant to record that she received their wholehearted support in the new production of this work, and therein lies its excellence.

George L. Frow
Sevenoaks, Kent
England

PREFACE ⟞

EVERY BOOK has its raison d'étre, and this revision of *From Tinfoil to Stereo* is no exception. Thirty years after its first appearance, *From Tinfoil to Stereo* is still the most comprehensive history of the phonograph and sound recording, starting with its inception in 1877.

This work has become the standard for early sound recording history for the casual reader and the serious scholar alike. Previous editions are now unavailable from publishers or clearinghouses, while copies surviving in libraries are worn and dog-eared. This revision covers in one volume the history of sound recording from its beginnings in 1877 to the time of the Great Crash in 1929.

When word spread through the sound recording community that a new revision was in the offing, Professor Raymond R. Wile of Queens College, Flushing, New York, kindly offered his thorough research work and writings for use in the chapters on the tinfoil phonograph, the talking doll, the Bettini story, the North American Phonograph Company and Bell-Tainter, the Columbia Phonograph Company, and, most importantly, the local phonograph companies. There is no one in the sound recording community who can come close to Professor Wile in his accomplishments in this respect. I wholeheartedly accepted his help and hoped that I would do justice to his efforts.

I must also mention Frank Andrews of Neasden, England, whose generous offer of help in the chapter on the international situation I most enthusiastically accepted. These two scholars represent a whole group of dedicated persons who have come forward to give advice and information for this revision. Further in-depth treatments of the subject can be found in individual articles in journals and other scholarly publications, most particularly those written by Professor

Raymond Wile, Frank Andrews, Bennett Maxwell, Allen Koenigsberg, Ronald Dethlefson, George Frow, Michael Biel, and A. R. Phillips, Jr. Charles Hummel provided some of the photographs, and for this I say thank you.

This book could never have come to be without the steadfast support of Dr. Frank Macomber, Department of Fine Arts, Syracuse University and the University of London. His unfailing confidence in us and in the project at every turn provided sustenance when it was needed. To him I owe a huge debt of gratitude for believing in the worthiness of our venture.

Leah Brodbeck Stenzel Burt
Hillsborough, North Carolina

CHAPTER 1

Before the Phonograph

OUR DESIRE TO add spoken words to inanimate objects has taken many forms. From the earliest times, we have tried to imitate the sounds of nature by mechanical means, something that children playing often spontaneously do. The first known serious attempt to simulate the human voice mechanically was in the colossal statue of Memnon at Thebes, built about 1490 B.C. during the eighteenth Egyptian dynasty. Carved in stone with a series of hidden air chambers, Memnon was supposed to emit a vocal greeting each morning at sunrise to his mother, the goddess of dawn. That the statue did produce some sort of sound was testified to by Strabo, who visited it in 7 A.D. Toppled by an earthquake in 27 A.D., when it was restored in 196 A.D. by Roman emperor Septimus Severus the statue had lost its alleged power of speech.[1] Questionable though the vocal capacity of Memnon may be, the Homeric poems further attest to the Greeks' belief that statues spoke. Before making important decisions, both the Greeks and the Persians consulted statues, oracles who probably spoke by means of a hidden priest.

During the Middle Ages a number of talking automatons were constructed. The first authenticated model was a talking head made by Friar Roger Bacon, the eminent medieval philosopher (National Phonograph Co., 1900). Automaton building reached its culmination in 1860, when Herr Faber of Vienna built an intricate talking man, although the Bell Telephone Company exhibited an electronic keyboard–operated talking man at the World's Fair in 1939.[2]

Building automatons is a far cry from applying pure science to the problem of sound reproduction, the "storing up" of sound that occurs in sound recording. A seventeenth-century science fiction writer forecast the functions of the phonograph, as Jules Verne did for the airplane and submarine. Savinien Cyrano de Bergerac's 1649 *Histoire Comique en Voyage dans la Lune*, a story of a visit to the moon via skyrocket, includes a detailed description of books "made wholly for the Ears and not the Eyes" that the narrator reported "hanging . . . to my ears, like a pair of Pendants, [when] I went to walking."[3]

Outside the world of fiction, Americans have held most of the patents on the various inventions incorporated into the modern phonograph, and Europeans have done most of the research in mechanics, acoustics, and electricity that has provided the basis for those inventions. This circumstance reflects the difference between the viewpoints and objectives of the great school of experimental scientists of eighteenth- and nineteenth-century Europe and the smaller but growing group of physicists in the new and opportunistic United States. European scientists were for the most part scholars, interested in exploring and expanding the frontiers of knowledge for its own sake. U.S. scientists of the period might better be described as teachers rather than scholars, more interested in the application of science than in pure science, destined to enter industry as executives or engineers.

Thus the stage was set for the great advances in applied technology in the United States of the nineteenth-century, of which the phonograph was but one manifestation. The goals of important figures in European research in electricity, such as Luigi Galvani, Giovanni Romagnesi, Georg Ohm, and Michael Faraday, or in acoustics, such as John Tyndall, Hermann Helmholtz, and Jules Antoine Lissajous, were quite different from those of the new class of practical experimenters and inventors beginning to rise in the New World.

In Europe, except for England, the first reaction to the industrial revolution was to attempt to insulate the leading schools and universities from the taint of commercialism. Scientific research was considered an adjunct to higher education and a leisurely pursuit reserved for gentlemen and scholars. Royalty, class distinctions, and the stratification of society helped isolate the learned class from the cycles of commercial and industrial development. Men working feverishly to advance industrial technics were often denied access to the discoveries resulting from research going on in a higher stratum of society.

Even though the corporate device of the limited stock company was coming into use, much of European industry in the eighteenth and nineteenth centuries was operated by families or as monopolies by royal appointment, a system that restricted competitive development in industry, retarded technological progress, and slowed the introduction of improved methods. Operating against the system was the zeal of a class of tradesmen who took pride in their work (an outgrowth of the feudal apprentice system) along with a trickling down of scientific knowledge from the learned class. These two factors were primarily responsible for the vast changes in European standards of living and cultural opportunity in these centuries. This progress was not the purposeful result of the activities of the European scientists, who remained aloof from the workaday world where necessity was the mother of invention. Others were free to make use of their discoveries, if they should be fortunate enough to become aware of them.

In the period just before the invention of the phonograph only one important U.S. scientist conformed closely to the European preference for theoretical science. Joseph Henry (1797–1878), professor of physics at Albany Institute, later curator of the Smithsonian Institution, was responsible for a remarkable number of experiments and writings on relationships between electricity, magnetism, and mechanical energy basic to our modern radio-phonographs and even television. Henry's theory of electromagnets was fundamental to the telegraph of Samuel Morse, to the telephone of Alexander Graham Bell, to the speaker systems of high-fidelity phonographs, to twentieth-century record-changing mechanisms, and, for that matter, to electric power plants. For this reason the story of the modern phonograph may be said to begin not with the first machine that would talk, but more truly with the telegraph, or the experiments of Helmholtz, or the phonautograph of Leon Scott.

The relationships of the evolving forms of the phonograph to the development of companion acoustical inventions such as the telegraph, telephone, and radio are a fertile field for investigation. The more important inventors of the first talking machines, for example—Thomas Edison, Bell, and Emile Berliner—had previously been engaged in telegraphic and telephonic invention.

The telephone itself came about only after prolonged experimentation by several independent workers, each seeking for the most part something quite different. Those in the forefront of this research were Edison, Bell, and Elisha Gray, not one of whom before the invention of the telephone had been trying to produce voice articulations over telegraph wires; all had been working on variations of the so-called harmonic telegraph. In the devices of these men, tuned resonators of one kind or another were employed so that multiple messages might be sent over a single wire. Dots and dashes were sent out as musical sound of a given pitch, with the receiving instrument tuned to respond to only those messages intended for it. In contrast, Charles Bourseul in France attempted to transmit speech over electric circuits as early as 1854.

Ironically, Philipp Reis of Germany, who in 1861 tried to transmit modulated vocal sounds over a wire, gave the name "telephone" to the instrument he was trying to invent but never succeeded actually in inventing it. Reis experimented with circuits made and broken by the vibrations of a diaphragm resulting in a similar movement of the receiving diaphragm, actuated by a magnet. Earlier, he had worked on the harmonic telegraph; if he had followed that up, he might have discovered that a continuous but undulatory current is required—not an interrupted current.

As an example of the magnitude of a single act of disassociation involved in making a basic invention, consider the following: when the telephone was invented by Alexander Bell, the language of his patent application left the invention's theory in considerable doubt. Bell still wrote in the terms of the harmonic telegraph, which afforded ample grist for the controversy that arose almost immediately as to who the true inventor of the telephone was. Both Count du Moncel and George Prescott, noted electrician and telegraph expert, questioned Bell's claim to the invention. (In a subsequent book covering the same subject matter, Prescott mitigated his skepticism somewhat.) [4] Edison always credited Bell as the first to achieve the transmission of articulate sounds, or the human voice, over wires, even though one of the devices Edison had made for the harmonic telegraph was later found capable of use for voice transmission.

Some authorities feel that, in inventing the tinfoil phonograph, Edison relied upon Bell's invention of the telephone a short time earlier. Perhaps the best way to analyze this possibility is to dissect the tinfoil phonograph and trace the origins of its components: trumpet, diaphragm, stylus, moving surface, feed screw, and wheel. The speaking trumpet is known to have appeared in a sketch by Leonardo da Vinci of a tube communication system that presumably was installed in a palace of the Duke of Milan. [5] Ear trumpets are believed to have been used from ancient times as an aid in hearing, perhaps originating with the cupping of the hand or perhaps with the conch shell. The diaphragm or tympanum has been known since the time of Hippocrates, through the dissection of human and animal ears, and its use as a sound resonator in drums and musical instruments predates written history. It was used by Scott in the phonautograph, and Bell reconstructed a telautograph using a tympanum from a human ear. The stylus had its origin, in name at least, in the engraving or embossing tool used for making pictographs and hieroglyphics by the ancient Assyrians and Egyptians. The tinfoil phonograph's stylus was actuated by the diaphragm, indenting its vibratory pattern into the moving tinfoil wrapped around the pregrooved cylinder. The moving surface, whether cylinder or disc, had been known in the making of lathes and other machines for years. Finally, the feed screw was invented by Archimedes, and the origin of the wheel is lost in prehistory.

The elements of the first phonograph are fewer and simpler than those of the first telephone; and the phonograph, from the start, worked much better.

It is surprising that the invention of both telephone and phonograph did not occur earlier, considering that by 1831 Henry had established the relationships of electrical coils, currents, and mechanical energy; that the Scott phonautograph of 1856 demonstrated the nature of complex sound waves; and that an ingenious toy called the string telephone had a wide popularity in European cities as early as 1867 (now often improvised by affixing a taut string to the centers of the round ends of two tin cans or cardboard containers, held at a distance). In the case of the telephone, the missing link was the analogy of the sound waveform to an electrical waveform of continuous variability. In the case of the phonograph, the only knowledge lacking was how to indent waveforms of sound into an amorphous substance so that the process could be reversed by mechanical means. In retrospect, however, one sees that a great step in thinking was required between the phonautograph, which traced sound waves for the purpose of visual analysis, and the phonograph, whose object was to recreate the original sound waves at any future time.

Edison's tinfoil phonograph was entirely an acoustical machine. Knowledge of acoustics available to those who first sought to record or reproduce sound was limited, but beginning about 1822 a series of notable advances occurred in the field. Joseph Louis Gay Lussac and Dominique-François-Jean Arago established the velocity of sound in air at given temperatures, while others ascertained the speed of sound through water and other media. Savart invented a toothed wheel for determining the number of vibrations per second for a given musical pitch. Helmholtz established the laws of harmonics. Lissajous, by means of a mirror attached to a vibrating body, projected light vibrations onto a screen as a series of sinusoidal curves. Tyndall investigated extensively the effects of interferences on the qualities of projected sounds; his writings would further popularize the study of acoustics.[6]

A few significant early contributions to the phonograph were made by Europeans. Jean Duhamel found that he could trace the simple, uniform vibrations of a tuning fork. Leon Scott perfected this idea by using a sort of resonating chamber or trumpet to collect complex air vibrations, which, impinging upon a diaphragm stretched across the smaller end, would convert the alternate air pressures and rarefactions into mechanical movements of the diaphragm. The diaphragm in turn actuated a bristle attached to its center, tracing the vibratory pattern as an undulating line upon lampblack-coated paper wrapped around a revolving cylinder. The cylinder was moved along by a screw as it rotated, much as in the later phonograph. Here the resemblance ends, for the movement of the bristle stylus of the Scott phonautograph was lateral. The movement of the stylus of the Edison tinfoil phonograph, in relation to the moving surface, was vertical.

Just as the telephone was named by an unsuccessful aspirant to the invention, Philipp Reis, the first to coin the word *phonograph* was not the inventor, but F. B. Fenby of Worcester, Massachusetts. In 1863 Fenby was granted a patent on his "Electro Magnetic Phonograph." As the device did not embody the essentially simple registering of the waveform, a feature of all successful sound recording and reproducing systems, it contributed nothing but its name to the development of the phonograph.

On July 30, 1877, Thomas A. Edison filed a provisional specification with the British patent office covering a telephonic repeater device. This was the same device that *Scientific American* would hail in a few months as the first machine that would store up and repeat at will the human voice—the first talking machine. Curiously, Edison seems to have had the same difficulty in taking the complete step of disassociation between his telephonic experiments and the invention of the phonograph as Bell had between his quest for multichannel telegraphy and the invention of the telephone.

On December 24, 1877, Edison filed application with the U.S. Patent Office for a patent covering the first phonograph to be built exclusively for the purpose of sound recording and reproduction at will. The patent, number 200,521, issued February 19, 1878, was for the tinfoil phonograph built for Edison by his Swiss machinist, John Kruesi, that repeated Edison's voice reciting "Mary had a little lamb."

Perhaps the closest idea both in time and concept to Edison's phonograph was that of Charles Cros, who had deposited a sealed packet with the Academie des Sciences de France in April 1877, three months before Edison's British patent office filing. There have been periodic attempts to dim the lustre of Edison's phonograph achievement, even to the extent of giving credit for the phonograph's conception to Cros, although the latter never built a machine.[7] There was in fact not the slightest resemblance between the proposed talking machine of Cros and either of the Edison phonograph concepts. It has been reported that it was at the insistence of Cros that the sealed packet he had left with the Academie be opened, after he learned a "successful experiment" had been run in the United States. Such action was hardly necessary, for a complete description of Cros's idea had been published in the October 10 issue of *La Semaine du Clerge* by Abbé Lenoir, who described it as a "phonograph." Edison's adoption of this term has been labeled suspicious, despite its coinage in 1863 by Fenby. There was also little similarity between the Cros concept and the cylinder and disc phonographs built in later years by Edison. (If anyone may be said to owe credit to Cros, it is Emile Berliner, who after several years of fruitless endeavor was forced to abandon the photoengraving idea.)

The phonograph was now an accomplished fact. Both laterally and vertically actuated methods of making sound records were described in Edison's fundamental phonograph patent dated February 19, 1878. This patent was granted by the U.S. Patent Office without a single reference, and its validity was never challenged.

It is interesting to note that Edison's approach toward science and inventing closely followed that of other great scientists he admired, most specifically Hermann Helmholtz. Edison's second wife, Mina Miller, much bemoaned the fact that she never got Helmholtz's signature in her guest book.

In summary, a period of complete saturation immediately precedes subliminal thought on a particular problem. This subconscious sifting of available information becomes an interval of fomentation. Suddenly an avenue of pursuit, an idea, evolves out of this subconscious thought. The idea becomes the creative venture of the inventor, and he follows it through to fruition.

CHAPTER 2

The Edison Tinfoil Phonograph

THE SUCCESSFUL transmission of articulate speech via the telephone developed by Alexander Graham Bell in 1876 may have provided the stimulus for the invention of the phonograph by Thomas A. Edison the following year. It must have been a jolt to Edison to have come so close to the secret of the telephone and the securing of what has often been described as the most valuable single patent in the world. It seems natural to suppose that he would rethink all his many experiments in harmonic telegraphy, which to a considerable extent had paralleled those of Bell. Certainly it is but a consecutive step in thought from the transmission of the vibrations of a diaphragm over an electrical circuit to the recording of those vibrations so that they may be repeated at will. Edison had already taken such a step in his telegraph repeaters.

Although he had not been the first to achieve voice transmission, Edison did not lose interest in the telephone. Drawing on his seemingly inexhaustible energy, he characteristically set to work to make it the practical instrument of communication it has since become. Within a few years he was granted upwards of forty patents dealing with telephonic improvements, including not only the vital carbon button transmitter but also several basic types of microphones, including the dynamic and electrostatic microphones. The importance of the Edison contributions to the success of the telephone in its earliest days is exemplified in the story of the carbon transmitter as told by Alfred O. Tate, at that time Edison's private secretary. Tate reported that the transmitter patent was first sold by Edison to Jay Gould for $150,000, payable in equal installments over a period of fifteen years. Gould later sold this key patent to Western Union, then in competition with the

Bell interests. In one year alone, according to Tate, the Western Union income from this patent was $900,000.[1]

A letter published in the November 17, 1877, issue of *Scientific American* announcing the phonograph seems further to tie the conception of the phonograph to the telephone. Despite laboratory evidence to the contrary, many have thought that Edison was forced to invent the phonograph in order to make good the boasts of his press representative, Edward H. Johnson, the writer of the letter. Both Johnson and the editor of *Scientific American* were personal friends of Edison, and so it was no surprise that Johnson's letter became the subject of an enthusiastic editorial headlined *"A Wonderful Invention—Speech Capable of Indefinite Repetition from Automatic Records."* In it, the editor extolled the marvels of the latest Edison device:

> It has been said that Science is never sensational; that it is intellectual, not emotional; but certainly nothing that can be conceived would be more likely to create the profoundest of sensations, to arouse the liveliest of human emotions, than once more to hear the familiar voices of the dead. Yet Science now announces that this is possible, and can be done. That the voices of those who departed before the invention of the wonderful apparatus described in the letter given below are forever still is too obvious a truth; but whoever has spoken into the mouthpiece of the phonograph, and whose words are recorded by it, has the assurance that his speech may be reproduced audibly in his own tones long after he himself has turned to dust. The possibility is simply startling. A strip of paper travels through a little machine, the sounds of the latter are magnified, and our grandchildren or posterity centuries hence hear us as plainly as if we were present. Speech has become, as it were, immortal.
>
> The possibilities of the future are not much more wonderful than those of the present. The orator in Boston speaks, the indented strips the tangible result; but this travels under a second machine which may connect with the telephone. Not only is the speaker heard now in San Francisco, for example, but by passing the strip again under the reproducer he may be heard tomorrow, or next year, or next century. His speech in the first instance is recorded and transmitted simultaneously, and indefinite repetition is possible.
>
> The new invention is purely mechanical—no electricity is involved. It is a simple affair of vibrating plates, thrown into vibration by the human voice.

It is crude yet, but the principle has been found and modifications and improvements are only a matter of time. So also are its possibilities other than those already noted. Will letter writing be a proceeding of the past? Why not, if by simply talking into a mouthpiece our speech is recorded on paper, and our correspondent can by the same paper hear us speak? Are we to have a new kind of book? There is no reason why the orations of our modern Ciceros should not be recorded and detachably bound so that we can run the indented slips through the machine, and in the quiet of our apartments listen again, and as often as we will, to the eloquent words. Nor are we restricted to spoken words. Music may be crystallized as well. Imagine an opera or an oratorio, sung by the greatest living vocalists, thus recorded, and capable of being repeated as we desire.

The invention, the credit of which is due to Mr. Thomas A. Edison, should not be confounded with the one referred to by us in a previous number, and mentioned in our correspondent's letter. That device is illustrated on another page of this issue, and is of much more complicated construction. Mr. Edison has sent us sketches of several modifications and different arrangements of his invention. These we shall probably publish in a future number.

As intimated by the editor, the device illustrated on another page of the same issue had little in common with the phonograph: the invention of a Dr. Rosapelly and a Professor Marey of France, its purpose was to record graphically the movements of the lips, veil of the palate, and larynx for the purpose of teaching deaf people to speak. Although it had been remarked in a previous article that it might be possible with the Rosapelly-Marey apparatus for the words of a speaker to be taken down by telephone wire at a distance, the invention no more undertook to reproduce a voice than had Scott's phonautograph.

The editorial was followed immediately by the letter from Edward Johnson:

To the Editor of the Scientific American:

In your journal of Nov. 3, page 273, you made the announcement that Dr. Rosapelly and Professor Marey had succeeded in graphically recording the movements of the lips, of the veil of the palate, and the vibrations of the larynx, and you prophesy that this, among other important results, may lead possibly to the application of electricity for the purpose of transferring these records to distant points by wire.

Was this prophesy intuition? Not only has it been fulfilled in the letter, but still more marvelous results achieved by Mr. Thomas A. Edison, the renowned electrician, of New Jersey, who has kindly permitted me to make public not only the fact but the *modus operandi*. Mr. Edison in the course of a series of extended experiments in the production of his speaking telephone, lately perfected, conceived the highly bold and original idea of recording the human voice upon a strip of paper, from which at any subsequent time it might be automatically re-delivered with all the vocal characteristics of the original speaker accurately reproduced. A speech delivered into the mouth-piece of this apparatus may fifty years hence—long after the original speaker is dead—be reproduced audibly to an audience with sufficient fidelity to make the voice easily recognizable by those who were familiar with the original. As yet the apparatus is crude, but is characterized by that wonder-ful simplicity which seems to be a trait of all great invention or discovery. The subjoined illustration, although not the actual design of the appara-tus as used by Mr. Edison, will better serve to illustrate and make clear the principle upon which he is operating.

A is a speaking tube provided with a mouthpiece C—, X is a metal-lic diaphragm which responds powerfully to the vibrations of the voice. In the center of the diaphragm is secured a small chisel-shaped point. D is a drum revolved by clockwork, and serves to carry forward a continuous fil-let of paper, having throughout its length and exactly in the center a raised V-shaped boss, such as would be made by passing a fillet of paper through a Morse register with the lever constantly depressed. The chisel point at-tached to the diaphragm rests upon the sharp edge of the raised boss. If now the paper be drawn rapidly along, all the movements of the diaphragm will be recorded by the indentation of the chisel point into the delicate boss—it, having no support beneath, is very easily indented; to do this, little or no power is required to operate the chisel. The tones of small amplitude will be recorded by slight indentations, and those of full amplitude by deep ones. This fillet of paper thus receives a record of the vocal vibrations of air waves from the movement of the diaphragm; and if it can be made to contribute the same motion to a second diaphragm, we shall not only see that we have a record of the words, but shall have them re-spoken; and if that second dia-phragm be that of the transmitter of a speaking telephone, we shall have the still more marvelous performance of having them respoken and *transmitted by wire at the same time to a distant point.*

The reproductor is very similar to the indenting apparatus, except that a more delicate diaphragm is used. The reproductor, B, has attached to its diaphragm a thread which in turn is attached to a hair spring, H, upon the end of which is a V-shaped point resting upon the indentations of the boss. The passage of the indented boss underneath this point causes it to rise and fall with precision, thus contributing to the diaphragm the motion of the original one, and thereby rendering the words again audible. Of course Mr. Edison, at this stage of the invention, finds some difficulty in reproduc-ing the finer articulations, but he feels quite justified by results obtained, from his first crude efforts, in his prediction that he will have the apparatus in practical operation within a year. He has already applied the principle of his speaking telephone, thereby causing an electromagnet to operate the in-denting diaphragm, and will undoubtedly be able to transmit a speech, made upon the floor of the Senate, from Washington to New York, record the same in New York automatically, and, by means of the speaking telephone re-deliver it in the editorial ear of every newspaper in New York.

In view of the practical inventions already contributed by Mr. Edison, is there anyone who is prepared to gainsay this prediction? I for one am satisfied it will all be fulfilled, and that too, at an early date.

(signed)
Edward H. Johnson, Electrician

Evident in this first published story of the phonograph is the influence of the embossing telegraph on the form the phonograph was to assume. From the first, separate recording and reproducing styli were envisioned, as well as separate dia-phragms and diaphragm assemblies for recording and reproducing. Clearly this first published concept of the phonograph was based on experimentation. In no other way would the fact that quite different qualities are needed in recording and reproducing diaphragms be known. In addition, from the viewpoint of the mod-ern phonograph the use of some form of electrical amplification is significant. This concept evolved out of the Edison invention of the loud-speaking telephone and his electro-motograph principle.[2] This principle rested on the discovery that the resistance between a pad moistened with acid and an alkali surface was reduced by the passage of a weak electrical current. It was made an actuating device for the telephone diaphragm by a central lever to a pad resting on the slowly revolving chalk cylinder partially immersed in a container of acid.

Charles Batchelor, British-born technical assistant to Edison, wrote from Paris to E. H. Johnson at 57 Holborn Viaduct, London, on January 13, 1882, verifying this earlier work on the phonograph:

My dear Johnson,

Your article on the phonograph for the "Scientific American" of November 17, 1877 I believe to be the first published account of the phonograph, therefore I think you are mistaken in the date of your little handbook which might have been at the same time but not before this. I believe however the experiment which we tried and was successful that is of pulling a strip by hand through a groove and producing thus a note that had been sung on it before by the same operation was done in *July or August* 1877.

I know among our telephone drawings at Menlo there was one in July 1877 that shewed the phono used as a telephone receiver.

Yours truly, Chas. Batchelor [3]

The little handbook was *The Telephone Handbook* by Edward H. Johnson, privately published in New York in 1877.

Before the announcement in *Scientific American,* the earliest evidence of Edison's thinking on the phonograph is a sheet of paper containing notes and sketches made by him and dated July 18, 1877. The sketches are of a cylinder device with batteries, diaphragms, membranes, and contacts arranged to act as a telephone repeater or amplifier of telephone voice vibrations. Its function was similar to that of a telegraph repeater: to receive and reinforce signals and then send them on to the next station. The sheet was captioned "Speaking Telegraph," as were contiguous sheets. But in this case the handwritten notes are of particular significance. For example, the note delineating one sketch reads:

X is a rubber membrane connected to central diaphragm at the edge, being near or between the lips in the act of opening it gets a vibration which is communicated to the central diaphragm and then in turn sets the outer diaphragm vibrating hence the hissing consonants are reinforced and made to set the diaphragm in motion—we have just tried an experiment similar to this one.

The development of Edison's thought leading to the next experiment was described but not illustrated by a note at the bottom of the sheet:

Just tried experiment with a diaphragm having an embossing point and held against paraffin paper moving rapidly. The spkg [speaking] vibrations are indented nicely & there is no doubt that I shall be able to store up & reproduce automatically at any future time the human voice perfectly.[4]

Charles Batchelor later testified in a deposition regarding the sequence of same events, as he remembered them:

The first experiment, as I remember it was made in this way: Mr. Edison had a telephone diaphragm mounted in a mouth[-]piece of rubber in his hands, and he was sounding notes in front of it and feeling the vibration of the center of the diaphragm with his finger. After amusing himself with this for some time, he turned round to me and he said: "Batch, if we had a point on this, we could make a record on some material which we could afterwards pull under the point, and it would give us the speech back." I said, "Well, we can try it in a few minutes," and I had a point put on the diaphragm in the center. This I had mounted on a grooved piece of wood that had been used for an old automatic telegraph. [Strips of waxed paper that had been used for making condensors were then prepared.] I pulled it through the groove while Mr. Edison talked into it. On pulling the paper through a second time, we both of us recognized that we had recorded the speech. We made quite a number of modifications of this the same night.

We tried a great many different experiments on this machine, such as different thicknesses of wax, different shapes of the knives, and also different depths of the knife for talking. We also put in paraffine paper that was crimped in the middle so that the knife would cut out on the crimp, making its record in that manner. We also took this paraffine paper and placed it edgewise under the same diaphragm, but with another wooden base made to correspond with the thickness of the paper instead of on the flat surface. We also pulled through metallic foils, and made special points for that, and

a great many other experiments. This was the only device that we had for
trying experiments for at least a couple of days.[5]

Edison was prone to manipulate the press whenever the occasion arose. At
times his boasts about forthcoming inventions were somewhat beyond the capabilities of his laboratory and staff. One such boast that occurred on September 7,
1877, fortunately remained in-house:[6]

Edison Phonograph.
An apparatus for recording automatically the human voice, and reproducing the same at any future period. Mr. Edison the Electrician has not only
succeeded in producing a perfect articulating telephone, which comparative
tests upon the lines of the Western Union Telephone Co. have proved to be
far superior and much more ingenious than the telephone of Bell and has
been adapted for use upon the 1300 private wires operated by the Gold &
Stock Telegraph Company of New York but has gone into a new and entirely
unexplored field of acoustics which is nothing less than an attempt to record
automatically the speech of a very rapid speaker upon paper from which he
reproduces the same speech immediately or years afterwards preserving the
characteristics of the speaker's voice so that persons familiar with it would
at once recognize it.

It would seem that so wonderful result as this would require elaborate
machinery; on the contrary, the apparatus, although crude as yet, is won-
derfully simple. I will endeavour to convey the principle by the use of an
illustration which although not really the apparatus used by Mr. Edison will
enable the reader to grasp the idea at once.[7]

Friend and politician Benjamin F. Butler advised Edison to maintain secrecy
regarding his new invention. As a member of Congress, Butler was in a position
to initiate or act favorably upon patent legislation that eventually might benefit Edison.[8] It was common knowledge that a foreign patent specification could
not be filed prior to a U.S. application, but it is conceivable that a widely read
news article might have preempted such a restriction. The secretive in-house announcement of September 7 suddenly appeared in the November 17, 1877 issue
of *Scientific American.* Indeed, the press immediately trumpeted Edison's newest
invention.

Both the handwritten 1877 diary of Charles Batchelor, Edison's meticulous technical assistant and draftsperson, and the payroll sheets of John Kruesi note December 4 as being spent entirely on the phonograph.[9] The machine was fully operable at the end of the day, as an entry in Charles Batchelor's laboratory notebook for December 4, 1877, indicates:

> This machine we devised for the recording and reproduction of the human voice; it consists in moving a sheet of tinfoil in front of a diaphragm having an indenting point in its centre, which when vibrated by the voice indents the number of vibrations accurately on its surface, this indented sheet is afterwards moved in front of another diaphragm to which is attached a point on a delicate spring. The movement of the spring in passing over the indents on the tinfoil transmits to its diaphragm the rates of vibrations recorded there and the diaphragm gives forth the sounds originally spoken.
>
> The machine proper shown in Fig. A is a cylinder fast on the shaft B. This shaft has a thread on one end which engages in bearing and the other end slides freely in bearing C. The cylinder A has a groove or thread cut on its face to allow the tinfoil which is put round it to be indented. E is the speaking diaphragm provided with an indenting point F. G is the reproducing diaphragm which receives its vibrations from spring H. This works well and the plain "How do you get that" comes very plainly. Chas. Batchelor.

From Batchelor's notebook entry it can be surmised that Batchelor and machinist John Kruesi tested their newly fabricated device before handing over the finished phonograph to Edison. Batchelor's words "How do you get that" thus may have been the first spoken into the phonograph, not Edison's "Mary had a little lamb," as has been thought.

More than thirty years later, however, on August 14, 1918, Edison wrote a letter in the West Orange Library at 3:30 P.M. witnessed by C. B. Hanford, H. A. Altengarten, and Charles Bottomford in which he seeks to dispel any doubt as to the first words spoken into the phonograph:

> Dear Carty:
>
>   In reply to your question, let me say that I was the first person to speak into the first phonograph. The first words spoken by me into the original model, and that were reproduced, were "Mary had a little lamb," and the other 3 lines of that verse.
>
>   Yours sincerely,
>   Thomas A. Edison[10]

In Batchelor's diary entry for December 6, 1877, is the notation: "Finished the Phonograph. Made model for P[atent] O[ffice]." Even though the first phonograph was operable by December 4, Batchelor added finishing touches on December 6. The next day Edward Johnson telegraphed his friend and mentor Uriah Hunt Painter: "Phonograph delivered to me today. Complete success. Inform Henry and Butler." On December 8 the new machine was exhibited in the New York offices of *Scientific American.*, as Johnson wrote Painter: "The Scientific American was all ready to go to press when I took the machine up there yesty. They stopped it—took a sketch of the machine. Made an Engraving of it last night & will issue one day later in Consequence." [11] Johnson showed his characteristic unbounded enthusiasm for the new machine. It would be a welcome addition to his lecture appearances.

It became obvious that a model for demonstrations or exhibitions would be necessary if the phonograph were to be shown at its best. Butler suggested that Edison provide a means for recording telephonic communications. In April 1878 Edison met with a brilliant reception in Washington, D.C.: President Rutherford B. Hayes roused the ladies in the White House at 1:00 A.M. to receive and listen to the phonograph, and Congress was without a quorum for nearly an hour as Edison and Batchelor exhibited the phonograph before the Committee on Patents. Senator Beck and Representatives Garfield and Cox of New York were among those who tested the instrument. [12]

Edison wrote on December 3, 1877: "Have tried lot of experiments with different thickness of tin foil. It's the best material yet for recording." In January 1878 he wrote W. J. McDonald, manager of Union Mills in Virginia, "that the third phonograph ever made was a disk and that disks are harder to mail than cylinders or sound boxes." [13] The next spring the *New York Sun* of April 29 and the *Washington Post* of May 20 described among Edison's improvements on the 1878 phonograph the substitution of a flat circular plate as large as a tambourine for the cylinder, with a sheet of tinfoil placed upon the plate and a well-tempered clockwork mainspring providing the movement. E. H. Johnson noted that the clockwork mechanism much improved the sound reproduction; otherwise the words "were snapped out like a fishwoman's."

Edison's attention was now fixed on marketing his phonographs, applying for a patent, and selling the rights. Laboratory drawings show only slight modifications during this period, but clearly difficulties surfaced: the rotational speed had to be controlled, a proper recording medium had to be developed, the diaphragm had to be made more sensitive and responsive to increase the amplification, and a method of removing the record when finished had to be devised. Also, he needed to think about how to duplicate recordings.[14]

By early 1879, Edison's inventive abilities were focused on developing the incandescent light. Improvements on the tinfoil phonograph would be in abeyance. In less than three years, the world had witnessed the birth of the phonograph, its rise to prominence, and its decline to has-been status.

CHAPTER 3 ➤

The North American
Phonograph Company and
the Bell-Tainter Graphophone

ON APRIL 24, 1878, the Edison Speaking Phonograph Company was organized under the laws of Connecticut to exploit the tremendous popular interest created by the announcement of the invention of a machine that could talk. (On the same day an important patent was issued in England to Edison covering numerous projected improvements on the phonograph, but this patent was not assigned to the new company.) Edison was paid $10,000 for his tinfoil phonograph patent and guaranteed 20 percent of the profits.

The five stockholders of the company were Uriah H. Painter, Gardiner G. Hubbard, George L. Bradley, Charles A. Cheever, and Hilbourne L. Roosevelt. Painter was a Washington reporter who came from West Chester, Pennsylvania. Hubbard, an eminent jurist and financier, was the father-in-law of Alexander Graham Bell and the chief organizer of the Bell Telephone Company. (Without Hubbard's assistance and encouragement, Bell might neither have reaped the rewards of his invention nor even have received the credit due him as the creator of the first articulating telephone.) Bradley was a metallurgist and financier, organizer with Hubbard of the New England Telephone Company and the National Bell Telephone Company of New York City. Cheever was a businessman of indomitable will, making and spending fortunes in spite of an accident as an infant that meant he had to be carried about by an attendant. As a young man, Cheever had secured an option on the New York City rights to the Bell telephone, but his father refused to loan him the necessary funds, so the option was dropped. Cheever was so certain of the success of the telephone enterprise that he persuaded Hilbourne Roosevelt, a cousin of Theodore Roosevelt, to back him, and together they secured the New York City rights from Hubbard. Thus some of the men closest to Alexander Bell were also associated with Thomas Edison and sponsored the commercial introduction of the phonograph.

When the phonograph came on the commercial scene, the telephone business had yet to show its first dollar of profit, so it was an economic convenience for the embryonic industries to share office expenses as well as certain officers and backers, and the two occupied the same offices at 203 Broadway in New York. During the first year of the Edison Speaking Phonograph Company, Hilbourne Roosevelt, who was a manufacturer of pipe organs as well, arranged demonstrations of the phonograph in and around New York City. These gatherings were attended by thousands eager to pay the admission charged. James Redpath, later of Lyceum Theatre fame, divided the country into territories and leased demonstration rights. The phonographs at first were leased to the demonstrators, not sold, which explains why few have survived from this period.

The elemental phonograph, using tinfoil for the recording surface, was a simple and crude affair, and the reproduction was generally poor. Yet contrary to the telephone, the phonograph was a commercial success from the first, paying its own way handsomely for the first few years. It was inevitable that people would tire of the novelty of hearing the human voice reproduced on the spot, and thus it became evident that there would have to be further technical development of the instrument if it were to continue to be profitable. It had to be developed into a useful machine rather than just a show business novelty. Edison had intended this from the first, but now his time was committed to other projects of more immediate importance. As the telephone began to show promise of becoming commercially feasible, the phonograph wore out its initial welcome.

When it became apparent that the demonstration phase of the tinfoil phonograph was nearing a stalemate, Edison bought the assets of the Edison Speaking Phonograph Company to prevent loss to the stockholders and to ensure that, when time permitted, he would be able to develop the necessary modifications.

At the same time word came from the U.S. Patent Office that his 1878 phonograph patent application had been disallowed, even though it was identical to his previously granted British patent, on the grounds that the British patent constituted prior publication. The decision was appealed, but the patent examiners were adamant, holding that Edison's interests were adequately protected under international agreements covering patents and copyrights. Edison always felt that this decision was most unfair. Perhaps the Edison attorneys protested too much, for on occasion portions of other patent claims had to be abandoned by Edison.

The examiners held that the subject had already been covered broadly in his 1878 British patent.[1]

One of the great mysteries in the history of the two related industries, the telephone and the phonograph, is that, with a collaborative beginning and cordial relationships between the principals, a schism should eventually develop. That the Edison and Bell family relationships were initially cordial is indicated by a letter from Mrs. Alexander Graham Bell to Thomas Edison congratulating him upon the invention of the phonograph. There is another such congratulatory letter from Gardiner Hubbard, Bell's father-in-law, chief backer, and one of the original stockholders of the Edison Speaking Phonograph Company.[2]

Yet the patent for Edison's carbon transmitter, vital to the successful development of the telephone, was transferred to the up-and-coming rival of the Bell Telephone Company—Western Union. Although Edison had sold many telegraphic patents to Western Union in past years, it may be that Bell thought Edison should have desisted from experiments with the telephone, or that he should have discontinued his association with Western Union as competition with the Bell interests developed. Perhaps these considerations were what stimulated Bell to begin his own work on the phonograph.

It was at this crucial point that a decision made some years before by Napoleon III of France played a decisive role in the future of the phonograph. The emperor had created an award for scientific achievement in honor of the distinguished French scientist Alessandro Volta. In 1880 a committee of the French Academy of Science granted this award to Alexander Graham Bell, in recognition of his invention of the telephone. Bell received $20,000, with which he established the Volta Laboratories in Washington, D.C., to engage in electrical and acoustical research. For assistance Bell brought from England his brother Chichester Bell and Professor Charles Sumner Tainter. The three men were known henceforth as the Volta Laboratory Associates.

At this point the Bell telephone needed a successful telephone transmitter, and patent rights to the Edison carbon button transmitter had already been transferred by Jay Gould to rival Western Union interests. Alexander Bell with Charles Sumner Tainter invented a photophone transmitter capable of producing a voice-modulated current by means of a light-sensitive selenium cell, in turn activated by a reflected variable beam of light attached to the speaker diaphragm—too complicated to compete with the Edison carbon button transmitter.

The first notations in the laboratory notebooks of Charles Sumner Tainter over this period are on the phonograph rather than on the telephone. The notations show that early phonographic experimentation stemmed from information and sketches contained in Edison's British patent of 1878. Tainter appears to have been responsible for the change in direction of research at Volta Laboratory Associates. If the circumstances surrounding the founding of Volta Laboratories may be described as dramatic, then the steps taken by the associates to protect the results of their phonographic achievements can be characterized only as fantastic.

On February 28, 1880, Alexander Bell and Charles Sumner Tainter deposited a sealed envelope with the Smithsonian Institution containing a caveat—an intent to invent or statement of conclusions—on early phonographic experiments. More than a year later, on October 20, 1881, they also deposited with the Smithsonian a sealed wooden box that contained two Washington newspapers of a day or two previous, a roll of forty-seven pages of notes and sketches traced and copied from Tainter's notebook, an eight-page statement by Tainter and Chichester Bell describing their invention of reproducing sound from a phonogram record by means of a jet of compressed air, and a recording device. A typed card affixed to the box with sealing wax stated:

> The following words and sounds are recorded upon the cylinder of this graphophone—
>
> > "G-r-r-G-r-r-There are more things in heaven and earth, Horatio, than are dreamed of in our philosophy
> > —G-r-r-I am a graphophone and my mother was a phonograph."
>
> Speaking mouthpiece and length of tube. Deposited October 20, 1881.

Upon the opening of the sealed box in 1937, it was claimed publicly that the recorded message on this first "graphophone" had been perfectly reproduced on that day in 1937. Examination of the machine fails to indicate how this could have been accomplished in view of the condition of the air-jet reproducing mechanism; a tag attached to the machine indicates that the glass nozzle was missing. Is it possible that the recorded message was simply quoted from the yellowed card attached so long ago with sealing wax? Or was special equipment brought in to play it? In any case, the instrument and reproductions of it that appeared in advertisements for the Dictaphone Corporation in 1937 under the heading "The voice that was buried for 56 years" may be identified easily as the 1878 Edison tinfoil phonograph. The only modification was that, instead of tinfoil, wax had been embedded in the grooves of the iron cylinder, and into this wax the voice vibrations had been incised rather than indented. No reproducing mechanism was shown in the advertisements, nor was any mention made as to the method of reproduction used on the celebrated occasion of the 1937 opening.

Although this instrument had been deposited with the Smithsonian in 1881, it was June 27, 1885, before the first applications for patents were made by the Bells and Tainter. Why the long delay? Volta Associates may have decided to wait until the original Edison patent had expired, depositing their notes and experimental apparatus in order to prove priority of conception. Or they may have wished to forestall an adverse decision by the patent examiners on the basis of the Edison British patent of 1878. At the very least, the delay gave the patent examiners an opportunity to forget the parallel of the 1878 Edison U.S. patent application that had been refused.

Of the five patents applied for by the Bells and Tainter on June 27, 1885, and granted May 4, 1886, the only one to become important in later patent litigations was 341,214.[3] This patent substituted for the indenting stylus of the Edison tinfoil phonograph an incising stylus for recording, and for the tinfoil recording medium, a wax-coated cardboard cylinder.

The unique contribution of patent 341,214 was that it clearly defined the difference between indenting and incising. Edison had done experimental recording with wax-coated surfaces, for he claimed that an indenting point, not a style or cutter, would become clogged upon a wax surface if not first covered with foil. A recording stylus used to indent tinfoil could also cut a groove of variable depth in a wax surface. As this difference was as obvious to physicists then as now, it should not seem strange that Edison failed to see anything of patentable value. Chichester Bell and Tainter did not themselves realize the importance in this matter of semantics, but later their attorney, the astute Philip Mauro, did. Tainter's notes show that Volta Associates was incising from the very beginning. In any case, with this one exception, all the Bell-Tainter improvements used in the industry were anticipated by the Edison British patent of 1878, including the method of amplifying the sound in reproduction by means of a jet of compressed air.

One real contribution resulting from the Bell-Tainter research has been completely overlooked: a turntable capable of variable speed in revolutions per minute (rpm) for recording and reproducing disc records, turning slowest when the stylus was at the outer circumference and progressively speeding up as the stylus approached the center, permitting a constant speed for the surface passing under the stylus.

Upon the issuance of the 1886 patents Bell and his associates organized the Volta Graphophone Company at Alexandria, Virginia, undoubtedly because of the restrictions on manufacturing in Washington, D.C. Headquarters remained in Washington, and influential members of Congress heard the graphophone in operation. One was Andrew Devine, reporter for the U.S. Supreme Court and later destined to become the president of the American Graphophone Company. In a deposition filed in a phonograph patent case in February 1896, Devine said he was immediately impressed with the potential of the machine for dictation. He added that the Volta Graphophone Company seemed more interested in exploiting the graphophone for music reproduction than for dictation; in fact, company executives let it be known they doubted the machine could ever be used successfully for business purposes.

Devine interested a fellow Supreme Court reporter, James O. Clephane, in developing the graphophone as an aid for business purposes. Clephane was the right man to talk to, for he was already involved in financing development work on a typewriter (later to be commercially produced as the Remington typewriter), and he was interested in the Mergenthaler Linotype. A demonstration was arranged, with one of the reporters, John H. White from the House of Representatives, in attendance. White, who had considerable inventive ability, later contributed and patented a number of minor improvements to the graphophone.

At the time of this demonstration and for some years thereafter, the graphophone employed removable cylinders of cardboard coated with ozocerite, 6 inches × 1 ^{5}/₁₆ inches. A separate speaker was required for recording and reproducing. The motive power was a hand crank, and the listening was accomplished through stethoscopic ear tubes. A feature that may have attracted Devine was the ease with which any passage of a recording could be located. Owing to the extremely small diameter of the record cylinder as compared with the earlier tinfoil cylinder or even the later wax type, the lateral displacement was much greater for a given number of words recorded. The ease of replacing the record was also important, for in the earlier phonograph the tinfoil recording was often damaged or destroyed in removal and subsequent replacement.

Andrew Devine, knowing that the Edison patents were basic and that the Bell-Tainter patents had not yet been tested in the courts, proposed that the Bell-Tainter interests should pay a visit to the Edison laboratory with the idea of joining forces. Devine, Clephane, and Tainter thus made arrangements to meet with Edison in Orange, New Jersey. According to an article in the July 1, 1888, *Electrical World,* because Edison was ill and unable to see them the meeting did not take place. Tainter said that instead he exhibited to several members of the Edison Speaking Phonograph Company in New York a graphophone "on which records were engraved and reproduced from cylinders of wax, in substantially the same manner as the so-called Improved Phonograph of Mr. Edison."

Edison by himself could not have consummated an agreement with the graphophone contingent, for the 1878 Edison patents were owned by the Edison Speaking Phonograph Company. That the stock of this company was still outstanding is proven by an annual certificate and the original phonograph contracts, found in Edison's desk in 1947. The certificate, dated February 14, 1888, contained the following items of information:

1. paid in capital stock $600,000
2. cash value of real estate $0
3. cash value of its personal estate, *exclusive of patents* about $5,000
4. amount of debts $0
5. amount of credits $0

It appears from these facts that Edison might have felt that his first duty was to his own stockholders, who still retained rights even though the enterprise had been dormant for some time. In any event a review of the patents issued to Edison before and after the graphophone promotion attempt leaves little doubt that Edison decided to renew his efforts to improve his phonograph. When he resumed this work in the latter part of 1886, he may have been irked to find so many of the improvements projected in his 1878 British patent now incorporated in the Bell-Tainter devices and patented by them in the United States. In 1888, however, seventeen U.S. patents were issued to Edison on phonographic devices; in 1889, nineteen more.[4]

By a fateful coincidence, just at the height of this activity Jesse Lippincott, former Pittsburgh glass magnate, approached Edison with a proposal to merge the rival graphophone and phonograph forces through a combined sales agency. About the only things the opposing camps had in common by this time were mutual feelings of distrust and suspicion. Naturally, under these circumstances, both sides hedged in negotiating with Lippincott but nevertheless reached an agreement. That Lippincott had millions to invest may have had something to do with the success of the venture. Lippincott's decision was to approach Edison through Thomas Lombard, a friend and partner in some mining ventures. The approach came at a crucial moment, for Edison and his associates had just formed a new company to manufacture the improved Edison phonograph, the Edison Phonograph Company.

As president of the company, Edison gave an old telegraph buddy, Ezra T. Gilliland, a contract for exclusive U.S. sales rights for the Edison phonograph in exchange for services rendered. By the terms of the contract, Gilliland would receive a commission of 15 percent on all phonographs sold. It was a valuable contract, and both Edison and Gilliland knew it. Under the contract, Gilliland formed a sales company and set the price of the stock.

On June 28, 1888, two companion agreements were drawn up by Edison's attorney. The first, between Edison and Jesse Lippincott, provided for the purchase of the Edison Phonograph Company stock held by Edison for $500,000, to be paid in installments over four months. Included was a stipulation that Edison would try to repurchase 150 shares that he had previously sold to Mary Hemenway, a Boston philanthropist. The second agreement was between Ezra Gilliland and Jesse Lippincott, providing for the purchase of the stock of Gilliland's sales company for $250,000, to be paid in five equal monthly installments. The Edison-Lippincott contract provided that the stock involved would be placed in escrow until paid for in full, and it is reasonable to assume that the same course was followed for the Gilliland Sales Company stock. Edison, however, evidently felt that Gilliland should have turned back into development work some of the $50,000 cash he had received. Instead, Gilliland and Edison's attorney sailed for Europe on a holiday, both terminating their association with Edison.

By these contracts, Jesse Lippincott's North American Phonograph Company became the sole proprietor of the Edison phonograph patents in the United States, with manufacturing and development to be carried on by the Edison Phonograph Works. Lippincott then returned to negotiations with the American Graphophone Company officials, one of whom was Colonel Payne. Payne shrewdly refused to make anything other than a personal, nontransferable agreement with Lippincott, which made Lippincott the exclusive U.S. sales agent for the graphophone, with the proviso that he agree to purchase a minimum of 5,000 graphophones a year. Payne drove a hard bargain, for Lippincott also gave the American Graphophone Company an option to purchase at any time within five years the stock of the Edison Phonograph Company for the price Lippincott was paying Edison. The basic Edison phonograph patents were still owned by the old Edison Speaking Phonograph Company, and Lippincott also agreed to try to purchase control of that company. This he never did, for reasons that will become apparent.

Through these involved transactions, Lippincott's North American Phonograph Company became the sole U.S. sales agent for the Edison phonograph, and Lippincott, personally, became U.S. agent for the graphophone, except in the District of Columbia, Virginia, and Delaware. This area had already been granted to a group of men in Washington, some of whom were officers and stockholders in the American Graphophone Company, and who were to organize the Columbia Phonograph Company. The tentative scheme of organization for the Columbia Phonograph Company was set up in February 1888, and the company incorporated in January 1889. As its name implies, Columbia Phonograph was to operate as a Washington-area company licensed by the North American Phonograph Company, with territorial sales rights to the Edison phonograph.

The Columbia organization was carried out principally by two U.S. Supreme Court reporters, Edward D. Easton, who later became president of the American Graphophone Company, and R. F. Cromelin. The predominance of court reporters and lawyers in the organization of American Graphophone and Columbia Phonograph may have lain behind the phenomenal success of the two companies in later battles over patent law and jurisprudence. It is not surprising that these bright young men had envisioned a great opportunity for the useful employment of phonographs for stenographic work in the courts, in the offices of members of Congress, and for general business purposes. For Jesse Lippincott, however, this maze of corporations and opportunity would become an entangling and destructive web.

CHAPTER 4 ➼

The Local Phonograph Companies

WHEN THE North American Phonograph Company proposed licensing local companies to conduct the talking machine business, it was suggesting the use of a tested concept. In 1878 the Edison Speaking Phonograph Company had often arranged state licenses for its traveling exhibitors.[1] Likewise, the licensing structure within the telephone industry revealed a parent company and local companies.

In the same tradition, Ezra T. Gilliland, general agent for the Edison Phonograph Company, had in 1878 proposed dividing the country into thirty-eight areas, with an additional three in Canada. Only one such company was actually organized—the Pacific Edison Phonograph Company, representing California, Oregon, Washington, and Nevada.[2]

The same type of organization had been proposed for the graphophone when Jesse Lippincott acquired the right of exploitation from the general agents of the American Graphophone Company. Lippincott knew that it would be impossible to conduct business until accommodation was arranged with Edison. His acquisition of Edison patents through the purchase of the Edison Phonograph Company made it possible for him to form the North American Phonograph Company in the summer of 1888. American Graphophone in turn insisted that Lippincott's license could not be transferred, and so Jesse Lippincott became sole licensee of the North American Phonograph Company.[3]

Lippincott proposed licensing a number of local companies whose primary function was to lease and furnish supplies for either the phonograph or the graphophone. Several promoters and syndicates underwrote the organization of the local groups, usually paying $100,000 for the privilege.[4] More than thirty companies were organized. Holland Brothers of Ottawa was appointed as agent for Canada and Alaska. Only two areas did not have local companies: North Dakota, which may have been serviced by South Dakota, and Indiana, which was always operated through an agent.[5] The earliest companies organized and the two with the most complicated contracts were the Metropolitan Phonograph Company and the New England Phonograph Company. Both were organized by the same syndicate, and both held the right to go elsewhere for supplies, if North American should be unable to furnish a sufficient quantity.

In all cases the local company was to pay the organizational fee to North American and was to deposit 12.5 percent of its capital stock with the parent company for a five-year license to operate. At the end of five years it was to increase its stock deposit by an additional 25 percent, thus extending its license to ten years. While one may question the rosy projections of the promoters, one cannot fault them for confidence. The preliminary prospectus of the Metropolitan Phonograph Company, probably issued in the fall of 1888, indicated:

> In the case of the telegraph, telephone and electric light, local companies are by no means assured of success by a franchise from the parent company vesting them with exclusive control in particular territory. The consents of municipal authorities to run wires and erect plants are indispensable. The phonograph and phonograph-graphophones being supplied by the parent company, there is eliminated the necessity of large outlays for extensive plants. The company has to do only with the individual user, and the rental is placed so low that the machine is brought within the reach of all.

The following is believed to be a careful and conservative estimate of the probable business of the Metropolitan Phonograph Company:

> Phonograph and Phonograph-graphophones. —When 10,000 phonographs and phonograph-graphophones are placed at a net annual rental to the Company of $2 each the amount will equal, annually . . . . . $200,000 Cylinders. —Each instrument using an average of 30 cylinders per day, would equal 300,000 cylinders per day for 10,000 phonograph-graphophones, which, at a profit of 6/10 of a cent per cylinder (20% of selling price), would equal $1,800 per day, or at

> 300 working days per year, annually $540,000
> Total income $740,000
> Expense of conducting this business $75,000
> Net profit per annum $665,000

The profit was estimated to be an amount of over 66 percent upon the capital stock.[6]

The New England Phonograph Company had an even rosier series of projections, estimating an annual rental on 20,000 machines at $400,000 and a sale of 400,000 cylinders yielding $720,000. With projected business expenses estimated at $120,000, an income of $1 million per year was visualized, a net profit of 50 percent upon the capital stock "exclusive of income that may be derived from other applications of the invention."[7]

North American Phonograph held great expectations for each of the organizations, as the phonograph was envisioned recording dictation in businesses. The instruments were to be rented to the local companies for $20.00 and in turn be rented out for $40.00. Each company was required to keep the machines in good operating condition, a burden that would prove onerous as the relatively untested machines broke down. In addition, North American was so certain of the probable success of the business that it included a clause concerning the rental amounts:

> [It] reserves the right in its discretion to reduce rentals whenever the net earnings shall be in excess of 12% per annum. In case of reduction the amount of same shall be equally divided between this Company and your Company. The profit to you on cylinders, or on special extras which are sold as extras, such as duplicate records of music, orations, novels, &, will be 20% of the selling price.[7]

Problems developing between Edison and Gilliland over the sale of Gilliland's agency contract with the Edison Phonograph Company and over rights of the old Edison Speaking Phonograph Company were to affect both the parent North American Company and the local companies. Adding to the confusion were difficulties encountered by both the Edison Phonograph Works and the American Graphophone Company in producing machines. The early phonograph and the early graphophone both exhibited fundamental shortcomings, making maintenance and repair a prime concern for the local companies. Customers experiencing difficulties often returned their machines or failed to renew their leases.

Edward Easton, intrigued by the phonograph since first seeing the Edison tin-foil phonograph in 1878, was convinced the machine would aid in his business but soon discovered that the tinfoil model was impractical. His interest was not re-kindled until he saw the Bell and Tainter graphophone in operation on March 31, 1887. The first graphophone that he used was a "Type A" graphophone acquired in March or April 1888. Upon the organization of the North American Phono-graph Company, Easton signed an agreement on January 15, 1889, to organize a local company for the District of Columbia and Maryland within six months. On the same day the Columbia Phonograph Company was organized in West Virginia.[8] With a group of stenographers in control who had used the grapho-phone extensively for transcribing debates in Congress, Columbia Phonograph was assured of success, dependent on the parent company only for machines and equipment.

With a limited number of machines available and the future uncertain, the Metropolitan Phonograph Company decided to explore other sources of income:

> A request was presented by Mr. V. H. Emerson, formerly in the employ of the Company, to have the privilege of exhibiting the Phonograph within our district and to charge an admission fee therefore.
>
> It was voted to give this privilege on the following terms. The Company to furnish the instrument and Mr. Emerson to keep it in repair and pur-chase his own supplies, that his territory be in Westchester County and the portion of New York north of Harlem River, that he pay the Company one fourth of the gross receipts, and that on all signed orders he may secure for the instruments which the Company accepts, he be allowed a Canvasser's commission of $2.00 each.[9]

Neither the phonograph nor the graphophone were mass produced, and both were largely untried. The local companies soon found that the ozocerite-covered paper tubes used for recording on the graphophone developed cracks as a re-sult of the unequal coefficient of expansion between paper and wax, making them unusable. The high moisture content of the ozocerite dulled steel recording needles, which not only caused chattering but tore large chunks from the tube surface. Users found the "sewing-machine type treadle" that moved the machine unwieldy.

The problem with the phonograph lay with the batteries, which showed a dis-concerting tendency to spill acid onto surrounding areas. An illustration from

Western Electrician that appears on the front cover of the reprint of the first convention of the local phonograph companies shows a battery placed on a small carpet in order the protect the rug underneath, which exhibits staining from repeated overflowings and spills. Local company experts were hard-pressed to keep up with the situation.

In 1887, as Edison and Gilliland resumed work on the phonograph, Gilliland approached Albert K. Keller, a former employee, with the idea of developing a coin-operated phonograph, as Gilliland later testified:

> In the summer of 1887, when we were engaged in perfecting the phonograph at Edison's Laboratory, in East Newark, I suggested to him that it might be very profitable to put the phonographs out, when they were perfected, on exhibition, connected with a nickel in the slot device. After the experiment on the phonograph was carried to the point of perfection where we were ready to manufacture them for commercial purposes, the factory was established in Bloomfield, and Mr. Keller was made the superintendent, and at my personal request and on my personal account, Mr. Keller undertook experiments and made models for many improvements on the phonograph, and among them was experiments on the nickel in the slot attachment for the phonographs.[10]

In order to remain afloat and maintain public interest, many of the local companies turned their attention to nickel-in-the-slot instruments. Starting with demonstrations of machines at hand, it was a short step to regular installations of coin-operated machines. By the first local phonograph company convention the slot business had grown sufficiently to warrant a session on these slot machines. Louis Glass of the Pacific Edison Phonograph Company reported that all of the money made by his company was from slot machines.

The North American Phonograph Company was quick to point out the potential of the coin-operated business in one of its circulars:

> The following is an extract from the *Cincinnati Commercial Gazette,* dated July 25, 1890:
> "The Musical Phonograph, which is now to be seen in every restaurant and bar downtown, is knocking the business of all the other Drop-a-nickel-in-the-slot machines into a cocked hat. When a man can hear the 7th Regiment Band of New York play the Boulanger March, a Cornet solo by Levy, or

the famous song, The Old Oaken Bucket, for five cents, he has little desire to pay five cents to ascertain his weight or test the strength of his grip. That is the reasons the musical machine has killed the business of the other automatic machines." [11]

As many of the local companies rushed to open phonograph parlors, the demand for musical phonograms increased, a demand Edison had reserved the right to supply in his contract with Lippincott. By January 1890 North American had issued a formal catalog of musical selections it proposed to keep in stock. Columbia Phonograph on February 7, 1890, reprinted North American's list, adding that "quite a number of other musical records are also kept in stock," including some "from the best soloists of the Marine Band. In addition to the music above set out, this company has arranged with Mr. Henry Jaeger, the celebrated flute and piccolo soloist of the Marine Band, to keep us constantly supplied with records of his best solos, which will undoubtedly prove a great attraction to subscribers." [12] Columbia was not alone. By 1891 the infant industry publication *Phonogram* carried references to other local companies producing and advertising their own selections.

It did not take long for another company to attempt to regularize the coin-operated scene. On February 8, 1890, the Automatic Phonograph Exhibition Company was organized "to manufacture, lease, use, and sell a nickel in the slot machine, by means of which the dropping of a coin in the slot will operate a mechanism which will cause a phonograph or phonograph-graphophone to produce the sound recorded upon its cylinder, and after such reproduction cause the diaphragm to return to its original position." [13] Almost immediately Automatic began to enter into agreements with the local companies, first with New York Phonograph, which at the time owned the rights for all the territories of New York excepting Westchester, New York, Kings, Queens, Suffolk, and Richmond. Automatic contracted to pay a rental on the phonograph or phonograph-graphophone of forty dollars for the first year and thirty dollars for each year thereafter for four years. Any profits were to be divided equally between the local company and Automatic. Also, "any and all revenues from advertisements, boards, or advertisements signs, used in connection with the Coin Slot machines" would be divided equally. [14]

With numerous applications for coin slot attachments before the Patent Office, it became increasingly obvious that Automatic must either control as many as

possible or enter into as many exclusive agreements as possible. Automatic encountered another problem in the form of Charles A. Cheever, Jr., who was allied
with Gilliland in wishing to reserve at least a portion of the Automatic cabinet
contract for Gilliland. To this Edison adamantly refused assent.[15]

By the middle of April 1890 the major points of contention were settled,
with three separate agreements entered into on April 19. The first, "The Six-
Party Agreement," involved Edison, Lippincott, Thomas R. Lombard, the North
American Phonograph Company, Louis Glass, the Exploiting Company of California, and the Automatic Phonograph Exhibition Company. Under this agreement the first six parties agreed to transfer and assign all inventions, applications
for, and patents relating to coin-operated phonographs to Automatic. Automatic
agreed to issue all its recently increased capital stock (15,000 shares with a total
par value of $1.5 million). The holders of the original 10,000 shares agreed to
another contract pooling their stock with that of the six parties so that all the
holdings would be in the hands of Felix Gottschalk as trustee, with the exception
of 1,000 shares that the trustee would attempt to sell at $25 per share. The new
shares were to be distributed in the following amounts: 5,500 to Edison, 5,500
to Lippincott and his associates, and 11,000 to Cheever and his associates.

In the second agreement Gilliland's firm was allowed to produce 500 cabinets,
bridging the gap caused by the gearing up of the Edison Phonograph Works.
Nothing had really been accomplished by October 17, when a memo from Gilliland to Edison pointed out ambiguities in the official model of the Automatic
machine, whether supplied by Edison or by Automatic. The memo also charged
that Gilliland had already exceeded his limitation of 500 cabinets by at least 200.[16]

Upon the urging of the North American Phonograph Company an informal
meeting of the local phonograph company managers was held on November 6,
1889, which led to the first formal meeting of all of the companies in Chicago on
May 28–29, 1890. The conduct of the meeting was recorded by stenographers
using the phonograph and the graphophone, then set in type by linotype operators working directly from the dictation cylinders, the whole process touted by
the *New York Times* on July 24 as an "unprecedented performance."

By now the graphophone was rapidly losing out to the phonograph, so that at
least among the local companies there was some standardization. North American, bound by Lippincott's contract to accept a stated number of new graphophones each month, arranged to pay a royalty on new phonographs instead.[17]
Graphophone usage by the local companies steadily declined, even though the

American Graphophone Company was supplying its machines with improvements patented by John White. To arrest this trend, the Graphophone Company commissioned Edward Easton to tour the local companies to instruct employees in the best methods for using their machines.

Even with all of this activity, North American and the local companies continued to decline. Both the phonograph and the graphophone had been improved, but North American's tight finances made it impossible to introduce the improvements. The first casualty occurred in New York State, where both the Metropolitan Phonograph Company and the New York Phonograph Company had seen their cash positions decline alarmingly. They received permission to merge from their stockholders and North American in hopes that by reducing overhead they might survive.[18]

North American itself was staggering under a heavy load of debt to Edison and the Edison Phonograph Works. Since Jesse Lippincott had been furnishing close to $25,000 a month to keep the operation afloat, it was decided that North American should begin selling machines December 15, 1890. Lippincott was now seriously ill; were he to die, North American would fail. On December 10 Automatic learned that plans to market phonographs and graphophones were afoot at North American and lodged a formal protest that sales should not be restricted. "If it is deemed desirable to sell phonographs the sale should be made in such a way, as the control of the machine should remain vested in the North American Phonograph Company, and through them in the local Phonograph Companies who have purchased franchises from the North American Phonograph Company. This could be done in several ways." North American simply replied, "Your favor to the Executive Committee of this Company was submitted yesterday afternoon, and I was instructed to say, that in their opinion it would be unwise to delay the sale of machines commencing upon Dec. 15th." Automatic immediately turned to the federal courts, filing a bill of complaint on December 13, and a restraining order was issued. On January 21 Judge Lacombe continued the injunction "but with an express reservation of the graphophone."[19]

In that same inauspicious month *Phonogram*, the official organ of the National Phonograph Association, which represented the grouping of local phonograph companies, made its debut. Because of the declining fortunes of North American, the publication was destined to lead a hand-to-mouth existence for the next two years.[20]

By the time the delegates to the local phonograph companies' second annual convention met in June 1891 in New York, the industry was clearly in transition. The number of phonographs out on rental was in growing disproportion to the number of graphophones: 2,000 phonographs to 65 graphophones. Many delegates continued to call for a merger of the better features of both the phonograph and the graphophone. Conscious of the growing potential of the "duplicate cylinder market," Edison representatives invited attendees to visit the Edison Laboratory in West Orange, where they saw, among other features, a smartly designed "duplicate cylinder with a slot designed to hold a paper strip giving the title of the record." [21]

Financial problems continued to plague Jesse Lippincott. The failure of North American to begin selling machines meant no income from this source. As Lippincott's health continued to decline, his absences from North American board meetings grew even more frequent. When eventually he was forced to assign his remaining assets over to his creditors, the May 10, 1894, *New York Times* reported the company's debt at over $1 million.

The ban on the sale of phonographs caused by the Automatic Phonograph Exhibition Company suit was lifted in July 1892. North American hoped to use the money generated from sales to reduce its indebtedness to Edison. Not all the companies agreed with the concept of selling machines; New York Phonograph and New Jersey Phonograph were prominent among the holdouts.

When by the beginning of 1893 the last two companies finally agreed to sell instruments, they unwittingly became involved in one of the early court cases involving the phonograph. George S. Tewksbury had purchased a supply of phonographs from the New Jersey Phonograph Company, as had Leonard G. Spencer. Tewksbury and Spencer took the machines to Washington, D.C., where they hired the U.S. Marine Band to make recordings. The Marine Band, however, had been a main staple of the Columbia Phonograph Company since late 1889 or early 1890. Columbia had established a wide market for its marches and therefore sought a restraining order from the Supreme Court of the District of Columbia. Tewksbury testified two days later that he had taken the "records for his own private use, and neither directly nor indirectly for the North American Phonograph Company. He claimed that as a citizen owning these phonographs, he had the right to use them in any manner he chose and that he intended to take the records so made on said phonographs of the music of the Marine Band and vend the same." Justice Cox refused to vacate the restraining order: "I think there is no right to bring machines here and undertake to use them in the way of trade, and really in that way to compete with the business of the complainants who have a prior right to the use of the inventions here."[22]

As North American sold more phonographs, large numbers seemed to be required by several distant companies. On October 18, 1892, the board of directors authorized the sale of 205 machines at $50 each. On the same day an additional 100 machines were sold to the Nebraska Phonograph Company at $70 each. Soon numbers of phonographs began to appear in England in direct competition with the Edison-Bell Company. The Edison United Company through Theodore Seligman lodged a protest requesting that all machines sold carry a notice limiting their use to the United States. On January 24, 1893, North American's board of directors refused to accede to the request.[23]

Thomas Lombard and A. O. Tate knew that by reducing North American's indebtedness and consolidating an unwieldy substructure they would be able to place the company on a more even keel. One solution would be to consolidate as much of the daily business as possible in the hands of the parent company. Thus, a series of suspension agreements materialized beginning in July 1892. On July 29 A. O. Tate, Edison's representative at North American, wrote to Edison, who had been voted titular head of the North American Phonograph Company:

> On Sunday morning Mr. Lombard and myself leave for Chicago, where we will meet the representatives of the first Companies which we expect will enter into the new arrangement. Mr. Bush has prepared a contract based upon the memorandum assented to by the Committee of sub-Companies and the Committee of the North Am. Phonograph Co., which I believe we will be able to put into effect without serious difficulty. If we are successful in putting this contract through with the Michigan Company and the Illinois State Company, our work with the balance of the sub-Companies will be greatly facilitated. The reason for this is that the two men who control these Companies are the actual representatives of all the other licensees.
>
> I am not prepared at the present time to make any report to you with respect to the stockholders of the North Am. Phonograph Company and how far we can count upon control. If we succeed in making the proposed contract with the sub-Companies, your control of a very large majority of the stock of the North Am. Phonograph Co. will be absolutely assured, for the reason that you will have behind you the power of the licensees.[24]

By February 1893, Tate was able to report to North American's board that some sixteen of the local companies had signed suspension agreements, varying in size and importance from such companies as the Colorado and Utah to such organizations as the Eastern Pennsylvania and the State Phonograph Company of Illinois. In a new spirit of confidence, the directors voted at the same meeting to expend up to $1,000 on exhibiting at the World's Columbian Exposition in Chicago.[25]

Meanwhile, because Jesse Lippincott had been forced to assign his assets to creditors, North American had not paid monies due to the American Graphophone Company. Claiming breach of contract, American Graphophone decided to market the machine on its own, in direct competition with North American and the local companies.[26] At the same time the company was undergoing an internal power struggle. The new management installed was basically the same as that of the Columbia Phonograph Company, with whom a close relationship developed, since it was one of the more successful local companies.

> With small sums of money borrowed from the last remaining friends of the [American Graphophone] Company, whose judgment and tenacity of faith in ultimate success have since been fully justified, a few machines of an improved design were built in a little factory at Bridgeport. By using to the best advantage our remaining material, this borrowed money sufficed for the purpose, and every energy was concentrated in the effort to increase cash receipts. Manufacturing was done only to meet requirements, and practically at no more rapid rate than the returns from the sales of the existing machines would permit. The business was conducted in this cautious and tentative way until 1895.[27]

In the context of the series of business failures and suspensions that became known as the Panic of 1893, the caution of American Graphophone and North American is understandable. The last known issue of *Phonogram* was published in March–April 1893, as local companies went under and economic conditions worsened, and the fourth and last annual meeting of the National Phonograph Association took place the same year.

In June, Edison formally assumed the presidency of the North American Phonograph Company, while the responsibility of its day-to-day operation was placed in the hands of his private secretary, A. O. Tate, who was made vice president. Thomas Lombard, the previous vice president, became general manager. As sales of machines continued to the independent subcompanies and were shipped to England in violation of Edison's agreements with the Edison United Phonograph Company, North American was repeatedly asked to furnish its machines with a plate limiting their use to the United States. Just as often, the company refused to do so. In December 1893, suit was brought in the New Jersey courts, the supporting papers citing the delivery of a machine by one Holland to J. Lewis Young.[28]

Steven F. Moriarty, the chief figure reporting to Theodore Seligman, was certain that Tate was behind the sales, and in March 1894 he succeeded in having Tate dismissed; he was replaced by William Gilmore. Strictures placed upon the sale of machines to England caused the situation to worsen for North American and the local companies. Edison received a promissory note for $78,518.37 on April 1, 1892, on which North American regularly paid interest. In addition, a series of bonds had been issued upon which interest was due on May 1, 1894. The terms of the notes and bonds made the principal due even if the interest was not paid. North American was unable to meet those payments.

Discerning that North American would never straighten out its tangled finances, Edison saw a way to free himself of the company and recover his Edison Phonograph Company stock. He secretly arranged to have suit brought to appoint a receiver and to wind up North American's affairs. Suit was brought in the name of Walter Cutting, the executor of the estate of R. L. Cutting, on August 16, 1894, and John R. Hardin was appointed receiver on August 21, 1894.[29]

As Hardin got to work, some of North American's creditors made their opinions known. Michael W. Nolan wrote to the receiver on April 9, 1895, demanding that he take immediate steps to abrogate the pretended sale of the Edison Phonograph Company stock of 1894. Nolan's petition could not have come at a worse moment for Edison, as he had just responded to an offer circulated by the receiver to entertain bids on the assets of the North American Phonograph Company. The value of the phonographs, graphophones, parts, and appliances as recently as 1894 had been placed at $40,000, according to the circular, which also specified that the purchaser would obtain title to all stocks of the local companies that had been deposited or due for North American. The offer contemplated the sale as a profitable one: "All the good will of the business of the North American Phonograph Company, the same having been preserved by the Receiver by prompt and faithful attention to all legitimate demands of the trade from the time of his appointment until now, the Company being, for business purposes, a going concern." Edison had bid $125,000. As a result of Nolan's petition, the sale was not only voided, but Edison was also required to abrogate the courthouse sale and return the title to his patents to North American.[30]

As the *New York Tribune* reported on May 29, 1895, other developments complicated the North American situation. New England Phonograph sued the receiver for its 6,000 shares deposited with North American for rights that were to exist through July 1, 1895. New York Phonograph sued for monies due at the time of the initiation of the receivership and for additional sums due on phonographs and supplies sold in New York thereafter. It looked as if it would be some time before the affairs of North American could be settled.

Edison was forced to bide his time, an exercise that must have proven particularly painful in light of a letter American Graphophone Company sent to most of the principals in the phonograph industry soon after North American's receivership was instituted:

> Notice is hereby given that ALL who USE, BUY or sell the so-called EDISON PHONOGRAPH are INFRINGING the PATENTS of the AMERICAN GRAPHOPHONE COMPANY, and are subject to PROSE-CUTION in the Courts.
>
> The American Graphophone Co. preferred to settle first with the larger infringers, but their disappearance renders this course impossible. It has therefore been determined to give notice to all who use or deal in the phonograph that they must immediately cease so doing or answer to this company in damages.[31]

American Graphophone became an even more formidable adversary in October 1895 when a new slate of officers was elected, and president and counsel became Edward D. Easton. In the early part of 1895, the *Washington Post* reported on October 19,

> there was a practical consolidation of the American Graphophone Company and the Columbia Phonograph Company, by the acquirement of the capital stock of the latter. From this point full advantage could be and was taken of the ability and organization of the Columbia Company. This step was soon followed by the acquirement of the Columbia Phonograph Company, General. The American Graphophone Company then assumed the position of

a manufacturing company only, with the two Columbia Companies as the distributors of its product.

Borrowing money for factory enlargements, American Graphophone was able to retire a bonded indebtedness of $60,000.[32]

At the same time, American Graphophone began to modify the cylinder carriers to accommodate the solid "wax" Edison cylinders and spring motors. Local companies also incorporated the spring motors, which meant it was now profitable for them to trim their North American machine inventories.[33]

The Edison Phonograph Works found itself blocked in its efforts to resume manufacturing phonographs. Only machines incomplete in November 1895 could be completed and sold through North American, with the stipulation that they were for use in the United States and Canada only. The following individuals and companies were banned from engaging in any of the transactions: "James Lewis Young, R. M. Leonard, George E. Tewksbury, Victor H. Emerson, S. S. Ott, Kansas Phonograph Company, United States Phonograph Company, Walcutt, Miller & Company and Holland Brothers." In a related action the Edison Phonograph Works was enjoined from manufacturing and selling directly within the United States.[34]

It was now even more important for the Edison forces to seek a solution to the North American receivership. If matters were allowed to drag, the graphophone interests would corner the market—either through court challenges or through marketing strategies. Edison now made agreements with Michael Nolan and Charles Boston, two of the chief objectors to the 1895 sale of North American assets. He promised each a specified amount plus a portion of the amount that he promised to pay North American's creditors.[35]

On January 29, 1896, John Hardin again offered the assets of North American for sale, specifying sale by the receiver "subject to all claims and litigations affecting the property to be conveyed, and the Receiver will not guarantee the property so sold against patent or other litigation. The right, title and interest of the North American Phonograph Company and of its Receiver is all that the Receiver undertakes to sell and all that he will expect to convey, and the purchaser buys at his own risk." [36]

Edison was willing to take that risk and made a bid on February 8, 1896, the result of another series of moves by the Edison forces. In January 1896 a new firm, the National Phonograph Company, had been established. On January 28 its board of directors had received and accepted the following proposal from Edison:

> I am the owner of allowed claims against the North American Phono-
> graph Company aggregating Five Hundred and Sixty Thousand Nine Hun-
> dred and Five Dollars and Ninety One Cents constituting about 95% of
> the total claims against that company allowed by its Receiver. The Receiver
> has on hand now about $30,000 in cash and owns a number of Phonograph
> patents, and stock in other phonograph companies. I offer to sell and assign
> to you the said claims and all my right, title and interest therein, for $10,000;
> $1,000 in cash and the balance in full paid stock of your company.[37]

The receiver refused to allow the Edison group to split their bid. As soon as the sale went through, however, it was requested that the property be split into two parcels. To the National Phonograph Company would go the patents, the Edison Phonograph Company, the supplies still owned by North American, and any cash paid on the final settlement of the North American accounts. The other parcel consisted of the local phonograph company stock and the contracts with them. In this way, Edison's advisers apparently tried to insulate the transaction from later attack.[38]

Even after North American's assets were sold, the receivership continued until litigations against it were settled. The claim of the New York Phonograph Company was settled, the receiver being ordered to pay a 10 percent royalty on all phonographs and supplies sold in the state of New York. A compromise was reached in the American Graphophone Company suit directed against North American and its receiver when North American admitted infringement and paid $1,750. On September 1, 1896, the New England Phonograph Company petition for the return of its stock was disallowed. Almost all of the outstanding litigation had now been settled except the suit of the Edison United Phonograph Company, which would continue to prevent the North American Phonograph Company from being laid to rest.[39]

A year and a half later, on April 28, 1898, an appeal of the Edison United Phonograph Company was disallowed, an action that caused the receiver to apply for final distribution of assets and extinction of North American. On August 2, 1898, it was "ordered, adjudged and decreed that the said North American

Phonograph Company be and the same is hereby dissolved, and its charter forfeited and void."[40]

Even though the Edison group obviously intended to abrogate the local companies' exclusive contracts, they used one in their battle with the American Graphophone Company. Numerous infringement suits had been brought against American Graphophone as a counter to suits against the Edison Phonograph Works. In mid-1896 an action was brought by the Edison lawyers: *The New York Phonograph Company vs. the American Graphophone Co.* Previous successes of American Graphophone in the courts made it extremely problematical that the Edison groups would prevail. Consequently the Edison groups and American Graphophone agreed to settle their differences in early December 1896. Each agreed to admit infringement of the other's patents and to cross-license the other. As a portion of the general agreement, all suits were discontinued.[41]

Once the suits were settled, the local companies soon awoke to the fact that they were in serious trouble. The National Phonograph Company was perfectly willing to sell to them, but only as a dealer, not as an exclusive dealer, in their territory. The U.S. Phonograph Company continued to do business with National, but at the end of 1897 U.S. Phonograph lost its privileged position. Soon a new dealer and exporter, Prescott, in conjunction with Stevens, assumed the position. Apparently worried about possible problems, National and the Edison Phonograph Works froze Prescott out, with the result that Prescott sued Edison.[42]

The New York Phonograph Company on several occasions attempted without success to meet with Edison to determine his future plans. The former Ohio Phonograph Company was forced into receivership and eventually sold—reemerging as the Edison Phonograph Company, with headquarters in Cincinnati, which proclaimed that it had retained the former rights of the Ohio Phonograph Company. The new company opened branches in Chicago and Dayton.[43] Ohio's promoter, James L. Andem, complained about Ohio's territory being thrown open after the North American bankruptcy. In the fall of 1899 he brought suit against a Cincinnati firm, Ilsen and Company, claiming they had been invading the territory of the former Ohio Phonograph Company for the past three years.[44]

Andem also took measures that were to prove momentous for the National Phonograph Company. His company became the first of the "Local Phonograph Companies to bring suit for an enforcement of territorial rights. They sued the National Phonograph Co. for $50,000 damages." The suit was still pending in

September 1900, "the court having refused to dismiss on demurrer of defendant's counsel." The Columbia Phonograph Company, also involved with the courts, successfully maintained its territory from "unlawful intrusion . . . and thereby protected its revenues." With this background a call was sent out by the Executive Committee of the old National Phonograph Association for the local companies to meet and consider "the present condition of the local phonograph companies' contracts terminating March 26, 1903 and the best method for enforcing same." The meeting was scheduled for September 25, 1900.[45]

At the convention a special committee was established to carry out a plan of concerted action. The committee consisted of A. W. Clancey, the former chair of the association; James L. Andem; Edward D. Easton; Robert C. Kinkead of the Kentucky Phonograph Company; and Lemuel E. Evans of New York City (presumably representing Charles A. Cheever of New England Phonograph and New York Phonograph).[46] Armed with a resolution, Andem entered into agreements with many of the local companies to act as their agent in bringing suits against the National Phonograph Company and Thomas A. Edison, to enforce their rights. The major litigants were New York Phonograph, New England Phonograph, and New Jersey Phonograph.[47]

With the prospect of litigation before them, Edison and his colleagues attempted to insulate themselves from possible consequences. In the 1890s Edison had begun using the talents of Joseph P. McCoy to act as a general jack-of-all-trades and what would now be called an industrial spy. In the guise of a stockbroker, McCoy acted for Edison's lawyer, Howard W. Hayes, and began secretly to buy shares in the three major companies as they appeared on the market. By 1904 the Edison forces had acquired enough stock to give them effective control of New Jersey Phonograph and New England Phonograph. In spite of contracts that Andem had made with these companies, he found it difficult to continue the suits. Without access any longer to the New Jersey Phonograph seal, in one instance Andem filed papers to which a blank wax wafer was attached. The Edison group saw their opportunity and brought Andem's action to the notice of the local federal attorney, who put Andem on trial for his actions. Following extensive testimony, the jury was directed by the judge to return a verdict of not guilty. In other instances, there were court challenges concerning the annual meetings of both New England Phonograph and New York Phonograph. At one point Edison's agents stole meeting minutes and at least some of the financial reports of New

York Phonograph. Edison was not alone in taking such questionable actions—the entire talking-machine industry was in a rough-and-tumble phase.

By the end of 1908 a multitude of suits was directed against Edison and his phonograph companies as well as local state actions against dealers and distributors:

> In the U. S. Circuit Court for the South District of New York:
>
> New York Phonograph Company against the National Phonograph Company, Thomas A. Edison, the Edison Phonograph Company and the Edison Phonograph Works.
>
> In the United States Circuit Court for the District of New Jersey:
>
> 1) Wisconsin Phonograph Co. against the same defendants
>
> 2) Minnesota Phonograph Co. against the same defendants
>
> 3) Illinois Phonograph Co. against the same defendants
>
> 4) New England Phonograph Co. against the same defendants
>
> 5) Missouri Phonograph Co. against the same defendants
>
> 6) Ohio Phonograph Co. against the same defendants
>
> 7) Kansas Phonograph Co. against the same defendants
>
> 8) Kentucky Phonograph Co. against the same defendants.[48]

The New York Phonograph Company suit was generally considered the major suit, and evidence gathered in that suit would be admissible in other actions. Suit was brought in January 1901 for damages and to restrain the National Phonograph Company from selling phonographs and supplies in the state of New York. The Edison forces demurred. The demurrer was overruled, and a special plea was entered. After a great quantity of testimony, this action was overruled and the defendants compelled to answer. The final court hearing was held on May 31, 1904, and on January 5, 1905, the court reached its decision. It directed an accounting for damages but denied an injunction. The complainant moved for a rehearing, and in April the court corrected its opinion and granted an injunction. The Edison group appealed, the circuit court of appeals upheld the judgment, and the Edison forces continued to violate court orders. A motion to punish for contempt was now entertained by the court, which agreed that the defendants were guilty of contempt and imposed a fine of $2,500. In view of the continuing legal maneuvers, it is not surprising that the head of the National Phonograph Company at this time was Frank L. Dyer, a patent attorney.[49]

The fine of $2,500 was appealed, but the circuit court of appeals affirmed the order on March 16, 1909. Dyer now wrote to Edison that they had exhausted all means of defense and that he could not see any way out except through a settlement. Even settling was not easy because the New York Phonograph Company had contracted with attorney Samuel F. Hyman to institute local New York cases against Edison distributors and dealers. Several hundred suits had now been brought. Hyman was to pay New York Phonograph a fee of $5,000 and was to receive 50 percent of the proceeds arising from any settlements.[50]

The settlement proposed by Dyer and accepted by the management of New York Phonograph was $405,000 for New York Phonograph and an additional $20,000 for Hyman. Any stock controlled by Edison was not to be included in the windfall. In addition, Edison's group was to acquire enough additional stock to control the company. After several additional complications, the long period of warfare with the local companies came to an end.[51]

At the end, besides Louis Hicks, the New York Phonograph Company was represented by John C. Tomlinson, who in 1888 with Gilliland had arranged the sale of the Edison Phonograph Company agency contract for a $250,000 payment in North American Phonograph Company stock. When Edison had discovered the secret agreement making it possible for Gilliland and Tomlinson to trade the stock in for a payment at par, he had objected to Jesse Lippincott. The delays thus occasioned in the sale of the North American stock and other delays occasioned by the dispute with the Edison Speaking Phonograph Company had slowed Lippincott and eventually led to the downfall of the North American Phonograph Company.

With the sale of controlling interest in the New York Phonograph Company, the local companies lost their raison d'être. The exact dates for the dissolution of the various companies is not known, except for the most prominent—the Columbia Phonograph Company applied to West Virginia for a voluntary dissolution. After the appropriate resolution by the directors and the proper period of advertising, Columbia ceased to exist as of June 1913.[52]

Thus the experiment of handling the talking-machine business through a parent company and local sales companies ended. The concept itself did not die, for large companies would subsequently operate through regional distributing companies who in turn would have exclusive rights within allotted territories.

CHAPTER 5

The Edison Talking-Doll Phonograph

THE EARLIEST mention of incorporating an Edison phonograph into a doll or other toy is November 23, 1877. On a laboratory note sheet Edison wrote:

I propose to apply the phonograph principle to make dolls speak, sing, cry, and make various sounds, also apply it to all kinds of toys such as dogs, animals, fowls, reptiles, and human figures, to cause them to make various sounds. To steam toy engines installation of exhaust and whistle, to reproduce from sheets, music both orchestral, instrumental, and vocal. The idea being to use a plate machine with perfect registration and stamp the music out in a press from a die or punch previously prepared by cutting in steel or from an electrotype or cast from the original on tin foil. A family may have one machine and 1000 sheets of this music thus giving endless amusement. I also propose to make toy music boxes and toy talking boxes playing several tunes and speaking several sentences. Also to clocks and watches for calling out the time of day or waking a person up for advertisements rotated continuously by clockwork to call the attention of passers by. I propose to make it loud by building up or enlarging the original vibrations or indentations by laying them out and cutting in steel or building up by electrolysis and other ways. The method for preparing a wheel or plate for toys is by stamping or casting of the same, if a wheel or band is stamped and put around it. It may replace a man on a telephone at either end by holding the telephone to the spkg. tube or the receiving magnet may be connected to work the iron diaphragm with toys or apparatus in which only reproduction is required. The character may either be indented or raised.[1]

As with other forms of the tinfoil phonograph, Edison seemed to have gotten sidetracked by the urgency of his work on the electric light. It was not until 1887 that a new impetus for phonographs within toys surfaced.

W. W. Jacques, a friend of Edward Johnson, experimenter, and electrical expert with the American Bell Telephone Company (95 Milk Street, Boston), became aware of the entertainment potentials of phonographic toys. His experiments in developing a workable internal mechanism were somewhat successful, for Johnson advised Edison on June 23, 1887, "My Boston friends are at work upon the toy application—they have been here today and showed me their apparatus."[2]

Licensing and contracting with the Edison interests was the next step, and on October 1, 1887, a contract was drawn up between Edison and Jacques and Jacques's co-worker, Lowell C. Briggs:

(1) The contract itself licensed the group under the Edison patent 200,521 and was "to use the invention or improvement . . . so far as the same may be applicable to dolls and toy figures."

(2) Edison authorized the signatories to enter into foreign marketing and manufacturing arrangements provided he received the same royalty—10 percent of the selling price.

(3) It was understood and agreed "that no right or authority was granted to use and employ the said invention in clocks or for any purpose useful in business or commercial transactions, or in the arts and sciences, or for any useful purpose other than the amusement of children as a part of the articles mentioned."

(4) The license would be in existence for nine months unless the group paid royalties as specified in the contract amounting to $4,000. After the initial period the foreign royalties were to amount to at least $10,000 a year or the contract would cease.

(5) Briggs and Jacques had the right to assign the contract to others so long as the internal details were maintained by the new principals.[3]

Jacques and Briggs were now in a position to organize a corporation for the purpose of "manufacturing, owning, buying and selling all kinds of phonograph toys and implements, to license others to manufacture, own, buy, sell, or otherwise deal in such toys whether made under such patents or not."[4] A second agreement between Briggs and Jacques and Edison outlined rights for foreign marketing.

Charles Batchelor, thorough experimenter and meticulous notetaker, detailed his own experimentation in a notebook entry on March 31, 1888, the following year: "Very good talking, but, in repeating, the work to be done by the needle is great and it shortly distorts the talking or it stretches the foil. The 2 ¼-inch diaphragm is too large as the travel it makes, added to its width, makes the apparatus too wide to go in the doll. 1 ½ inch is as much as we can allow." Besides tinfoil as the recording medium, Batchelor tried thin sheets of copper, which seemed to produce a loud and clear result. A cylinder made of a mixture of asphalt and hard carnauba wax gave loud, clear talking with no scratch. A 1:1 cylinder of lead and tin also gave good results. By April 16, Batchelor had decided to make the toy phonograph "like the regular phonograph, but provided with a cylinder to take a number of tin rings on. Thus we can talk at least 15 times and take them off and mount them on the toys, or we can have the words put on a cylinder a large number of times and then cut the cylinder up into small pieces and mount each piece in a toy."⁵

Increased experimentation caused Edison to extend contract limitations with Briggs and Jacques. The phonographic toy apparatus was not performing as it should. By January 10, 1889, Edison was prepared to furnish the Jacques contingent with toy phonograph mechanisms for 500 dolls. The cost of the mechanism was estimated at ninety-seven cents. In this experimental period Julia Miller was paid $2.60 (twenty-six hours at ten cents an hour) for speaking into the toy phonograph at the Edison laboratory.⁶

The new toy phonograph was much heralded in the press. The *Brooklyn Times,* June 13, 1889, claimed "that phonographic cats could now purr, meow, spit, and caterwaul; a horse, neigh and whinny; a sheep bleat in a way that would deceive the mother ewe. Melodies of the lark, finch, robin, and canary bird can be reproduced indefinitely. Thus an artificial canary can outsing a natural one, and the entire repertoire of high-priced birds be preserved." Yet six months later, Alfred Tate, Edison's private secretary, had to admit to Jesse Lippincott, president of North American Phonograph, that there were only several dolls that could talk well, while most got of order quite easily. The experimental period was not over.⁷

Jacques evidently did not consider an unreliable product reason enough to forgo the establishment of foreign rights. He contracted with William Hope Dean for rights in Canada and Newfoundland, and with M. O. Madden in Europe. Newly established factories in Paris and Geneva were to be managed by Edison's former friend, Ezra Gilliland, a choice that did not sit well with Edison, for he soon began to look for ways to revoke the toy company's license.

By July 1889, after much negotiation, agreements were signed between the Edison Phonograph Toy Manufacturing Company and both the Edison Phonograph Company and the North American Phonograph Company.[8] The phonograph factory at Orange now was set to turn out talking-doll mechanisms for inclusion in imported doll bodies. Charles Batchelor admonished Edison Phonograph Toy Manufacturing for not seeing that the dolls were sewn in such a manner that they could be taken apart, in order to put the phonograph inside. He also said that the head should be made with a hole in the top, covered by hair, to let out the sound.[9]

Benjamin F. Stevens was chosen as president of Edison Phonograph Toy Manufacturing, edging a disgruntled Jacques out of company management. Jacques noted that British patent 20,257 had been issued to him on December 17, 1889, for "Improvement in Phonographs," and that under a series of foreign applications covering a much simpler and more economical construction of the talking doll, he would now have exclusive rights to manufacture and sell the talking doll in England, Germany, and the United States. Tate expressed the fury of the Edison group by cabling that Edison's British representative had filed one week previous and that the best course of action for Jacques was to resign his directorship. Jacques did resign on April 26, 1890.[10]

Although Jacques had foreseen the problems of imperfect dolls in his many patents on talking-doll mechanisms, it became clear that the strained relations between Jacques and the presiding officers of the toy company would prevent many of his constructive ideas from being put into practice.[11] As a result, no successful domestic or foreign toy business was established. Manufacture was suspended in May 1890, a month after Jacques's resignation. Prospects for an invigorated approach faded, and S. B. Eaton, Edison's lawyer, drew up the formal revocation of contract with the toy company based on the nonpayment of royalties:

I, the said Thomas A. Edison, hereby elect to exercise the option given me by the said second paragraph of the Second Section of the said agreement, in the event of the non-payment of the guaranteed royalties as therein and thereby provided, and do hereby terminate the aforesaid contract and all rights of the said Edison Phonograph Toy Manufacturing Company, of every kind of nature whatsoever thereunder, as of the 23rd day of March, 1891, because of the failure of the said Edison Phonograph Toy Manufacturing Company to pay the royalties aggregating Five thousand dollars, due under and by virtue of the provisions of said agreement on or before the 31st day of October, 1890.[12]

On November 20, 1895, an agreement was reached between Edison Phonograph Toy Manufacturing and Edison Phonograph Works and Thomas A. Edison and John W. Mackintosh, mortgagee, and John W. Mackintosh and William E. Gilmore, trustees, as follows:

> *FIRST:* All said dolls, both disjointed and fitted with metal bodies, now at Orange aforesaid, are hereby bargained, sold and conveyed [to representatives of the toy company and of Edison], . . . the same to be held in trust by them and sold by them without any compensation to them, to the best possible advantage. All phonographic apparatus in the bodies of any of said dolls shall be taken out of the same and destroyed by and at the expense of the said parties . . . before such dolls are delivered. . . .
>
> *SECOND:* All contracts and suits would be cancelled.
>
> *THIRD:* The Edison Phonograph Toy Manufacturing Company in case it shall resume business, is to change its name so that the name "Edison" shall no longer be part of its corporate title.
>
> *FOURTH:* Edison to relinquish all of his shares in the Company for cancellation.[13]

Edison's toy company thus concluded its tenure of operation after only a few years of manufacture, albeit under extremely volatile circumstances.

CHAPTER 6

The New Graphophone

IN 1893, after the Detroit convention of the local phonograph companies had tentatively approved Thomas Lombard's plan for restoring all sales rights to the North American Phonograph Company, nearly a year was required to straighten out difficulties and to put through contracts with each of the companies. The only company that refused to sign an agreement, Columbia Phonograph, was in a unique position by virtue of its having acquired sales rights for the graphophone for the District of Columbia, Maryland, and Delaware *prior* to the organization of North American and the resulting acquisition by Lippincott of the graphophone sales rights for the rest of the United States. This situation enabled Columbia Phonograph to claim that these rights, conceded to Lippincott when Columbia was functioning under the local company plan in exchange for equal sales rights for the Edison phonograph in the same territory, now reverted to the Columbia Phonograph Company.

Edward Easton, Columbia's shrewd president, saw the opportunity of a lifetime. He and his associates, among whom were R. F. Cromelin, Andrew Devine, and James Clephane, agreed upon a plan, which if successful, would put them in control of a great industry. To assist them in their new scheme, Easton enlisted the aid of brilliant Washington attorney Philip Mauro. Briefly, the plan was this. If these men, some of whom already possessed stock in the American Graphophone Company, could gain control of that company and its Bell-Tainter patents, they might well be able to take advantage of the demoralized state of the industry. After all, Edison was not in possession of his own patents on phonographic achievements.

As American Graphophone stock was at the time practically worthless, it was fairly simple to execute the first step of the plan. On May 1, 1893, the new group assumed control of American Graphophone, with Easton as president.

The next step was the appointment as factory manager of Thomas H. Mac-Donald, who had attracted the favorable attention of Easton through improvements he had made on the earlier Edison phonograph, improvements that Edison had adopted. Thousands of inoperable Bell-Tainter graphophones in the factory were promptly scrapped. Through economizing and borrowing from company friends, MacDonald was able to produce a new type of machine that would work satisfactorily.[1] The machine had a tapered mandrel, solid metallic wax blanks, sapphire recording and reproducing styli, and a spring motor. For the first time cylinders were employed that were interchangeable with those of the Edison phonograph, and the recorded cylinders were cut to the Edison-established standard of 100 threads to the inch.

By late 1896, with the aid of Philip Mauro, the American Graphophone Company was able to resolve patent problems between the Edison interests and Columbia Phonograph. Delays in the settlement of North American Phonograph's liquidation gave the graphophone faction added impetus, for the Edison interests did not fare well.[2]

Knowing that it would be easier to establish an imposing record of validity for the Bell-Tainter patents against people who had no patents than against those who had, Mauro brought suit against a number of firms that had been manufacturing machines or blanks without benefit of patents. One of these precedent-setting cases was *American Graphophone Co. v. Edward H. Amet of Waukegan, Illinois.* Amet had been making and selling a machine allegedly for reproducing graphophone records, thereby infringing on the Bell-Tainter patents. Amet claimed that he was not infringing because he did not make cylinder or sound records but merely reproduced them, and that the art of so doing was available to the world. Judge Grosscup in the U.S. Circuit Court for the Northern District of Illinois granted a permanent injunction and ordered an accounting of Amet's profits and the Graphophone Company damages. This case was destined to be cited in case after case brought by American Graphophone against other purported infringers.

With the more important portions of the Bell-Tainter patents sustained by the courts, American Graphophone now was in a position to broaden its base. By the latter part of the year the company was ready to unveil its own inexpensive machine, the Eagle, designed to cost one American gold eagle—ten dollars. National Phonograph was not to be outmaneuvered and introduced its own ten-dollar machine, the Gem. It was fortuitous that a slough in economic activity occurred in June 1897. The two new machines could be introduced in the environment of a recovering economy.[3]

American Graphophone's new MacDonald graphophones were designed primarily for the home market, although some models were made for dictating purposes and coin operation. To compete, Edison put out in April 1896 his first spring-motor phonograph, which the *New York Electrical Review* described in its April 8 issue:

The recent announcement that Mr. Thomas A. Edison had bought back from the receivers of the North American Phonograph Company his own property and rights is followed by the placing on the market of the new Edison phonograph, here illustrated. This machine is being built at the Edison Phonograph Works at Orange, N. J. and will be handled by the National Phonograph Company, which is now establishing agencies everywhere for its sale.

The new machines conform in a general way to the older type, but it has two decided elements of novelty. One is that it is operated by a spring motor, the other is that it is to be sold for about $40, thus placing the instrument within the reach of everybody, as a formidable rival to the music box.

The thread on the main shaft is 100 to the inch, so that standard music cylinders, of which there are now thousands, can be used. It is so arranged that multiple tubes can be employed, enabling several persons to listen at once, and it is also furnished, when desired, with a large horn and stand, answering the needs of a large audience. . . . The machine is fitted for reproducing only, but for a small extra charge it is built also to record, or to do both.[4]

Sales of the new spring-motor Edison phonograph were brisk, which led American Graphophone attorneys and publicists to prepare a circular for wide distribution to the trade warning against buying Edison goods:

American Graphophone Company
           Washington, D.C., Oct. 15, 1896

The American Graphophone Co. owns the fundamental patents which created and cover the talking machine art as it is known and practiced today; and every so-called "Edison Phonograph," unless it indents in tinfoil, infringes these patents. All of the so-called improved Edison Phonographs manufactured in 1889 were made under a license from the Graphophone Co. and paid the Graphophone Co. a royalty until Jesse H. Lippincott, President of North American Phonograph Co. became bankrupt. Since then suits for infringement, injunction, accounting, etc. have been vigorously pressed against the Edison Phonograph Works, the United States Phonograph Co., the Ohio Phonograph Co., the New England Phonograph Co., and others. Already, several judgments have been entered in our favor, the latest being against the Receiver of the North American Phonograph Co., who voluntarily submitted to an injunction and paid damages.

The suit against Edison, the U. S. Phonograph Co., and others was argued in Sept., 1896 before Judge Green in the U.S. Circuit Court in Trenton, N. J., although the defendants did everything in their power to retard trial, and for a time succeeded in postponing a hearing by urging upon the court that no phonograph had been made since 1889, and that they were doing substantially no business.

Shortly after final hearing Judge Green died suddenly, leaving the case undecided. This delay has emboldened the infringers, and they are now reembarking in the business with a hastily constructed type of phonograph, some of which they hope to market before another judge can rehear and act upon our suit, leaving the purchasers of these machines to settle with us. We are pressing the matter with all possible haste in the courts, and meanwhile give public notice that every individual, firm or corporation who sells or uses the so-called Edison Phonograph, or appliances therefore, does so unlawfully and will be *legally accountable* to this company in damages.

                    American Graphophone Co.
                    E. D. Easton, President

Naturally, the Edison camp had to reply:

National Phonograph Co.
Orange, New Jersey[5]

Our attention has been called to a circular letter dated Oct. 15, 1896 and signed and distributed by the American Graphophone Co., warning the public against the use or sale of Edison phonographs and appliances.

It is generally known beyond dispute that Mr. Edison, and not the Graphophone Co., invented the phonograph. Most persons and concerns interested in the talking machine enterprise understand the controversy between the two interests too well to be misled by the Graphophone Co.'s reckless statements.

As to the Graphophone Co.'s claim that its "fundamental patents" created and cover the talking machine art, it seems sufficient to call to mind the dismal failure which met the graphophone, made some years ago under those patents—a failure which continued up to the time the Graphophone Co. appropriated the Edison improvements which made the phonograph a success.

The entry of the "several judgments" in the Graphophone Co.'s favor, as referred to in the circular letter, was upon consent and in no ways affected the merits of the Graphophone Co.'s patents. Particularly is this true as to the decree against the Receiver of the North American Phonograph Co., which was consented to in order to expedite the distribution of the assets in the receiver's hands. The Graphophone Co. has never yet obtained a judgment at final hearing and upon a full showing of the facts. It did obtain, in Chicago, a final decree upon two of its claims, but this case was tried upon affidavits, and not on the customary oral evidence, and the case was manifestly so incomplete that on Nov. 10, 1896, the U. S. Circuit Court for the Southern District of New York, refused to follow the Chicago decision, and denied a motion made by the Graphophone Co. for a preliminary injunction under the same claims.

The Graphophone Co. has never sued Mr. Edison, nor the Edison Phonograph Co. as stated in its letter to the public. One of the suits argued before Judge Green in September has been pending nearly four years. If the Graphophone Co. had confidence in its patents this case would have been tried and decided long ago.

Suits are now pending against the Graphophone Co.'s factory and selling agents for infringements of the Edison patents on the phonograph improvements which the graphophone was forced to adopt to keep before the public. We believe that a decision on these suits will set the present controversy at rest for all time. Then the only persons or concerns "legally accountable" will be the handlers of the graphophones who have invaded our patent rights in the Edison Phonograph.

> National Phonograph Co.
> W. S. Mallory, President[6]

Hereafter, the progress of the battle may be followed in *Phonoscope,*[6] the first independent publication devoted primarily to the phonograph field. Coincidentally, *Phonoscope* was launched when this furor was at its height—November 15, 1896. The editor would comment in the April 1897 issue:

> We have had many inquiries relating to the cause and result of the late legal trouble between the Phonograph and Graphophone Companies. We print the claims of both concerns as put forth in circulars issued by their parent companies of the rival parties during the recent controversy. We are pleased to say, however, that the trouble has been amicably settled, and both concerns are now working for the general interest of the talking machine.

An uneasy truce between the two factions was to prove not more than a lull in the ongoing battle, although neither side seemed willing to risk an all-out court decision on patent superiority. Statements concerning the settlement were issued by American Graphophone's legal staff to the press on December 18, 1896, and a story in the *Brooklyn Eagle* the following day is in substantial agreement with the known settlement terms:

> The litigation which has been proceeding for several years between the American Graphophone Co., of Washington, D.C. and Thomas A. Edison and the Edison Phonograph Works relative to the talking machine patents, has been brought to an amicable conclusion. Edison, it is stated by counsel for the Graphophone Co., admits the fundamental character of the graphophone patents, and that they control the commercial art of sound recording and reproducing as it is practiced today, and agrees to a decree of injunction in the principal case pending in the U. S. Circuit Court for the District of New Jersey. The American Graphophone Co., on the other hand, admits the validity of patents for various improvements which Edison has taken out

since the issuance of the graphophone patents, and consents to decrees in favor of Edison on those patents.

Shortly before such news stories appeared, Columbia Phonograph offered a spring-wound graphophone at the then unheard-of low price of twenty-five dollars, with discounts to the trade as high as 40 percent. It was a maneuver to keep Edison from getting a foothold in the home talking-machine market. Now, with the settlement of court cases making the adoption of Edison improvements legal for the first time, American Graphophone interests made use of another strategy. Columbia Phonograph had not surrendered its contract with North American, maintaining that the contract provisions were still enforceable upon Edison and the Edison Phonograph Works. Columbia Phonograph could thus still represent itself before the public as agents for the Edison Phonograph and demand that it be sold merchandise under the contract provisions.

In January 1897 Columbia Phonograph moved its main offices from Washington to New York City, where its chief sales activity was then centered. A three-story building prominently located on Broadway was secured, with offices and recording studios on the upper floors and the main floor given over to a large salesroom for machines and records. Large, electrically lighted signs the entire width of the building were placed above each of the three floors, as follows:

EDISON PHONOGRAPHS

THE PERFECTED GRAPHOPHONE

THE COLUMBIA PHONOGRAPH CO.

The stock of American Graphophone was soaring. Charles Sumner Tainter, who had not been with the company since its collapse, now secured himself a position there, as announced in the daily papers, including the *Washington Star* of July 30, 1897:

Prof. Charles Sumner Tainter, who with Prof. Alexander Graham Bell and Prof. Chichester Bell, invented the Graphophone, has entered the service of the American Graphophone Co. to conduct experiments looking to improvements in sound-recording and sound-reproducing apparatus. Prof. Tainter since the original invention has contributed much towards the improvement and perfecting of the talking machine. The talking machine as it is represented in the graphophone, was invented and improved in Washington and as a business enterprise the graphophone has been developed largely by Washington capital and energy.

The campaign of Easton and the Washington court reporters was succeeding handsomely, at least in a financial sense. The Edison interests meanwhile were in a bad way. In October 1897 Edison was forced to mortgage the Edison Phonograph Works for $300,000 to finance operations. The contrasting prosperity of American Graphophone was further emphasized when Washington, D.C., newspapers headlined Andrew Devine as a "Noted House Stenographer" and announced that he was leaving that remunerative post to accept the vice presidency of American Graphophone, of which he had been a founder and director, and to which he would henceforth devote all his time.

Philip Mauro and his staff were now so busy narrowing competition by eliminating the many opportunists who had entered the talking-machine field that Mauro felt an advertising department should be organized. Outstanding men in the newspaper business were brought in to prepare advertising and publicity, headed by Harry P. Godwin, then editor of the *Washington Star.* Mauro's ability to translate technical information and the legal phraseology of the courts into simple and meaningful English was never surpassed by his hired publicity experts, as talented as they were. From this time forward, however, the success of the graphophone seemed assured.

Not until 1898, with the introduction of the Edison Home Phonograph, did National Phonograph begin to compete successfully with the graphophone in the home market, employing a different marketing strategy than Columbia's. Columbia had gained much of its early success by opening showrooms in urban areas such as Boston, Chicago, Philadelphia, and St. Louis. In contrast, National Phonograph, finding the big-city competition too difficult because of the lower prices of the graphophone, concentrated on securing outlets in the smaller towns or through farm mail-order houses, such as Babson Brothers, Chicago. Two other influences helped establish the Edison phonograph in rural areas: first, the isolation of farmers in remote areas made for ready acceptance of the more rugged, dependable Edison machine; second, the admiration of rural people for Thomas A. Edison, the great inventor, knew no bounds. Magazines and papers received in rural homes carried little anti-Edison propaganda. When a luckless graphophone salesperson did venture into a farmhouse to deliver the Columbia sales pitch ("Did you know that Edison was not the inventor of the phonograph?"), he was fortunate to escape without bodily injury. These influences that shaped the growth patterns of the cylinder industry were to affect the disc talking-machine industry later. For similar reasons, the disc gramophone and its successor, the Victor talking machine, were to have their initial success in urban areas, while the phonograph continued to expand its market outside the large cities. The American Graphophone Company, trying to ride both horses, was caught in a stretch of its own making.

CHAPTER 7

The Bettini Story

TO ENTERTAIN READERS, authors may understandably tend to seize upon the more fascinating or dramatic episodes of a period and develop them out of proportion to their actual importance. Such is the case in stories of the phonographic achievements of Gianni Bettini. Born in 1860, in Novara, Italy, to a family of the landed gentry, Bettini received, as was the nineteenth-century custom for young men of his class, a gentleman's education, stressing languages, classical literature, and a grounding in the arts and music. Not particularly scholarly, he gravitated toward an army career; a dashing and handsome young man with a turned-up military mustache, he was striking in the uniform of a lieutenant in His Majesty's Italian cavalry.

The life of an Italian cavalry officer in those days offered considerable opportunity for travel and social enterprises. While on a visit to Paris Bettini met a vivacious young socialite, Daisy Abbott, of Stamford, Connecticut. Lieutenant Bettini gave up his military career, followed Daisy back to New York, and persuaded her to marry him. For a short time the newlyweds settled in Stamford, the home of the bride's parents. Perhaps Bettini grew bored with the somewhat staid existence of a country squire, for he soon began to evidence a great interest in mechanical contrivances and turned to inventing. The first product of his efforts reflected his musical background—a mechanical page turner.[1]

Sometime during the latter part of 1888 Bettini secured an improved Edison phonograph. Like others produced at that time, it was designed to serve as a business machine. Consequently, Bettini found it totally unsuitable for recording and reproducing the singing voice and music. From the beginning Bettini's purpose in recording was to make realistic and pleasing reproductions of the voices of accomplished singers. It was a worthwhile, if expensive, avocation; in its pursuit, he determined to move to New York where there were many great singers whom he might persuade to sing into his recording horn.

In analyzing the poor quality of the vocal records he made, Bettini came to the conclusion that the difficulty lay in the single point of contact of the cutting stylus with the diaphragm. He therefore designed a more flexible diaphragm made of mica, instead of the thin French glass, and attached four radial spurs from the stylus to the diaphragm. His device changed both the recording stylus and the reproducing stylus assemblies. His first phonograph patent describes the operation:

> Taking vibrations off a vibratory body at several points or places, communicating them to a common or central point or place by independent conductors, causing a record to be made from this common point or place, and then causing this record to act at the common or central point or place, communicating vibrations to a vibratory body at several points or places.[2]

Bettini found it difficult to get an audible impression in the cylinders, and consequently the quality of the reproduction lacked the clarity of timbre that would allow a listener to distinguish one voice from another. He found it unpleasant to use ear tubes, and a metal horn made the reproduction even poorer and lacking in musical quality.

Scientific American in its April 26, 1890, issue explained Bettini's purpose and theory with respect to his invention:

> Any reader of the daily papers must have noticed within the last few months frequent mention of a new instrument of the phonograph type, invented by Lieut. Gianni Bettini, an officer in the Italian navy, at present residing in this country. This gentleman conceived the idea of constructing a phonograph so as to be exceedingly sensitive to the different qualities of the tones of the human voice, and to reproduce those tones with the original qualities, so that the voice of the speaker could be easily recognized; and furthermore to produce uniformly good records without regard to the quality of the speaker's voice, also to secure a volume of sound which would compare favorably with that of a voice engaged in ordinary conversation, so that the words could be heard and understood without the necessity of employing stethoscopic ear tubes.

Every student of acoustics knows that vibrating membranes, strings, rods, columns of air, and thin plates of various kinds have active points and neutral points, and Lieut. Bettini has taken advantage of this fact in the construction of his instrument. He connects his recording stylus with the diaphragm at various points, to insure contact with one or more of the actively vibrating parts or centers of the diaphragm, thus avoiding the points of rest or nodes where little or no vibration occurs.

A further description of the Bettini method appeared in *Electrical World,* April 26, 1890:

The Micro-Graphophone.
An ingenious modification of the phonograph has recently been devised, that gives remarkable results in reproducing the human voice. The inventor is Lieut. Gianni Bettini, and he calls his improved apparatus a micrographophone. The object of the modification he has introduced into the existing phonograph was, to secure a reproduction of speech or music without the metallic tone sometimes so troublesome, and to secure a sufficient volume of sound to obviate the necessity of hearing tubes.

To secure these ends he employs several independent non-metallic diaphragms instead of the one diaphragm of the usual instrument. These diaphragms are all operated from a single stylus, which is supported on a spider, one leg of which rests on the center of each of the diaphragms. Lieut. Bettini's theory with regard to this arrangement of diaphragms is, that when each individual plate is small it vibrates as a whole instead of being thrown into forced segmentary vibrations that change the quality of the tone produced. Of course, in any vibrating diaphragm set in motion from the centre the vibration is of a very complex character. If the diaphragm be large, the vibration in the predominant vibration would be that of the whole; and, while overtones will undoubtedly exist, they will be of a less prominent character. In particular, anything like forced vibrations will be in a great measure avoided. In any large plate thrown into motion from a single point, that point might happen to be so chosen that it would fall at a vibration node of the plate, in which case it would fail to produce a proper motion of the whole.

This is Lieut. Bettini's theory, and the results he has obtained in practice are such as to render it exceedingly plausible. To secure a sufficient volume of sound while still using diaphragms of small size, several of them are, as we have said, connected by a spider, and act from a single stylus. The result appears to be that the effective vibrating surface is very much increased without a corresponding increase of the segmentary vibrations that produce a false tone color.

The arrangement of the instrument is, as will be seen from Fig. 1, very similar to that of the phonograph in ordinary use. The peculiarity exists in the arrangement of the diaphragms. These are non-metallic. In making the record in this machine, the single stylus receives the united impulses from all the diaphragms, and when this record is reproduced, all the diaphragms are correspondingly thrown into strong vibration. The result of this is that the micro-graphophone speaks with a volume of sound that is really remarkable. With a short and small trumpet it can be heard distinctly over a good-sized hall, the articulation being clear and non-metallic in spite of its loudness. When the trumpet is entirely removed so that the sound comes simply from the face of the diaphragms, the tone is still clear, and distinctly audible over an ordinary room.

It is hard to estimate the loudness of the sound, but the volume poured out by the four small diaphragms of this instrument is most amazing. They seem to work in perfect unison, and their tendency appears to be to reinforce rather than to deaden each other. The reproduction of the human voice is singularly clear and free from any harshness or metallic sound. By the use of a non-metallic trumpet the tones are still further softened. In reproducing music the notes of different pitch come out with singular distinctness, and the *timbre* of the voice is admirably preserved. It appears that by making the individual diaphragms small enough, so that the vibration produced by the stylus is the vibration of the whole, unusual loudness and a remarkable degree of distinctness have both been secured. While making the record, a comparatively low tone of voice is reproduced with remarkable distinctness. Even a whisper is whispered back from the diaphragms very clearly.

Bettini's "musical spider" legs were generally placed concentrically, not haphazardly. Only one of his models shows a random disposition of the legs.

If Bettini had indeed fashioned something of outstanding merit, one of the leading companies would probably have adopted it. Will Hayes of the Edison staff said that one of the Bettini attachments was available there but that the Edison experts considered it weak, though it produced good results.

Russell Hunting, the editor of *Phonoscope*, himself a prolific recorder, wrote in the November 1896 issue that "the records taken with the Bettini Micro-phonograph Diaphragms are wonderful for their solidity of tone and resonant carrying powers. Records of the female voice taken with the attachment are truly marvelous." Another commentator in the same issue wrote on the voice repro-duction accomplished by Colonel George Gouraud and Theodore Wangemann:

> Recently the writer had occasion to attend a phonograph recital. Among the cylinders used that night were some whereon Hon. W. E. Gladstone and the venerable Bismarck had recorded their voices. . . . I have read the speeches of Gladstone and Bismarck, but I did not know their spirit until I heard their voice on the cylinder of a phonograph. The body, the strength, the soft modulation, the emphasis, so faithfully reproduced by the delicate mecha-nism, the life thus imparted to the words, made them sink indelibly into my soul, showing to me the fullness of their power, the men whom till then I had only known vaguely.[3]

Of course, the comment referred only to the speaking voice.

J. Mount Bleyer, surgeon to the New York Throat Infirmary and editor of the *Electrical Review*, left important comparative information in a paper he entitled "The Edison Phonograph and the Bettini Micro-Phonograph—The Principles Underlying Them and the Fulfillment of their Expectations." Employed as a vocal consultant by many of the famous vocal artists of the time, Bleyer collected recordings (none of which have survived) of their voices much as Bettini had, but as a means of studying vocal-cord functioning and singing technics.

> It is a known fact that in instruments made in exactly the same way there is still perceptible a certain difference in the shade, the quality, or the timbre of their tones. So we find it with the human voice. A certain standard is necessary in order to judge the proper timbre, pitch and quality in a tenor, baritone, and a basso voice, as well as in a soprano, a mezzo-soprano, an alto, and a contralto. By bestowing some further experimental study on this subject, I am certain that shortly I can bring forward a standard as well as an additional new art to aid the learning of singing, etc.
>
> Some of the records which served me for my purpose were taken from celebrated tenors of the Metropolitan Opera House, as Julian Perotti, Andreas Dippel, Carl Streitman, Mr. Koppel, etc. Also singers Theodore

Reichmann, Emile Steger, Conrad Behrens, Felicia Koshofska, F. C. Nicolini, Nina Bertini, Helen Mora, Bertha Ricci, and many others less educated in the several arts.

Mr. Thomas A. Edison has interested himself in my behalf regarding these studies, and has specially built for me a phonograph which has many new attachments, besides a number of fine diaphragms on a new principle; with its recorder I shall be able to receive the fine tones and reproduce them.[4]

About this same time Edison sent an improved phonograph to Lionel Mapleson, librarian of the Metropolitan Opera Company, who set out immediately to secure recordings of live performances from the stage of the Metropolitan Opera. He at first concealed the recording phonograph in the prompter's box near the footlights, but its large horn blocked the view for some seatholders, resulting in numerous complaints. He then rigged the phonograph up on the catwalk just behind the proscenium arch, with the recording horn hanging below. Snatches of historic performances were secured, including some artists never available on commercial records, such as Jean DeReszke.

Mapleson also rigged up telephone wires to opera manager Fry's bedside at 38 Union Square from the Academy of Music about a quarter of a mile away. Thus, Mapleson had seen to it that bedridden persons could hear opera as it was being performed.[5]

Perhaps the best way to arrive at an impartial judgment today on the comparative merits of the Edison and Bettini machines would be to compare the records and the machines themselves. These are extremely hard to find, particularly those of Bettini, to say nothing of amassing sufficient quantities in one place to make direct comparisons. A former columnist of *Hobbies Magazine,* however, Stephan Fassett, expressed great disappointment upon hearing some of the Bettini recordings, when fifteen Bettini cylinders turned up in Mexico City in 1945. Fassett's disappointment may have stemmed from the fact that these recordings were principally of lesser artists. Another factor may have been that all Bettini recordings offered for sale were duplicates, not original recordings. All were dubbed from the one original master cylinder Bettini kept in his studio at 115 Fifth Avenue.

Bettini made a proposal to the New York Phonograph Company on February 19, 1892:

Having invented a process for making duplicates of musical and other Phonograph records from a Phonograph cylinder or cylinders having records thereon, I hereby make the following proposition.

On receipt of $100 I agree to give you the sole right to manufacture or make duplicate Phonograph or Phonograph-Graphophone records by means of my process, for which I am about to make application for a patent in the U.S., and I give you exclusive right to use my invention in the U.S. except as hereinafter mentioned, during the life of my patent.

If my patent is allowed, and if my invention works in a manner satisfactory to you, then when my patent is allowed to me, you are to pay me a further sum of $250, also one cent on each record manufactured by you through my patented process, and 10% on all records sold by you that have been so manufactured.

If my patent is not allowed, then the payment of $100 to me shall be received as payment in full for all demands.

In granting you exclusive right to use my invention referred to in the U.S., I reserve the right to duplicate Micro-Phonographs records, but if I do so at any time, I bind myself, and my Company, and Assigns, to pay to you one cent for each duplicated record made, and 10% on all duplicate records sold. If my patent is not allowed and you use my process, you are still to pay me one cent for each duplicate record made by my process, and 10% on all sales of such duplicate records, so long as my process is not used by other parties, but if it is used and known to other parties, then this percentage and any agreement contained herein shall become null and void.

If my patent referred to above for making duplicates of Phonograph records, is allowed, and I receive the sums of moneys referred to above, namely $100 referred to in the second paragraph of my letter and the $250 referred to in the third paragraph, then you shall be entitled thereafter, without further payment, to the use of all further improvements that I may make that can be applied to the manufacture of duplicate Phonograph records, excepting an electric heating process, which I am perfecting for the duplication of my Micro-Phonograph records, but this process, nor any other duplicating process shall not in any way affect or change my agreement referred to in paragraph five of this letter, to pay you one cent for each duplicate made and 10% on all duplicate records sold by me, or my Company, or my assigns during the life of my patents.[6]

On May 14, 1892, Bettini applied for a patent on his method of duplicating cylinders. The plan involved the use of opposed cylinders, similar in principle to the device for recording both sides of a sound wave, one side on each of two parallel cylinders, with a double-pointed stylus between as would be patented by Hall in 1899. Bettini's device was so arranged, however, that gravity assisted in cutting the cylinder located diagonally below the mandrel holding the master record.

Bettini and his wife, Daisy, were popular with the New York musical set and often played their Edison phonograph with the Bettini microdiaphragm attachment for their distinguished guests. Pleased to hear themselves as others heard them, the artists would then willingly consent to record a song or two. In this manner Bettini built up over a period of three or four years a fabulous collection of recordings. Without question his recording technique improved with time. He was greatly assisted in his work by two of his best friends—Emilio de Gogorza, destined himself to become one of the most famous of recording directors, and Rosa Chalia, a South American soprano who sang many solos for Bettini, as well as duets with de Gogorza, de Bassini, and others.

In April 1897 Bettini filed an application for an improved duplicating machine, indicating that his former device left something to be desired. The new model provided means for adjusting the pressure on the cylinder being cut, to match the volume of the master cylinder being copied. Bettini made the records to order on standard commercial blanks, using his microphonograph attachments.

The large number of recordings made by de Gogorza beginning with the Bettini era and lasting through the electrical recording era offer a rare opportunity to compare recording techniques and materials. Bearing in mind variables caused by wear, the necessity of securing a proper matching of takes, and the changing voice of the singer, comparisons are still quite revealing. At least three authentic Bettini/de Gogorza cylinders have been compared with de Gorza cylinders made for Columbia and discs recorded by Berliner, Eldridge R. Johnson, Victor, and Zonophone. There is no question but that the Victor records are the best. As more Bettini cylinders were probably made after 1896, with the development of his improved duplicator, additional caches still to be discovered may reveal a better quality than those found in Mexico City.[7]

It is rather amazing that Bettini was able to persuade so many great artists to record for him. The cost of such talent, had he paid it, would soon have terminated his recording activities. Very likely it was the enterprising Gramophone

Company, Ltd., venturing in 1900 into the recording of celebrities for fees that brought this phase of Bettini's career to a close. Still, as *Phonoscope* reported in August 1898, Bettini had by then recorded on wax a galaxy of stars:

> The collection is unequalled anywhere. There are songs by Yvette Guilbert, who sang into the phonograph on her recent visit to this country. When the writer visited the studio lately, Yvette's voice sounded from the phonograph, one of her English songs, "I Want You, My Honey." Then the voice gave "La Soularde" and an imitation of Bernhardt's style of delivery in a favorite character. Then followed a selection from "Izeyl," by Bernhardt herself, with all the passion in which the passage was recited on the stage.
>
> . . . The next cylinder was one labelled "Melba," which was truly wonderful; the phonograph reproducing her wonderful voice in a marvelous manner, especially on the high notes which soared away above the staff and were rich and clear. . . . Among [the singers] were Victor Maurel, the well-known baritone singer, . . . Tomaso Salvini, who rolled out a grand passage from "Otello" in the Italian translation; M. Coquelin, the famous French actor, whose visit to this country will be remembered; Pol Plançon and Mme. Saville, the beautiful French woman, who warbled a bit from the opera of "Rigoletto," and another from "Carmen" . . . Sigrid Arnoldsen's voice was heard in a cylinder to which the artist sang three years ago.[8]

Despite all the publicity and free talent, there is considerable doubt as to whether Bettini actually made money. He dabbled in things other than the phonograph. In 1893 he invented a nickel-in-the-slot machine, not for playing phonograph records but for dispensing gum or candy balls. In 1897 he had a patent on an acetylene lamp. That same year he published a twelve-page catalog of cylinders for sale. The next year, with the addition of popular songs, the catalog contained more than 400 selections.

By 1899 Bettini was offering for sale records by such famous artists as sopranos Nellie Melba, Frances Saville, Sigrid Arnoldsen, and Marie Engel; tenors Dante del Papa, Albert Saleza, Ernest Van Dyke; contralto Eugenia Mantelli; and the noted bassos Pol Plançon and Anton Van Rooy. He also advertised for sale dramatic recordings by Bernhardt, Rejane, and Salvini. Some artists may have asked Bettini to refrain from advertising their names, for in his 1899 catalog the following paragraph appears: "We have in our collection many records from celebrated artists, not mentioned in this catalog, and we are constantly adding new ones."[9]

From newspaper and trade articles it appears that Bettini also produced records by both Jean and Edouard DeReszke, Italo Campanini, Emma Calvé, Francesco Tamagno, Lola Beeth, Ellen Terry, Mark Twain, John Drew, Lillian Nordica, and Lillie Langtry.

In 1897 Bettini filed a patent on a small spring-motor phonograph and sold the patent to the Lyraphone Company of West Virginia. Subsequently he designed two other chassis for small spring-motor phonographs, some of which he had made up and advertised for sale. Not many can have been sold, as they are at least as scarce as the Bettini cylinders. Also in 1897 Bettini filed an application for a patent for copying records involving an electrical method. The specification shows a coil and an armature attached to the recording stylus and refers to the "transmitter," but there is no evidence that it was used commercially. In the March 1898 issue of *Phonoscope* a letter from F. M. Prescott, export and import dealer in phonographs and supplies, stated that Pathé in France was manufacturing the Bettini microphonograph attachment. The next month Bettini placed a notice warning purchasers against infringements being offered for sale in the European market. Evidently Bettini followed up this alleged infringement with a trip to France:

> Mr. G. Bettini, has sold his patent rights for France and the French Colonies to a newly organized company in France, called Compagnie Micro Phonographes Bettini, with a capital of 1,200,000 francs. Mr. Bettini is to remain in France some time in order to organize the company and take charge of the manufacturing plant.[10]

Bettini's last application for a U.S. patent was filed May 2, 1900, for a small spring-motored phonograph. By the time the patent was awarded in 1902, Bettini had apparently realized he was losing the battle against the industry giants that had outgrown him in every sense—in acquiring recording talent, maintaining continued research, and organizing and operating a business enterprise on a large scale. It is said that he sold his microphonograph patents to Edison; if so, Edison never made use of them.

Bettini chose to take his priceless collection of great voices to France, where they were destined to be destroyed during World War I. The company bearing his name continued until 1905, when it advertised a disc machine called the Hymnophone, made in Germany. In June 1905 the firm's U.S. counterpart was reorganized as Bettini Company, Ltd., with a capital of only $20,000; in December 1907 the firm went out of business.

In Paris Bettini continued making his attachments, phonographs, and recordings of great artists. In 1903 he recorded Pope Leo XIII shortly before the pope's death. Columbia issued a special brochure featuring cylinder recordings of the pope after his death, but whether these were duplicates of the Bettini recordings is not known.

After 1908 Bettini went into the motion picture business. He invented a motion picture camera that failed to impress the trade to any extent. Later, he was a war correspondent for a Paris newspaper. In 1917 he returned to the United States as a member of a military mission from the Italian government. He never returned to Europe and died in 1938. As far as the phonograph was concerned, Bettini had been at least its foremost dilletante. Like Jesse Lippincott, another man of wealth who had been fascinated by the machine's attractions, Bettini lost a great deal of money. Unlike Lippincott, he had a grand and glorious time doing so. On the other hand, Lippincott affected the mainstream of phonographic development; with all the glamour of his activities, Bettini left scarcely a mark upon it.

CHAPTER 8

The Concert Cylinders

THE COMPROMISE permitting the graphophone and the phonograph to coexist in parallel development was less peaceful for other entrepreneurs than for Gianni Bettini. The legal staff of American Graphophone that had permitted him free rein remained vigilant in regard to other inventors and contributors.

Some enterprising individuals made a start in the business by having the Edison phonograph copied by local machine shops. Complete instructions as to how to make both the Edison tinfoil phonograph and the later electric-motor wax cylinder Edison phonograph had been published in England and distributed in the United States. The manual provided complete working drawings, even to the details of the electric motor and the making of molds for molding cylinder blanks. Other service handbooks published in the United States for users of the Edison phonograph contributed later improvements.[1]

After Edison's experience in having his improvements "lifted" by MacDonald for the new graphophone, a certain class of discoveries were no longer patented. These changes included improved recording techniques, differing compositions of recording blanks, and methods of grinding and polishing styli. A period of trade secrets had arrived. Edison henceforth applied only for patents on definitive changes, amenable to protection in the courts.

The phonograph-graphophone story of the 1890s and well into the 1900s is one of ongoing espionage. The Edison and the American Graphophone interests maintained spies in each other's plants. Any change in the formula of Edison cylinder blanks was immediately reported to American Graphophone at its headquarters in Bridgeport, Connecticut. Employees of one plant who suddenly turned up missing reappeared as employees of a competing plant. One such employee was Victor Emerson, later founder of the Emerson Phonograph Company.

Both Edison and MacDonald worked feverishly to invent a commercially feasible molding process. Recording cylinders by the "round," where a singer might sing the same song over and over again into a bank of recording horns, did not preclude the duplication of cylinders. In the absence of a satisfactory molding process many experimenters developed methods of copying records from one to another, or dubbing. The third patent issued in the United States for phonographic devices involved dual-cylinder recording.[2] Edison, MacDonald, and others patented various forms of transcribing machines employing two mandrels, one to receive a recorded cylinder and the other a blank. Between the two cylinders was a lever with a smooth reproducing stylus bearing on the record on one side, while on the other side a cutting stylus bore down upon the blank. Even the Hall device could be adapted to make duplicate wax records, though wax cylinders were not in use at that time. Where a single lever arm was used, the sound wave configuration in the second record was the inverse of the original, although they sounded identical. Other devices were based on the principle of the pantagraph, which produced identical copies. Salespersons and publicists of the various companies would nevertheless invariably insist that all of *their* records were "originals."

There was some loss in dubbing from one record to another, and duplicated records varied widely in loudness and tone quality, prompting a continuing search for a material that could be added to wax blanks to make them stand up to reproducing. A harder playing surface would allow the copying of duplicates through any number of methods then in use. Edison experimented with many substances that would take the recording impression: "Sulfur is a good base to work with, melts about 250, limpid like water, takes beautiful impressions sharp and will make perfect record of the Record in brass mould for phono"; "on account of tenacity of transparent amorphous soaps there will be a tendency for knife to dig in and produce vibrations. What is wanted is a substance that has no cohesion, possibly trihydrate of alumina, amorp. silica, etc." He even had his chemist, Dr. Schulze-Berge, try chocolate for cylinder composition in November 1902.[3]

Phonoscope editor Russell Hunting told of discovering that unauthorized duplicates were being made of his records when Leeds and Catlin, one of the pioneer companies in producing entertainment records, engaged him to record ten rounds of his specialty, "Cohen at the Telephone," at five dollars per round. He had just finished the fourth round when a boy crossed the end of the studio with a tray of twenty-four cylinders. Curious, Hunting found that all these records were of himself reciting "Cohen at the Telephone." He had completed only four rounds, reciting into four recording funnels, which made a total of only sixteen cylinders. He therefore accused Leeds and Catlin of scheming to defraud him. Upon being threatened with exposure, Hunting reported, Leeds and Catlin made good.[4]

The economic importance of record duplication was apparent in a Bridgeport, Connecticut, *Farmer* article on March 26, 1898, reporting a visit of a group of recording artists to the American Graphophone plant there. The artists were George Gaskin, Russell Hunting, Len Spencer, Dan Quinn, George Schweinfest, George Graham, and the recording director of the Columbia Phonograph Company New York studio, Victor Emerson.

> The company arrived at the factory about noon, and were met by Assistant Manager W. P. Phillips. They were first treated to a lunch and then made an inspection of the plant. Of course, the visitors took the occasion to make some "master" records. Hunting made a Casey speech to the G. A. R. Gaskin song, "On the Banks of the Wabash"; a trio and other records were also made.
>
> The "master" record is made in just the manner one having a graphophone at his home would employ; the company, of course, has a special machine for the work, in which the recording of sound is quite pronounced, so much so that one hearing the "master" records is often surprised to hear the human voice in such strident tones in the upper register. All the harshness is eliminated in making the duplicates. From each record 25 to 100 duplicates are made, the number depending on the quality of the "master" record. The company turns out an average of 12,000 records a day from the "master" records sent them and yet are unable to keep up with the demand.

Edison discovered that the higher frequency sound waves could be captured with less distortion on a cylinder of larger diameter, traveling at a higher surface speed. He applied for a patent on a device for receiving cylinders of different diameters on December 3, 1890, which was not granted until September 13, 1898.[5]

In 1892 Leon Douglass, a former associate of Edward Easton in Washington, applied for a patent on a method of rerecording from one cylinder to another.

The patent was assigned to Easton, who in turn granted Douglass a license to manufacture records under American Gramophone patents. Douglass moved to Chicago, where he became associated with Babson in manufacturing large quantities of cylinders for the growing midwestern market. Douglass and his colleagues eventually manufactured machines, precipitating a court conflict with Easton and American Graphophone.

Edison's pantagraphic method of duplicating cylinders involved two mandrels on the same machine, one of which held the master recording and the other, a blank. A fine point fitted into the master record, the other end of which cut into the receiving cylinder. Thus the master record was literally traced by mechanical means upon the new record. This tracing of one cylinder into another was necessarily attended by many complications. In the first place, the cutting knives were always becoming worn, even though they were made of sapphire. The reproduced cylinder was never as perfect as the master record, and when it came to cutting a number of records one after another, the loss was even greater. In addition, the duplication process was extremely slow. Working at full capacity, the machines were seldom able to turn out more than thirty duplicate records per day from one master record.[6]

By 1898 Leon Douglass had applied for a patent on a phonograph that used dual reproducers in tandem, so that the stylus of the second followed closely in the same turn the grooved path of the first. When recorded and reproduced at a fairly high speed, the slight delay in response of the second reproducer was not particularly noticeable; in fact, the volume seemed more than doubled, probably because of the synthetic effect of reverberation introduced. Douglass realized that a larger cylinder was required for the best functioning of his polyphone, as the dual reproducer instrument was called.[7]

If a larger cylinder and higher speed made a better recording, why not simply reproduce the music from larger cylinders? MacDonald decided to place a large, concert-sized cylinder on the market. The November 1898 *Phonoscope* carried the first announcement of a private exhibition at the New York Bowling Green offices of the American Graphophone Company for a new instrument called the Graphophone Grand, a deluxe new machine designed to play the new large cylinders exclusively. (These cylinders were so unwieldy that it became necessary to build a lifting device into the storage cartons for removing them.) The demonstration was conducted by Philip Mauro.

The back cover of the December *Phonoscope* carried a full-page advertisement of the Graphophone Grand at $300, placed by F. M. Prescott, a jobber and exporter who had heretofore dealt in Edison goods and had also been closely associated with Hawthorne & Sheble, manufacturers of phonograph accessories in Philadelphia.

On December 24, 1898, an Associated Press dispatch to member newspapers announced that a suit had been filed against Hawthorne & Sheble by the American Graphophone Company, seeking to have that firm enjoined from allegedly converting Edison phonographs into Grands. The fact was that neither MacDonald nor any other person associated with American Graphophone had applied for a patent on a device using large-diameter cylinders. The only U.S. patent issued on such a device had been granted to Edison in October. The cleverness of Philip Mauro and other astute publicists in American Graphophone's employ was never more evident, for now Edison was forced to produce a similar product just to prove that he had the right to do so. The *Pittsburgh Dispatch* ran the Associated Press release on December 23, 1898, under the headline, "Not an Edison Invention":

> The American Graphophone Co. has entered suit in the U.S. Circuit Court here against Messrs. Hawthorne & Sheble, to enjoin an alleged infringement of the graphophone patents. The American Graphophone Co. has recently developed a new model of talking machine known as the graphophone Grand, whereby, it is claimed, acoustical results are obtained far exceeding in volume and quality anything heretofore obtained.
>
> It is alleged that Messrs. Hawthorne & Sheble have arranged to unlawfully construct graphophones of this type by reconstructing phonographs, making the necessary changes in the mechanism. The defendants, it is said, claim to be acting under the authority of the National Phonograph Co., which manufactures the so-called Edison Phonograph.
>
> The National Phonograph Co., it appears by the averments in the complaint, manufactured its machines under certain restricted rights under the graphophone patents, but these rights, it is claimed, were not transferable, and also do not include the right to make machines of the type known as the graphophone grand.
>
> The suit brings out the interesting fact that what is known as the Edison phonograph is manufactured under a license from the Graphophone Co. and is not an Edison invention. The Graphophone Co. patents, which cover

every successful device for recording and reproducing sound, have recently been firmly established by court decision.[8]

Pushing their publicity campaign to the utmost, American Graphophone officials arranged a demonstration of the new Graphophone Grand before the Washington Academy of Sciences on January 31, 1899. No less a personage than Alexander Graham Bell introduced the speaker of the evening, Philip Mauro. Surrounded by notable men of science, Mauro delivered a brilliant paper entitled "Development in the Art of Recording and Reproducing Sound." It was so successful that Mauro reread it before the Franklin Institute in Philadelphia, an occasion for which he received a citation. The free publicity was worth a fortune to American Graphophone interests.

Mauro, of course, had perpetrated a hoax on the Associated Press and the scientific societies, attributing every constructive development in the science of sound reproduction to his associates and their predecessors. His speech opened: "The graphophone had its inception in the Volta Laboratory, in this city, of which Professor Bell was one of the founders, but the perfection of the instrument in the form of the Graphophone was due to Thomas H. MacDonald of Bridgeport, Connecticut."

He went on to state that the invention of the phonograph had depended on the invention of the telephone the year before by Bell, who, of course, was on the platform. Mauro also said, in referring to the Graphophone Grand, "A notable result has recently been produced"—rather than "invented" or "discovered"—a truthful statement with a misleading implication.

In the fourth paragraph, Mauro indulged in another deceit: "So far there is nothing original in [Edison's] thought, for Leon Scott had, many years previously, devised an instrument, known to all physicists as the 'phonautograph,' whereby graphic representations of sonorous vibrations could be traced by means of a stylus in a film of lampblack." He did not mention that Scott's method had described a *laterally* undulating line without depth, whereas Edison's first phonograph indented, or embossed, a *vertically* undulating groove of variable depth that could be used to recreate sound—an entirely original concept.

Mauro in considerable detail outlined the work of the Bells and Tainter as having provided the essential basis upon which MacDonald developed his ideas. As has been pointed out earlier in this book, the graphophone had but one element from the original graphophone of the Volta period, and that was the idea of incising. All other methods and materials in the Graphophone Grand had been developed by Edison in 1887 and 1888 and incorporated into the graphophone in 1893 without permission, which made the graphophones illegal until the cross-licensing agreement of 1896.

With respect to the large-diameter cylinder Mauro went on: "But within a few months a new development has taken place, which produces results in volume of sound and fidelity to the original far exceeding the limit of what was previously, and by those best able to form an opinion, deemed possible." He then emphasized the importance of the jewel recording stylus in achieving the excellent results, neglecting to point out that the jewel stylus was an innovation patented by Edison in 1892, applied for in 1890.[9]

The only patent ever issued to MacDonald on a concert-size graphophone was applied for on March 14, 1901, and granted on July 23, 1901. It was for a graphophone that would permit the playing of both the standard-size and concert-size cylinders on the same machine by means of one mandrel telescoping within the other. In retrospect, it was the introduction of the Graphophone Grand and the accompanying publicity that forced Edison into manufacturing the Edison Concert Phonograph.

The situation gave added impetus to the production of the Berliner disc. Although the concert-size cylinders had volume and sound quality, they could not stand up to the inexpensive little hard-rubber disc. The easy-to-handle Berliner discs had plenty of volume but not much quality. By 1898 the quality of reproduction from the discs was improving, because of the substitution of wax for zinc in the recording and of shellac for rubber in the records.

The difference in space required by the concert cylinders and the Berliner discs was appreciable. Four standard cylinders could be stored in the space occupied by one concert cylinder, but fifty of the thin improved Berliner discs filled the same space. At five dollars each, the concert cylinders were much more expensive. Most of the Graphophone Grands were sold for exhibitions to which admission was charged.

Disc records from the beginning were all pressed, or molded, duplicates. The company that made the Berliner Gramophone (see chapter 11) also controlled the making of its disc records. The advent of the discs therefore redoubled the intensity of the search for a process that would do for the cylinder what Berliner had done for the disc. Very early there had been a search for a recording surface that would be soft when recorded upon but hard enough to make duplicates.

Also envisioned was a way of making the surface of the wax electrically conductive, so that it could be used in electroplating. Edison had a number of patents for making the surface of the wax master conductive by dusting on finely divided graphite or plumbago, or by depositing gold through vaporization. He also received patents on various types of molds of one or more pieces. The multiple-piece molds proved unsatisfactory because of the virtual impossibility of casting without a seam. The one-piece mold meant developing a record medium with sufficient shrinkage to permit its withdrawal from the mold.

There were so many problems involved in the cylinder-molding processes that not until 1901 was Edison able to market molded records in commercial quantities. (The first molded cylinder records on the market were of pink celluloid, produced by the Lambert Company of Chicago in 1900.) The gold-molding process, patented in principle as early as 1892, did not become a viable commercial method until almost a decade later. At about the same time, the American Graphophone Company began producing molded records that they called Columbia High-Speed XX records. Both companies adopted 160 rpm as the standard speed, instead of the former 120-rpm speed.

The harder composition that could be employed for the molded cylinders, plus the Edison button-shaped stylus, made these new cylinders superior to the earlier concert-size cylinders. Consequently the large-cylinder machines were now obsolete. The damage had been done; by early 1902 the Victor Talking Machine empire had begun its phenomenal growth. From this time forward the concert cylinders were only made to order.

Pathé-Frères, operating under Edison licenses in Europe, for years used the Edison device or an adaptation of it in all of its European studios. Master records were made on large-diameter cylinders and then transcribed on smaller-diameter cylinders in three different sizes for sale to the public. Even after the introduction of molding methods, Pathé recorded the originals on the large-size cylinder and reduced them to the smaller sizes for processing. Pathé even recorded on cylinders for transferral to discs into the 1920s. Many great European artists had their voices recorded by this means, and many of these Pathé cylinders still exist in Europe, as contrasted with the comparative dearth of such material available on cylinders in the United States. By 1902 Columbia and American Graphophone contrived to enter the disc talking-machine business—by the back door, another chapter in this story of intrigue, chicanery, corporate manipulation, and the use of high-pressure publicity methods.

CHAPTER 9

The Celluloid Cylinder
and Molding Patents

THE SEARCH for a record surface that would harden, or that could be hardened after recording, began nearly as early as did the effort to find a satisfactory molding method.

The first record surface that would harden after recording was covered in a patent applied for by George H. Harrington of Wichita, Kansas, on June 18, 1887, and granted February 12, 1889. Harrington assigned the patent jointly to himself and Edward H. Johnson. The most important element of the device, which used a moving-strip format, was the composition of the tape. Two different formulas were covered in the specification: one of celluloid mixed with molasses and beeswax; the other of glue, molasses, and wax. Smooth-surfaced tapes of these compounds could be temporarily softened by applying a solvent such as alcohol, recorded upon while soft, then allowed to harden.

In France somewhat later M. Lioret experimented with methods for softening celluloid in preparation for impressions of sound waves. Plunging a celluloid ring of the proper diameter into hot water rendered the surface soft enough for recording. A concept that later won Lioret a patent in the United States (patent 528,273, October 30, 1894) required softening a celluloid ring by plunging it into hot water and upon removal inserting it into a mold. The pliant celluloid ring was then forced into the recorded undulations within the mold using a tapered plunger mandrel. Successive cooling caused the celluloid to shrink and allowed it to be withdrawn from the one-piece mold.

Lioret evidently had difficulty in perfecting his idea, for in November 1897 an article that appeared in *Scientific American* about his phonograph made no mention of his record-molding process. The making of the records was described only as the result of "a secret softening process."

In 1901 in the United States a patent interference case that dealt with recording on celluloid was brought by Frank J. Capps against A. N. Petit of Newark, New Jersey, both former employees of Edison. Petit claimed that while employed at the Edison Phonograph Works in 1896 he had conceived the idea of recording on celluloid softened by a solvent, and that he had conducted experiments at that time with only fair results. He claimed that later he discovered that "acid of oil" with an alcohol solvent produced excellent results and that patents on his process had been taken out all over the world. Capps entered a claim in interference. The court decided in favor of Petit.

Since the only method then in commercial use for making cylinder duplicates was through rerecording, it became obvious that there was a need for a harder reproducing surface. The harder reproducing surface would in turn give more volume. Discs already had considerable volume, though not much quality.

During these years the manufacturers of cylinder talking machines considered their machines' capability to record anywhere a great sales advantage over the new disc talking machines; the disc machines could not provide such capability. Experience soon showed that this advantage was more than offset by the lack of control over the record market. Disc records were easily reproduced, whereas cylinder reproduction was complicated. A laboratory-processed record would have been an asset to the manufacturers of cylinder machines.

From the first, Edison had envisioned making molds, beginning with the idea of plating the tinfoil and copper sheets used for the recording surface. His experiments along these lines included experiments to back up the recorded foil with plaster of Paris or asphaltum compounds. As early as 1888 he filed a caveat— that is, notice of intention to invent—on a method for molding celluloid records. Because numerous snags had to be eliminated in order to make the process commercially feasible, Edison did not file a patent application for the process for another decade. In the meantime, Capps and Petit, his former employees, independently conceived the idea of recording directly on celluloid blanks.

On August 14, 1899, Thomas B. Lambert of Chicago applied for a patent on a process for making a copper mold by electroplating a graphite-dusted master wax cylinder and subsequently using this mold for making duplicate records of "cellulose" or a similar plastic. As a result, the Lambert Record Company was organized and began production and sale of molded celluloid musical cylinder records for use on both the standard Edison and the Columbia machines. The patent was granted on December 18, 1900. Edison's patent on a celluloid record molding process was finally issued on November 11, 1902, patent 713,209. This patent, together with patent 713,863 issued November 18, 1902, on an improvement to his gold deposition or "sputtering" process, completed the basis for his caveat of 1888. Lambert's pink celluloid cylinders were the first molded records manufactured for the trade. In contrast, in 1901 the first records to be molded in commercial quantities by the National Phonograph Company were not celluloid, but a metallic soap compound.

National Phonograph filed suit against Lambert for infringement on its patents. The case was brought before the Circuit Court of the Northern District of Illinois, where the decision and subsequent appeal both went against Edison and National Phonograph. The first decision was to the effect that a patent for a process is not infringed by the sale of a product. It was held that the proof offered by the plaintiff—that the defendant sold an article a month or two after the patent had been issued to the plaintiff—was not sufficient to establish that the article had been made after the date of patent issuance. So the motion of the plaintiff for an injunction was denied. The defendant, Lambert, continued to infringe on Edison's patent, according to National Phonograph. In August 1905 the Seventh Circuit Court of Appeals handed down the decision that the 1902 Edison celluloid patent, applied for in 1898, was void because he had used the process described therein for nine years before the patent was issued. The basis for the decision of the court apparently lay in the testimony of F. Schulze-Berge and Charles Wurth of the Edison staff, who had explained in great detail a series of seemingly endless experiments preceding the application for a patent. The judge in this decision stated that the production of a great many matrices and a great many copies in this manner constituted public use and thereby disqualified the patent. The decision of the judges Grosscup, Baker, and Seaman was that Edison patent 713,209, dated November 11, 1902, for a process of duplicating phonograms, was void by reason of prior publication of the invention.

One of the most costly and important developments in cylinder phonograph manufacture thus became the property of persons other than the originator. The sequel to this story is that in July 1906 the Indestructible Record Company was organized under the laws of Maine, to operate under the Lambert patents and others, including one issued to W. F. Messer, July 29, 1902. Edison could not now use celluloid as a record surface. He had lost the keystone patent.

The National Phonograph Company made one more attempt to stop the Lambert Company, this time on the basis of the Edison tapered-bore patent. As the Lambert cylinder made contact with the mandrel only at either end of the cylinder, where the celluloid was turned in for about a quarter of an inch, this Edison patent was held not infringed. In other words, even though the Lambert cylinders were made to fit on the Edison tapered mandrel, it was decided that the Lambert did not have a tapered bore.

It was several years before Edison was legally able to return to the expanded plastic impressed into now perfected molds. He was forced to fall back on the metallic soap composition cylinder, fragile and much less durable. The inevitable result was a cylinder with a volume limit at a time when volume was a critical factor in the competition with the rapidly improving discs. The first 200-thread Edison record was made in 1894, using a .025-inch-diameter stylus made by George McIntosh, and the first 400-thread record was made April 24, 1895, by Charles Wurth, using a stylus .010 inch in diameter.[1]

The recording studio and headquarters of American Graphophone at the corner of New York's Twenty-seventh Street and Broadway occupied the ground floor, basement, and part of the second floor. The whole of the ground floor, one large room, was used for exhibitions. A brass-railed platform in the center contained a display of goods and a small office area. Around the room were arranged kinetoscopes and nickel-in-the-slot graphophones supplied with the latest records. The basement rooms accommodated bookkeepers, a repair shop, and the record department. On the second floor, besides the commodious salesrooms, were the offices of Edward Easton, president, William H. Smith, general manager, and Harry Godwin, advertising manager. The upper floor was devoted entirely to the record-making department under the guidance of Victor Emerson. There, bands, orchestras, and soloists performed before the big horn. American Graphophone operated its extensive factory at Bridgeport, Connecticut.[2]

National Phonograph also claimed patent infringements of its molding methods by its old archenemy, American Graphophone. Both companies had begun producing molded records at about the same time. One case involved the same celluloid molding patent cited in the Lambert litigation. In two other cases, Judge Platt of the Connecticut circuit court on March 17, 1905, handed down decisions against the Edison patent. In one, he held that the patent was limited in its application to the process of expanding the blank within the mold and was not infringed by a casting process. In the other, he held that Edison patent 667,662 for a process of duplicating cylinder phonograph records was entitled to only a narrow construction in view of the prior art and so was not infringed by the process of MacDonald patents 682,991 and 682,992.

One substantial factor affecting the disc-versus-cylinder competition was the introduction of a twelve-inch disc by Victor in 1903, increasing playing time to three and one-half minutes, compared with two minutes for the cylinders. Edison delayed putting out a grand-opera series until 1906, but by then most opera selections were on the longer-playing discs. In their fragile form and with their restricted playing time, the cylinders could not begin to compete with discs in the field of serious music.

As Victor gained the attention of opera lovers and urbanites with its recordings of great opera artists and top-flight entertainers, Columbia Phonograph Company's mostly urban cylinder business began to fade. To stem the decline and revive interest in cylinders, American Graphophone purchased the rights to a new mechanical amplifying system invented by Daniel Higham, of Boston. By means of a simple little amber friction-wheel device, the mechanical pull upon the diaphragm from the stylus was augmented by power from the spring motor, greatly increasing the volume from the cylinder. The technical flaw, as with the floating weight by Edison, was that the wear upon the record was increased proportionately. Combining Higham's contrivance with a longer mandrel increased playing time. The resulting machine was introduced in 1905 and named the Twentieth Century Graphophone. Records six inches long were cut with the standard 100 grooves to the inch, thus increasing playing time by a little more than half.

The new Columbia record was probably the reason Edison decided to launch the four-minute wax Amberol, whose increased playing time was the result of doubling the number of grooves from 100 to 200. The difficulty lay in its composition: the same soft, fragile metallic soap compound. The closer-spaced smaller grooves also necessitated the sale of special reproducers and a new feed mechanism for existing phonographs. Still, the Edison Grand Opera Series was recorded on the Amberol four-minute records, for it was thought that the increased playing time would be appreciated. Instead, the advantage of the longer playing time disappeared when the purchaser found the beautiful high notes of Leo Slezak singing "Celeste Aïda" from the opera *Aïda* cut off after only a few playings. Even for Slezak, a two-dollar record that played only a few times was too expensive. Jobbers began to report that dealers and customers were complaining that the new records would not stand up to use.

National Phonograph's challenge to the longer-playing Twentieth Century Graphophone and the discs boomeranged. In September 1908 *Talking Machine World* announced the organization of the U.S. Phonograph Record Company in Cleveland, capitalized at $300,000. Indestructible records soon appeared on the market as U.S. Everlasting Records. Two-minute cylinders were made in 1908, four-minute in 1909. The Columbia Phonograph Company announced that it was taking over the sales of the celluloid cylinder records made by the Indestructible Record Company of Albany. National Phonograph's effort to provide longer playing time had served only to focus attention on the fragility of the Edison cylinders. The experiments that got underway when Edison asked his associates Jonas W. Aylesworth and Walter H. Miller to find a new record composition eventually led to the manufacture of an entirely new type of disc record, for they failed to disclose a better material than celluloid for cylinder records.

Meanwhile, great damage was done to Edison's potential classical record market by this situation. Although the four-minute Amberol impasse was solved by buying the rights to the celluloid process now owned by Brian F. Philpot in England, it was too late for Edison to compete; Victor dominated the classical market. The irony of this bitter experience for Edison was that the Philpot process had been developed from patents issued in the United States to a former Edison employee, A. N. Petit. Philpot had acquired additional information while trustee for the bankrupt Lambert Company, which a decade before had thwarted Edison in a contest over molding method patents. Now there was little difficulty in perfecting a factory system for celluloid record production—Edison and his colleagues had been through all that before, and they even found that they could use the Amberol molds. The new celluloid records, with their rich cobalt blue exterior and an inner core of plaster of Paris, were christened Blue Amberols. Playing time, as with the wax Amberols, was four minutes or more at 160 rpm. The records were unbreakable, among the most durable ever made. A celebrity series was introduced later in a brilliant fuchsia.

Ernest Lippelgoose of the Edison staff described the dyeing process of the celluloid cylinders: "It was a baffling process as temperamental as the weather. If it was too sultry, too moist, the dye would run. The weather had to be just right. I would lie in bed, look up at the stars and know the time had come to dip.

It often would happen in the early morning hours. I would walk from Bloom-field to Orange—there were no automobiles in those days—wake up a few sleepy workmen along the way and take them with me to the 'dipping' party."[3]

Following the lead of Victor with its Victrola, Edison phonographs were re-designed with internal horns and labeled Amberolas. The high point in the de-velopment of the Edison acoustic cylinder phonograph came with the Concert models of the Amberola. These had a fixed, airtight tone passage with constantly expanding bore from the diaphragm chamber to the flare of the horn. The record moved horizontally beneath the stylus on the principle of a lathe. The early Con-cert Amberolas, before the introduction of the Blue Amberol records, played both two- and four-minute wax records by an ingenious turn-over reproducer. Acoustically, the external-horn Concert was superior to the internal-horn model, although both were produced to meet the same general specifications. Function-ally, the open horn was and is always inherently superior to the enclosed horn.

In the search for a better record surface for the cylinders, Edison and his asso-ciates developed a material that included the desired properties but that was ap-plicable only to a disc process. This new thermoplastic material was called Con-densite.[4] The decision to develop a disc record marked the end of the long series of experiments to develop better cylinders. The Twentieth Century Grapho-phone, in the end, aroused but little interest. Although it was advertised until 1909, Columbia filled its diminishing demand for longer-playing cylinders by taking over the sales of Indestructible Records, made in both two- and four-minute formats. Within a few years Edison had the cylinder field virtually to himself.

The last Edison two-minute metallic soap cylinders were made in September 1912. Although a few two-minute Edison cylinders were molded in blue cellu-loid shortly thereafter, the first four-minute Blue Amberol cylinders appeared in October 1912. With a dependable rural area trade Edison converted many thou-sands of machines to play the new celluloid cylinders, but World War I marked the beginning of the decline of Edison cylinder sales in the United States and abroad.

CHAPTER 10

The Coin-Slot Phonograph Industry

THE YEAR 1889 marked the beginning of the use of the phonograph in conjunction with a coin-in-the-slot device, formerly used only in weighing machines and gum dispensers. The coin-in-the-slot phonograph preceded the era of the home phonograph.

The organizers of the early phonograph and graphophone companies had imagined leasing their wares mainly to businesses. When Jesse H. Lippincott organized the North American Phonograph Company to operate as sales agent for the improved Edison Phonograph, his intention was to promote the use of both the phonograph and the graphophone for office work, giving lessors a choice between the instruments. Although the organizers of the Columbia Graphophone Company were themselves court reporters and aware of the needs of stenography, like Lippincott they were unable to make a success of the business of leasing the machines for office work. Substituting the Edison machine for the Bell-Tainter graphophone did not alleviate the situation. It was obvious that others less familiar with the stenographic field would be even less successful.

Resourceful Louis Glass, general manager of the Pacific Edison Phonograph Company, decided to change tactics entirely. He equipped one of his electric motor–operated Edison phonographs with a nickel-in-the-slot operating device so that it might be used as an entertainment machine. On November 23, 1889, Glass installed the phonograph in the Palais Royal Saloon in San Francisco, equipped with four listening tubes and a coin slot for each tube. For each play of a record, the machine would gobble up from five to twenty cents. Within a few months it was apparent to Glass and his associates that this setup was a money-making proposition. More than a dozen idle Edison phonographs were converted and placed into service. Glass designed a multitube attachment and applied for a patent on his coin-controlled mechanism.

In New York City, Felix Gottschalk, secretary of the Metropolitan Phonograph Company, arrived at the same brilliant conclusion by a somewhat different route. He organized the Automatic Phonograph Exhibition Company of New York, with capital of $1 million, to make the working mechanism and lease it to others on a profit-sharing basis. About this time Louis Glass met Gottschalk in New York, and a deal was consummated by which the Automatic Phonograph Exhibition Company would acquire the rights to Glass's multitube coin-slot mechanism.

Automatic began operations with a glass-topped cabinet holding a single-cylinder Edison machine in the top and a primary battery in the bottom. Ear tubes protruded from the front for listeners. The original coin device operated on the principle of making or breaking the electrical circuit.

At this time the phonograph and the graphophone were quite different instruments. As the graphophones generally were powered not by electric motor but by treadle, the phonograph came into greater use for entertainment. The graphophone cylinder was not interchangeable with the phonograph cylinder. When the National Association of Phonograph Companies was organized in 1890 to handle information exchange and intercompany problems, at least two circumstances were obvious to all: the advantages of standardization and the development of one machine to handle all usages. Louis Glass requested that the association resolve "that all parties, that is, the American Graphophone Co., the North American Phonograph Co., and Mr. T. A. Edison, shall direct all their efforts to that end; that they give us one instrument for correspondence, stenography work and for amusement." [1]

At the association's first convention Gottschalk exhibited one of Automatic's machines and offered the independent companies contracts by which Automatic would supply the cabinets and operating mechanism; the companies would use their own Edison machines obtained through contracts with North American. Gottschalk gave North American 15,000 shares of Automatic stock in order to secure the right to do business with the independent companies. By the contract offered to the companies, the machines were not to be sold, all servicing was to be done by the local companies, and profits were to be shared with Automatic.

The misapprehension that Thomas Edison opposed using the phonograph for entertainment purposes also appears to have been set in motion at this convention. Samuel Insull, Edison's representative at the meeting, knew of Edison's profound belief in the ultimate usefulness of the phonograph as an efficient aid to business. Loath to see this aspect neglected, Insull stated that Edison was not too enthusiastic about the slot machines and that their use might tend to discourage acceptance of the phonograph as a business machine. Insull warned the local company representatives that they should not neglect the original purpose of their companies' organization—the promotion of the phonograph as an adjunct to business. Meanwhile, Lippincott's North American as early as the 1890 convention was recording and selling musical records to the local companies.[2]

According to Fred Gaisberg, Columbia Phonograph Company executives Edward Easton and R. F. Cromelin's

> purpose was to exploit [the graphophone] as a dictating-machine for office use. In this respect, however, it proved a failure. I remember some hundred of the instruments being rented to Congress and all being returned as impracticable. The Columbia Company seemed headed for liquidation at this point, but it was saved by a new field of activity which was created, almost without their knowledge, by showmen at fairs and resorts demanding records of songs and instrumental music. Phonographs, each equipped with ten sets of ear-tubes through which the sound passed, had been rented to these exhibitors. It was ludicrous in the extreme to see ten people grouped about a phonograph, each with a tube leading from his ears, grinning and laughing at what he heard. It was a fine advertisement for the onlookers waiting their turn. Five cents was collected from each listener so the showman could afford to pay two and three dollars for a cylinder to exhibit.[3]

The machines returned by the members of Congress were Bell-Tainter graphophones, employing the $1\frac{5}{16}$-inch ozocerite-coated cardboard cylinders 8 inches long. The musical cylinders that Columbia then began making for the phonographs were the standard Edison solid-wax type, $2\frac{1}{8}$ inch in diameter and 4 inches long.

When Charles Sumner Tainter designed a coin-slot machine for demonstrations at the 1893 World's Columbian Exposition in Chicago, Gaisberg reported,

> the entire repertoire consisted of "Daisy Bell" and "After the Ball Was Over." His slot-controlled automatic phonograph was a truly remarkable achievement for that period but proved too delicate to stand the rough handling at the Chicago Fair Grounds. It was withdrawn and shipped to Wash-

ington where, acting on Tainter's instructions, I installed some dozens in the local saloons, restaurants, and beer gardens. They were not infallible and sometimes would accept a coin without giving out a tune. In carrying out my job of collecting the coins early in the morning and reloading the machines with cylinders, I would at times be badly handled by an irate bartender who accused me of taking money under false pretenses. With the failure of the World's Fair venture, I was free to work for the Columbia Phonograph Company which had begun to make musical cylinders on a large scale.[4]

This episode must have represented the last attempt to use the Bell-Tainter graphophone commercially, for by this time American Graphophone had ceased operation and was being reorganized by Easton and others. Tainter had evidently been working independently for some time, and the distinction Gaisberg makes between working for Tainter and for the Columbia Phonograph Company is important. The records that Columbia "had begun to make on a large scale" were for the phonograph—not for either the Bell-Tainter graphophone or the Mac-Donald graphophone, which had yet to make its appearance. A poll taken at the June 1891 phonograph convention showed that, of an estimated 400 machines Columbia Phonograph had out on rental, only 12 to 15 were graphophones.

In general, the preferred fare on nickel-in-the-slot machines seemed to be comic songs, monologues, whistling, and band renditions. In some saloons, hymns were popular. By September 1890 every leading hotel in New York had coin-operated phonographs in its main lobby. The *New York Press*, September 24, 1890, reported that most popular were songs such as "Annie Rooney" and "Down With McGinty," waltzes, banjo solos, violin performances, and recitations.

By the second convention of phonograph companies in June 1891, all but three of the remaining nineteen local companies were in the coin-slot business. New York Phonograph had 175 machines on location; Old Dominion Phonograph of Virginia, 142. Many of the local companies were reluctant to pay the 50 percent of gross demanded by Automatic in its contracts, especially as the locals had to do all the servicing. The machines were considered business boosters and placed with the owners of locations, usually without paying a percentage. Despite stern warnings to infringers by Automatic, several new types of nickel machines were offered for outright sale. They generally had a square, or slanting, glass top on a base cabinet of oak, cherry, or mahogany, with the ear tubes hanging from the front, and were to be used with the standard Edison phonograph and battery. They sold for an average of fifty dollars each, creating considerable competition for Automatic with its stiff percentage deal.

Receipts from some of these early slot machines were amazing, especially in view of the mediocre quality of the entertainment offered. Only phonograph parlors with a multitude of machines offered a choice of selections. The Louisiana Phonograph Company reported that one of its machines had taken in $1,000 in the two months following April 1891. Missouri Phonograph reported that it had about fifty machines on location, one of which took in $100 in a week.

The Edison Phonograph Works began to manufacture musical phonograms as early as 1890. The Works also made all blanks used by the companies, as it was entitled to do by contract. Many operators sought to keep a larger part of the profits by molding their own blanks in violation of Edison patent rights. Chief offenders were Columbia Phonograph and American Graphophone. New York Phonograph, New Jersey Phonograph, and Ohio Phonograph companies produced recordings. Although it was not illegal for the companies or anyone else to make records, it was illegal to make records on blanks made to fit Edison mandrels.

Many of the original records of exceptional drawing power sold for two to six dollars each. Operators with good locations made money; others lost their shirts. Machines were bootlegged, altered, imitated. Soon the industry was in a virtual state of anarchy. It was impossible for Edison or North American Phonograph to police the entire country.

The industry began by trying to police itself. By the 1893 phonograph company convention, American Graphophone was being reorganized by officials of Columbia Phonograph. It was common knowledge that Columbia was to be exclusive sales agent for the new graphophones. After the convention, the commission on any sales made by North American could be credited to the account of the local companies in whose territories the merchandise was sold. For a time it seemed that this new plan might work. The operators were really in command, however, not the local companies or North American. Irresponsible and lawless elements were in on the take. The manufacture of machines and blanks without regard to patents or territories continued. High shipping costs to the Midwest, Far West, and South for machines made at the Edison Phonograph Works in

Orange were an added stimulus to illegal manufacturing. It became apparent that neither the parent companies nor the local companies would be able to regain control.

Upon acquiring the assets of North American, the Edison Phonograph Works began to produce an improved line of coin-slot machines for the entertainment field. Operators could buy the machines as they had before, but now the Edison Phonograph Works was to receive the monies. American Graphophone reentered the field, using the MacDonald graphophone equipped with an Edison tapered mandrel and employing solid wax blanks. In 1896 both parent companies began to make spring-motored coin-slot machines.

The phonograph parlor idea spread throughout the world. In Paris, Pathé employed forty people in the most unique establishment of this type. On the spacious street floor were many desks equipped with listening tubes, with a chair before each desk. All customers had to do was seat themselves, order the selection they wanted played by speaking into a tube, deposit a coin, and listen through their ear tubes as the record was played on the phonograph in the room below. The customers had a choice of 1,500 cylinders—the first musical library.

The popularity of the phonograph parlor in the United States is illustrated in the planning of the first "deluxe" motion picture theater—the Vitascope Hall in Buffalo. In the theater vestibule, "a palace of pleasure itself," twenty-eight of the latest Edison phonographs were placed for "the diversion and instruction" of visitors, as well as a number of Edison peephole kinetoscopes, an early motion picture machine. Among the kinetoscope films being offered were *The Courtney-Corbett Fight*, *The New Kiss* with May Irwin and John Rice, *The Parisian Dance*, and *Bertoldi, the Contortionist and Perfect Woman*.

In order to compete successfully with other types of coin machines, operators of nonselective coin phonographs were forced to resort to gadgets. One combined changing pictures with the change in sound. The Mills Novelty Company of Chicago developed a machine that periodically dropped cards illustrating the song being played. Another picturized phonograph was the Illustraphone, made by Hawthorne & Sheble of Philadelphia. Other machines of this type were the Cailophone and the Scopephone, both made by the Caille Brothers, Detroit; and the Illustrated Song Machine, made by the Rosenfeld Company of New York. Later the Valliquent Novelty Company of Newark, New Jersey, made the Discophone, the first illustrated machine sold in the United States using disc records. Earlier the Universal Talking Machine Company made a coin-operated machine to be sold in Germany. Although the best locations were taken by automatic pianos and music boxes, the phonograph parlor persisted and, by the addition of other nickel- and penny-catching devices, were gradually transformed into the penny arcade.

Unique among attachments was the Multiplex, put on the market in 1896. The rotation of the Multiplex group was controlled by a compound reacting rachet lever, one movement bringing the next cylinder into position. The mandrels were numbered in regular order, enabling the patron to make selections from a numbered list on an announcement card. If the record in position did not suit one's fancy, a lever could be pulled back and forth until the desired recording revolved into position. At that point the patron dropped a nickel in the slot.[5] The $150-attachment had five mandrels made to fit over the standard Edison chassis and had the customary ear tubes.

The Automatic Reginaphone, made by the music-box manufacturers of Rahway, New Jersey, was a similar machine but designed as a complete unit with a glass front so the mechanism operation could be viewed. It held six cylinders on mandrels around a wheel, with the cylinders parallel to the center shaft of the wheel as in the Multiplex. When a coin was deposited, the wheel progressed so that the next cylinder would be in position for playing. For each coin deposited, one of six records played, with no preselection available. First produced in 1905, the machine came with optional ear tubes or speaker horn.

Also in 1905 the first truly selective automatic phonograph became available— the Multiphone. It held twenty-four numbered cylinders. The patron deposited a nickel and, with an external crank, selected a title, supplying the motive force by winding the crank of the standard Edison spring-motor machine. The machine had a huge overhead horn masked by a grille in the top of the rather grotesquely bulging mahogany cabinet. Customers were evidently being asked to work too hard for their entertainment, for the company went bankrupt in 1908.

Another unusual cylinder machine was the Concertophone, provided with a carrier that held twenty-five six-inch Columbia Twentieth Century Graphophone cylinders. It was operated by setting a dial at the side of the cabinet and manipulating a sliding bar to maneuver the desired record into place. First announced in the September 1906 *Talking Machine World*, it employed the Twentieth Century Graphophone loudspeaking mechanical amplifier invented by Higham of Boston. A later model shifted the records automatically. With its plate-glass front and mirror to reflect the machinery operation, it was the most spectacular of all the cylinder record players developed. In its original locations, the Concertophone earned up to ten dollars per day. Sold also for home use without the coin mechanism, it was probably the first automatic home record changer, as well as the last of the new coin-slot cylinder phonographs.

By 1908 coin-operated disc machines were fairly numerous. Julius Wilner of Philadelphia had invented a coin-operated phonograph that played twelve ten-inch discs in sequence, but with no preselection. In 1906 the Automatic Machine and Tool Company of Chicago produced John Gabel's Automatic Entertainer, which held twenty-four ten-inch records, twelve on either side of the turntable. Any record could be played by turning a knob. Although powered by a hand-wound spring motor, the operation otherwise was entirely automatic. A forty-inch-long horn protruded from the top of an oak cabinet five feet high glassed in on three sides so that the mechanism might be viewed. A magazine holding 150 needles was positioned directly above the sound box. The handle that wound the motor changed the needle and the record all in one turning. The coin device was also of advanced design, equipped with a magnetic coin detector. The Gabel Entertainer thus is looked upon as the progenitor of the modern jukeboxes.

By 1927 the Automatic Music Instrument Company of Grand Rapids placed on location a selective, coin-operated jukebox that played one or both sides of ten records. Other makers of coin-operated pianos and automatic musical instruments such as J. P. Seeburg and the Rudolph Wurlitzer Company were producing selective, coin-operated phonographs in the early 1930s. During the depression years, when economic conditions and the consuming interest in radio combined to push over-the-counter record sales to their lowest levels since 1900, the electronically jazzed up jukebox created a market most important in the rehabilitation of the recording industry.

In 1927 a letter from W. L. Pace of Beaumont, Texas, to Thomas A. Edison, Inc., stimulated Charles Edison, the inventor's son and by then head of the company, to consider a slot machine that had a selective device for records.[6] Pace divulged the secret of the operating game—"plenty of records of the type and style that take in resorts, restaurants, etc. where they like jazzy classy music songs." Amplification of musical recordings across a skating rink, theater, or pavilion caused distortion. Characteristically the Edison Company chose to take a conservative tack: the new automatic machines were to operate only in conjunction with vending machines and would thank the purchaser and give him a short message.

The idea of a machine saying thank you was not new. R. Barrett of London had written to Edison in 1890 to suggest that his automatic machine for testing the strength of the grip of the hand be fitted to emit a sound as nearly as possible like the words *thank you* upon the introduction of a coin.[7] In 1928 cigarette-vending machines began thanking customers and adding "Not a cough in a carload," "Mild as May," "Good and mild," or "Cork tips protect the lips." The record was of Edison manufacture, a 7¼-inch disc hill-and-dale (vertical-grooved) recording spoken by Ed Meeker; the machines were produced by the newly organized Automatic Merchandising Corporation of America, in which United Cigar Stores had a substantial stock interest. Joseph J. Schermack, the inventor of the machines, was president of the corporation. The records sold for ninety cents apiece.

By 1929 Automatic Merchandising was branching out into amusement parks, cafeterias, and department stores, and Meeker was earning twenty dollars for each satisfactory recording. Sample recordings included:

Thank you, Filene's growing on value.
Thank you, Katz pays the tax.
Thank you, Hershey's for health.
Thank you, you'll like all Beech-Nut products.
Thank you, now try the Pretzel Ride.
Thank you, there is a wonderful thrill on the Cuddle-Up.

The message had to fit within one revolution of the record, since each record had five concentric recorded grooves. Thomas A. Edison, Jr., suggested a joint venture with the Union News Company or similar newsstand controlling syndicates, with the Hearst International Group, or with the Coca-Cola Company, all of which would mean a broadening of the market. The possibilities were limitless. The Edison record was superior to others in the field for this sort of use. With proper amplification, even talking billboards were a possibility.

None of this would materialize. The Edison Company would be out of the record business in October 1929.

CHAPTER 11 ⟶

Advent of the Discs

AS THE PHONOGRAPH and graphophone interests battled each other in 1896 for leadership in the lucrative sound-recording business, another contender entered the field—Emile Berliner, a sometime inventor and business venturer.

Berliner was born in Hanover, Germany, in 1851. He immigrated to the United States in 1870, establishing himself in Washington, D.C. There he invented a microphone and patented it in 1877. Berliner's first experiments in sound recording used the same medium as Leon Scott's phonautograph, that is, a smoke-blackened recording surface. Berlin fixed the resultant wavy tracing on the smoke-blackened cylinder with shellac. Converting this original track into another usable form became a problem.

The photoengraving techniques developed by Charles Cros must have influenced the direction Berliner pursued, for it was not long before he abandoned the cylinder for the disc, which was easier to photoengrave. Berliner again let the stylus trace sound vibrations into a thin layer of lamp black, this time deposited on a film of linseed oil. The recording disc was held in an upside-down position, so that all the leavings would immediately fall away from the recording surface.

Berliner next tried a thin layer of beeswax adhered to a polished metal surface; in this case, zinc was but a short step. The recording stylus cut an undulatory groove only into the upper layer, exposing the zinc for later chemical etching with chromic acid.[1] Berliner now had a metal master with the sound vibrations accurately etched into the surface. The metallic disc could subsequently be reproduced through electroplating techniques.

Both the phonograph and the graphophone employed wax cylinders, each cylinder being sold as an original or transcribed record. Berliner's disc gramophone employed hard plastic discs made of a new material called Duranoid, made by the Duranoid Company of Newark, New Jersey.[2] These discs were much louder than wax cylinders, and a reproducing funnel could now be used instead of ear tubes for listening to the gramophone. The Berliner machine, designed to reproduce speech and music for home entertainment only, could not be used for dictation. In contrast, the cylinder machines were meant for office dictation, not for entertainment.

Another method of recording discs somewhat comparable to Berliner's was patented in the United States and England by Rev. A. C. Ferguson, a Baptist minister in Brooklyn. A diaphragm-controlled shutter varied a tiny beam of light aimed along a spiral path at a seven-inch glass plate coated with photographic emulsion. Developing and subsequent photoengraving onto a metal plate created an etched groove that could be used for sound reproduction by means of a Lightophone, whose stylus-diaphragm-horn assembly resembled that of the gramophone.[3] A matrix could be made for pressing duplicate discs, although as far as is known this was not done commercially. Ferguson claimed that, as there was no friction in the recording, there was no distortion, although the volume was not as great as that obtained by the Berliner method. Without doubt, if the use of wax disc recording blanks had come into being at this time, the Lightophone would have been commercially developed, as the idea itself was practical and the processing simple. A diaphragm-controlled shutter was later used to record sound on motion picture film.

Considering Berliner's limited background and facilities, it is amazing that he was the first not only to produce disc records commercially but to produce stamped, or molded, records commercially. As early as 1891 Edison had molded and demonstrated experimental wax musical cylinders, and the Bells and Tainter as early as 1885 had molded experimental vertical-cut discs, but none of them were able to bring the process to a commercially practicable state.[4] Berliner's gramophone did not have a motor, whereas Edison had in 1878 equipped an experimental disc machine with a spring motor.

If Berliner had been a more practical experimenter, his original carbon button transmitter might have been operative. Berliner himself admitted in a statement given in interference, March 4, 1887, that "a person heard sounds, but could not generally make out the words I spoke."[5] It was this Berliner transmitter, however, that caused the Bell interests to engage Berliner on a retainer basis, thus giving him time and money to develop the gramophone.

Berliner worked on the gramophone almost continuously from 1887 to 1895 before producing any machines or records for sale. Fred Gaisberg, one of Berliner's early associates, in his fascinating story of the development of the lateral-disc industry, *The Music Goes Round,* stated that he had established the first professional disc recording studio in Philadelphia in 1897. A small store was opened nearby, with Alfred Clark in charge of sales.

Gaisberg's experience in cylinder recording studios was undoubtedly of considerable assistance to Berliner, for Gaisberg and his brother, Will, were well acquainted with many of the popular vocalists and entertainers recorded on cylinders. Berliner put Gaisberg to work rounding up talent of a caliber that would attract capital. In 1895, singing for cylinders was by the "round," with up to twenty cylinders being recorded at a time, hard work for entertainers; their income from this process was limited by the few records that could be secured from each performance before the recording horn. The Berliner method permitted the making of an indefinite number of duplicates from one master, with increased volume to boot, decided advantages over any cylinder method.

Early entertainers contracted by Gaisberg included George Graham, a black member of an American Indian medicine troupe, and John O'Derrel, an Irishman who played the banjo and sang with the same company. Fred Gaisberg claimed he was the first to record on Berliner discs many of the great vocal artists of the operatic world, including Enrico Caruso, Sigrid Arnoldsen, Adeline Patti, and Mattia Battistini. According to Will Hayes, a veteran cylinder recording expert and European representative for Edison, however, it was Will Gaisberg who was business agent for Berliner, not his brother Fred, who played the piano accompaniments. Hayes, moreover, is of the opinion that Will Gaisberg deserves the larger share of the credit for the phenomenal success of this initial gramophone recording tour. Be that as it may, the zeal of these two converts to discs gave the popularity of the gramophone throughout the world its initial impetus.

Largely through the work of the Gaisbergs, Europe was to adopt the disc gramophone as a cultural medium—a means of bringing into the home the voices of great singers. In 1895 the gramophone was still hand driven. It appeared to be a toy and was largely sold on that basis. Even though Berliner produced a motor-powered gramophone in 1896, it was left to the Gaisbergs and Clark, together with William Barry Owen, another graduate of the cylinders and Bell-Tainter school, to promote disc usage in America. Fred Gaisberg quite logically thought that the Bell interests might be persuaded to back the commercial introduction of the gramophone in the United States, so, armed with a special exhibit, he and an assistant went to Boston to attend a meeting of the board of directors of Bell's telephone company. Although the financiers were amused, they were not inclined to invest.

Through the continued enthusiasm and efforts of the Gaisbergs, $25,000 was raised by the sale of stock to a group of Philadelphia investors, and the U.S. Gramophone Company was organized. The task of fitting a clockwork motor into the gramophone began. An advertisement for hand-wound spring motors to be used with sewing machines led Gaisberg to the Camden, New Jersey, machine shop of Eldridge R. Johnson, who was destined to play a powerful role in shaping not only the future of the gramophone but the entire course of the industry. The first order to Johnson was for 200 motors, with an advance from the funds that had been raised. The first lot failed to operate properly, and Fred Gaisberg prevailed upon Johnson to install a flat type of spring, similar to the one Edison was using in his spring-motor phonograph.

At the time Gaisberg opened his Philadelphia studio, all discs were seven inches in diameter, stamped from vulcanite. Later some were made from Duranoid, a semiflexible composition. The average playing time was about two minutes as against approximately three minutes for the slow-speed cylinders. Gaisberg rounded up more and more popular recording artists and soon had a considerable stock of recordings for Clark to purvey. In Atlantic City, Gaisberg met the handsome and popular tenor Ferruccio Giannini traveling with a small opera company. Gaisberg persuaded Giannini to record "La Donna e Mobile" and "Quest o Quella" at the Philadelphia studio. Highly successful recordings, these were the first operatic records to be made on discs.

Wax blanks were infinitely superior to any other medium for making a master recording, whether cylinder or disc. The problem lay in making their surface conductive to electroplating. There is some confusion as to who first discovered that wax could be rendered conductive by simply brushing it with finely powdered graphite. In *American Graphophone Co. vs. Emerson Phonograph Co.*, Eldridge Johnson testified that in September 1896 he had found that wax blanks could be copper plated by this method, and that it was first done for him by a friend named Dubois. Johnson stated that duplicate records were not actually produced commercially under this process until April 1898. He made every effort to keep his work secret until 1900, which is perhaps understandable in view of the tangled situation that had arisen in his relationships with Berliner and Frank

Seaman, the exclusive sales agent for gramophone products in the United States by contract with U.S. Gramophone.

By 1898 sales of Gramophones and records were zooming. Eldridge Johnson was quoted in the Camden, New Jersey, *Telegram* in October, saying he had been putting out 600 machines per week for some time and that he was planning to increase production to 1,500 per week by operating his shop twenty-four hours a day. With the Gramophone's commercial success seemingly assured, the avaricious proprietors of American Graphophone began to lay plans for getting into the disc market, a move that would inevitably test the relative value of certain key patents.

The basic patent, 564,586, issued to Emile Berliner July 28, 1896, applied for November 7, 1887, read in part:
"The original record, as well as the copy of the same, is thus obtained as an undulatory line of even depth, as distinguished from a line of varying depth, obtained from the ordinary phonograph and graphophone."[6] The question of the applicability of the Bell-Tainter incising patent with reference to a cutting stylus drew the battle lines between the proprietors of the Bell-Tainter patent and the proprietors of the Berliner patent, with neither side daring a frontal attack.

Early in 1899 the executives of American Graphophone mapped out a campaign to break into the lateral-disc talking-machine business. There appeared in the *Phonoscope* in August 1899 a half-page advertisement describing a new horn-type machine similar to the Gramophone, called the Vitaphone. This advertisement carried the statement "Manufactured under the basic patents of the American Graphophone Co." Berliner's U.S. Gramophone Company retaliated by publishing a notice in the September 1899 issue of *Phonoscope* that these Vitaphone machines and records were being made in violation of its patents. U.S. Gramophone further alleged that the bright red Vitaphone records were actually copies of Berliner records. In this same issue another article told of a disc machine, the Zonophone, similar to the Gramophone, offered for sale by a New York company affiliated with Seaman's National Gramophone Company, exclusive sales agent for the Gramophone in the United States. This affiliated company turned out to be the Universal Talking Machine Company, by a suspicious coincidence organized in February 1898 in Yonkers, New York, the location of National Gramophone.

The most conclusive evidence of the connection between these two corporations is molded into the first Zonophone records, which were seven inches in diameter and similar to the Berliner records in appearance: "Zonophone Record—National Gramophone Corp.—All Rights Reserved"; in relief on the back of the record, where "all rights" are also reserved to the "Universal Talking Machine Co.," the condition of lease states that "this record is leased upon the express condition that it shall not be copied or duplicated, and that the full right of property and possession immediately reverts to the *Universal Talking Machine Company* upon violation of the above contract."

As the records were thus leased and not sold, perhaps the conspirators felt that the courts would not be able to construe the subsequent use as a violation of Berliner patents, or of Seaman's exclusive sales agreement with Berliner and U.S. Gramophone. The absence of patent information on the record itself is significant. The product of the Universal Talking Machine Company was named the Zonophone, with F. M. Prescott as sole export agent. To make the tangle more complete, Prescott until then had been the export agent for the U.S. Phonograph Company of Newark—also exclusive exporters of Edison cylinder machines and supplies.

Prescott unexpectedly sued Edison, the Edison Phonograph Works, and its business manager for diverting the profitable export business he had formerly enjoyed under the U.S. Phonograph Company to a new distributing company, Edison's National Phonograph Company. U.S. Phonograph just as unexpectedly consented to a decree brought against it by American Graphophone alleging infringements of a Bell-Tainter duplicating patent. Undoubtedly the skids had been well greased in this maneuver, for Edison's attorneys made no attempt to defend his former export company and announced that its former manager, George S. Tewksbury, no longer had any relationship with the Edison Phonograph Works.[7] American Graphophone magnanimously announced it was making a shipment of blank cylinders to U.S. Phonograph so that it could wind up its business.

In November 1899 the *Phonoscope* carried a story criticizing the apparent duplicity of certain individuals. Attention was drawn to the issuance by Seaman's National Gramophone Company of circular letters calling favorable attention to the Vitaphone made by the American Talking Machine Company, but not to the Zonophone made by the Universal Talking Machine Company. C. H. LaDow was president and financial backer of the Universal Talking Machine Company and also secretary and general manager of the Seaman's National Gramophone Company. Suit was brought against the American Talking Machine Company by the Berliner Gramophome Company on the basis of the Berliner patents. Berliner Gramophone alleged that Frank Seaman had been assiduous in betraying Berliner interests to competitors. Seaman replied with a petition to have Gramophone Company enjoined from using the name "Gramophone" on its products. As the American Talking Machine Company had earlier been enjoined from using its own name on its own products, the result was a complete tying up of the disc industry. For a considerable time American Graphophone was stymied in its efforts to break into the disc business, and Berliner had to confine himself in the United States to the export business.

Nevertheless, in February 1900 Hawthorne & Sheble of Philadelphia introduced the Discophone, licensed under the patents of American Graphophone. Hawthorne & Sheble together with Prescott organized the American Record Company, opening its record-manufacturing plant in Springfield, Massachusetts. American Record's discs were a rich blue with a colorful label on a white ground.

The disc business remained thoroughly encumbered except for Eldridge Johnson, who continued to produce a limited number of machines and records, eliminating the name "Gramophone" from his products. At first the records bore the label "Eldridge R. Johnson Record"; later "Victor Record" was added. In late 1902 Johnson purchased the Globe Record Company, a little-known firm founded by G. H. Burt of the Burt Company, makers of billiards balls and poker chips, and suppliers of mixes for record making. Johnson had filed the name "Victor" as a trademark with the U.S. Patent Office in March 1901. The famous "His Master's Voice" trademark, which pictures a dog listening to a gramophone, had been registered by Emile Berliner in July 1900. The painting of little Nipper, the dog, was the work of Francis Barraud, an Englishman, who had painted it for exhibition at the Royal Academy. When the hanging committee refused it space, Barraud tried to sell it to the talking-machine manufacturer whose product he had originally portrayed. This manufacturer refused to purchase what now is generally considered to be the most valuable trademark in existence. Barraud then painted out the original cylinder machine and painted in the gramophone. William Owen of the newly formed Gramophone Company, Ltd., purchased the painting for £100. Later, Barraud made other copies for the company, but, according to Owen in the July 1906 *Talking Machine World,* the original painting graced the office of Eldridge Johnson in Camden. The astute Johnson made early use of the "His Master's Voice" trademark, adopting it even before the formation of the Victor Talking Machine Co.[8]

1. Original Edison tinfoil phonograph, 1877.

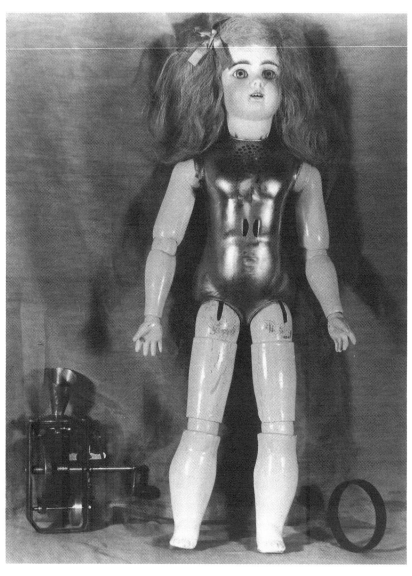

2. Edison talking doll, 1888–89. The internal recording mechanism for the doll is displayed on the left, a wax cylinder for that mechanism on the right.

3. Edison Phonograph Toy Manufacturing Company stock certificate.

4. Advertisement for the Universal Phonograph Company, 1897.

"COLUMBIA"

THE SYNONYM OF SUPERIORITY

THE EXECUTIVE OFFICES OF THE COLUMBIA PHONOGRAPH COMPANY are now located in the spacious buildings, *1155, 1157 and 1159 Broadway, New York City*, the largest and finest establishment of its kind in the world. Every modern facility for manufacturing and selling *everything in the Talking-Machine line*. Promptness and care in attending to orders are special features of our immense system. *We give the same attention to orders for one outfit or one cylinder as to orders for one thousand outfits or cylinders.*

GRAPHOPHONES : : :
AND PHONOGRAPHS

For the Home   For Public Exhibition
For the Store   For Office Use
For Pleasure   For Profit   For Instruction

The Columbia Graphophone

The most marvelous production in the art! Compact, simple, durable and attractive. Records and reproduces with astonishing perfection. Suitable for home entertainment or public exhibition. Not a "Cheap Talking Machine." but a superb Talking Machine *cheap.* Driven by clockwork or electric motor.

Price, $25 and upward

Complete Outfits from $35 upward.

The "Spring-Slot" Graphophone

YOU WIND IT! A prince of money earners. More profit in proportion to expense than any form of slot machine on the market. Only expense for maintenance is the purchase of new records occasionally. Mechanism simple and reliable, reproducing qualities unsurpassed. Splendid for stores, depots, hotel corridors—anywhere the crowd passes. Great trade bringer for stores. *No electricity needed.* Investigate it.

Only $50

"Columbia Records are Best!"

Do you use them? You should! We make and sell more records than all other manufacturers and dealers combined. We couldn't do it if "Columbia Records" were not THE BEST. We run our record-making department *twenty-four hours a day*. Have to do it to keep up with our orders. Dealers who sell our records report remarkable increase in trade and *are continually ordering more*. A sample order will convince you if you do not already know

"COLUMBIA RECORDS ARE BEST!"

Projecting Machines and Films

THE PHANTOSCOPE. A projecting machine suitable for exhibition in large cities or small towns and villages. Calcium or electric light may be used. Simple and satisfactory. Steady pictures, clear views. A Phantoscope and Graphophone make an exhibition combination that will "coin money." Catalogue free.
FILMS. For Kinetoscopes or Projecting Machines. Splendid subjects, clearly defined pictures, superb examples of photographic art. Send for list and prices.

GET OUR ILLUSTRATED DESCRIPTIVE CIRCULARS OF GRAPHOPHONES,
PHONOGRAPHS, RECORDS, AND SUPPLIES. MAILED FREE ON APPLICATION.

COLUMBIA PHONOGRAPH COMPANY "DEPARTMENT A₁"

1155, 1157, and 1159 BROADWAY, New York City

919 Pennsylvania Avenue, Washington, D. C.   110 East Baltimore Street, Baltimore, Md
720 and 722 Olive Street, St. Louis, Mo.

5. Advertisement for the Columbia Phonograph Company, 1897.

LIEUTENANT BETTINI'S

Micro-Phonograph

RECORDER AND REPRODUCER FOR

EDISON'S PHONOGRAPH

A TRUE MIRROR OF SOUND

♦

Just Out. THE IMPROVED MODEL, '97

With the Automatic Self-Adjusting Reproducer

Gives the most faithful reproduction in a loud, clear, and natural tone, *distinctly audible in the largest hall or theatre. The only machine that successfully records and reproduces the female voice.*

JUST OUT

BETTINI'S MICRO-REPRODUCER FOR GRAPHOPHONE

(Automatic Self-adjusting)

SPECIALTY: High-grade records, high-class music, and only by leading performers and world-famed artists. Send for catalogue.

Also on hand : Phonograph, Graphophone, Projecting Machine, etc., etc.

PHONOGRAPH LABORATORY 110 FIFTH AVENUE New York City

6. *Left*: Advertisement for the Bettini Micro-Phonograph, 1897.
7. *Below*: Advertisement for Edison phonographs, National Phonograph Company, 1897.

AT LAST!

Genuine—
―EDISON―
―Phonographs
$30.00

EDISON RECORDS
50c. Each, $5.00 per Doz.

WRITE FOR CATALOGUE 21

National Phonograph Co., Edison Laboratory, Orange, N. J.

8. Phonograph room in Edison's laboratory at Orange. Note the talking doll on the Weber piano. A recording horn and wax cylinder masters are in the foreground. Photo by W. K. L. Dickson, ca. 1888.

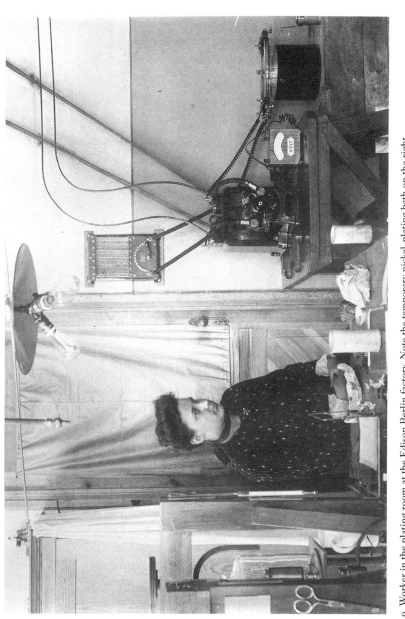

9. Worker in the plating room at the Edison Berlin factory. Note the temporary nickel-plating bath on the right.

10. Inspecting room at the Edison Paris factory. One worker is listening to a recording; the other is using a microscope to inspect records. Bell jars housing plating mechanisms are in the foreground.

11. Plating room at the Edison Brussels factory.

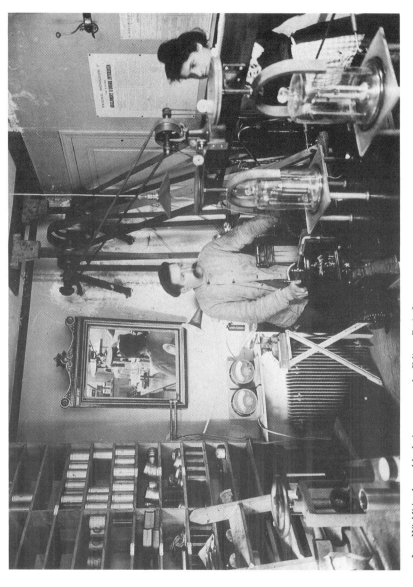

12. Jean Wickli in the gold-plating room at the Edison Paris factory.

13. Copper plating at the Edison Berlin factory.

14. Gold plating at the Edison Berlin factory. Note the gold-plated wax cylinder in the far right bell jar.

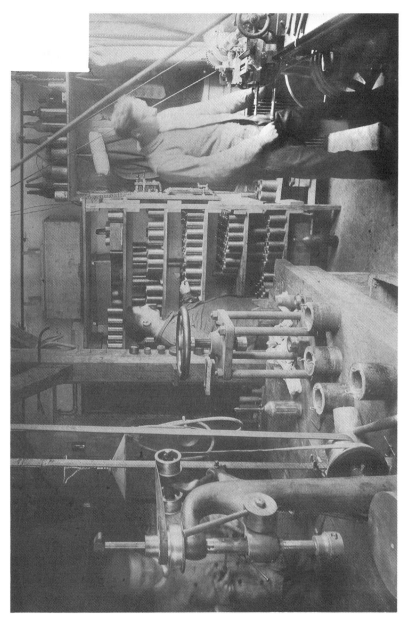

15. Machine shop at the Edison Paris factory.

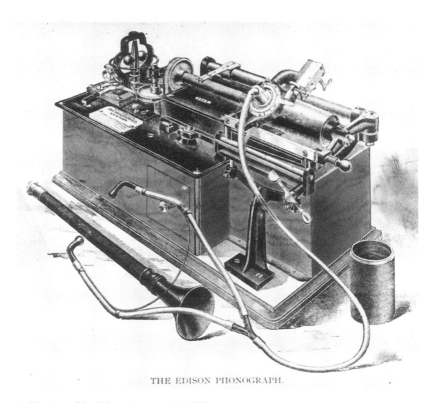

THE EDISON PHONOGRAPH.

16. Drawing of the Edison phonograph, 1888.

17. George Gouraud, left, supervising recording at Little Menlo, Beulah Hill, England, 1888–89. Note the recording equipment on the balcony; a recording horn is being held directly over the piano.

18. Mary Helen Ferguson typing from dictation recorded on an Edison phonograph, 1888–89. Note the primary battery on the table behind the phonograph.

19. Graham Hope using an Edison phonograph for dictation, March 3, 1889, Edison House, London.

20. Gouraud giving dictation into an Edison phonograph, 1888–89. A primary battery jar is on the table near the phonograph.

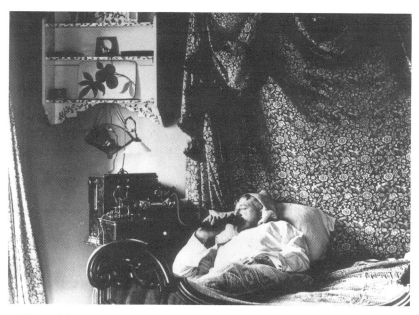

21. Gouraud dictating into Edison phonograph while lying in bed, Little Menlo, ca. 1888–89.

22. Gouraud dictating into Edison phonograph, 1888–89. Note the wax cylinders and the primary battery on the table, along with a photograph of Edison.

23. Phonograph parlor at a ferry juncture with the Pennsylvania Railroad, 1891–92.

Jacques Urlus and Soder's Orchestra recording at the Edison Studio, 79 Fifth Avenue, New York, ca. 1900.

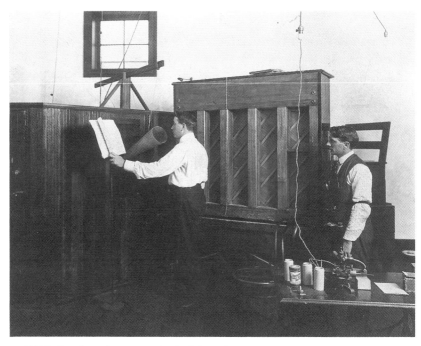

25. Ed Meeker, formerly a painter for the Edison Company, recording before the horn. Clifford J. Werner is operating the recording equipment, ca. 1903.

26. Edison cement phonographs, 1912. Note the relief ornamentation on the sides and front.

27. Statuesque Edison cement phonograph, barely showing the actual phonograph within the opening, 1912.

28. Edison listening to voice trials.

29. Edison Phonograph Works, Lakeside Avenue, West Orange, N.J., 1914.

). Advertisement for Edison talking pictures.

Interior of Edison Kinetophone studio looking toward entrance, May 1914. Note the Edison phonograph on the
f at right and the rug on the floor in the filming area.

32. The first talking picture studio in the world. Edison Kinetophone experimental recording and photographing were done simultaneously in this echo-proof tent in the yard of the Edison Storage Battery Works, Orange, N.J.

33. Music Room, building no. 5, Edison Laboratory, 1923. Note the Edison phonograph artist publicity shots lining the walls; the Victor machine in the center of the room was obtained for comparison purposes.

34. Three Edison recording artists posing for a tone test publicity shot: Blanche L. Dann, M. Felice Dann, and Rosalynd J. Davis.

35. Nat Shilkret, Gladys Rice, Douglas Stanbury, 1931.

36. Edison listening to a vocal performance by Helen Davis in the Music Room, building no. 5, Edison Laboratory. Noted pianist Victor Young accompanying.

37. Edison Recording Department employees performing in front of the Edison Laboratory, West Orange, N.J. Third from left, William Meadowcroft; third from right, Clarence Hayes; second from right, Edison.

38. Harold Lyman giving a tone test in Atlantic City, 1924.

39. Edison Recording Department employees Fred Burt (standing) and George Werner before a recording horn, 1913.

40. Treadle model North American phonograph, 1892, given to Mrs. Homer Page, Milan, Ohio. Mrs. Page was Edison's sister. A handwritten note by Edison dated January 28, 1892, reads: "Walter Miller: Have you anybody you could send out to Milan Ohio—to put up a treadle machine for my sister—if so let me know also if you can get a good treadle that will govern well for music. I want to send one of every duplicate you have made. Edison." Order no. 78, Mrs. Homer Page, Milan, Ohio.

CHAPTER 12 ➤

The International Situation

HENRY EDMUNDS, an English electrical engineer, was the first overseas entrepreneur to witness the demonstration of the phonograph:

> Before returning to Europe I called with Professor Barker one afternoon in
> November [1877] on Mr. T. A. Edison, at his then small laboratory in Menlo
> Park. Prof. Barker led the way, opening the door; in a dimly lighted interior we could just see Mr. Edison and his assistant working upon a small
> brass cylinder covered with tinfoil. Edison held up his hand dramatically.
> We halted. He slowly turned the cylinder with a handle and an unearthly
> metallic voice with a strong American accent spoke out the words "Mary
> had a little lamb." We had arrived just in time to hear the first reproduction
> of mechanically recorded speech.[1]

In January 1878 Edmunds returned to London, met with William Preece, the General Post Office chief engineer, and presented him with a letter of introduction from Edison. Preece was scheduled to introduce the telephone to the Royal Society on February 1 and wanted to include Edison's new phonograph at the same gathering. With drawings supplied by Edmunds, Preece had one of his assistants, Augustus Stroh, build a prototype. The Royal Society, counting among its attendees the eminent British physicist John Tyndall and poet laureate Alfred Tennyson, was indeed impressed. Edmunds conveyed to Edison that he hoped he would see fit to appoint him British agent for the phonograph.[2]

Royal Letters patent 2909 for "Improvements in Telephonic Communications" announced to the British scientific community Edison's discovery of sound recording and reproduction, although it did not mention the phonograph as such.

A second provisional specification for "Improvements in Means for Recording Sounds and in Reproducing Such Sounds from Such Recording," Letters patent 1644, was sealed on August 6, 1878. The tinfoil phonograph was to become available through the London Stereoscopic Company, in 1885 known as the London Stereoscopic and Photographic Company, Ltd.[3]

In 1888 the phonograph came to be publicized by a very colorful figure —Colonel George Edward Gouraud, son of François Fauvel-Gouraud, who had studied under Daguerre and who subsequently was the first to bring the daguerrotype process to the United States. That the flamboyant, socially aspiring Gouraud happened to be the man chosen by Thomas Edison to be his associate and representative in England for the phonograph was indeed fortuitous, for he was the right man at the right time. His personality and presence commanded attention and elicited an enthusiastic response from his listeners.[4]

As early as 1879 Edison conveyed to Gouraud powers of attorney in matters dealing with telephones and phonographs:

> Know all men by these Presents, that I, Thomas Alva Edison, of Menlo Park, in the State of New Jersey, United States of America, have made, constituted and appointed, and by these presents do make, constitute, and appoint George E. Gouraud, of No. 6 Lombard Street, London, England, my true and lawful attorney for me, and in my name, place, and stead, to represent me the said Edison, in connection with the contract between the London Stereoscopic Company, and myself, concerning my Improvements in Phonographs and Telephones.[5]

Gouraud's strategy in promoting the perfected phonograph of 1888 with its wax cylinder phonograms entailed an exchange of phonographic messages between Edison and noteworthy personages across the Atlantic.

> Edison: Your choice of Hamilton is good. Please be sure to caution him against showing [it] on the steamer, as anything of that sort done, especially if use were made of your original phonogram to me, before I received it, would tend to diminish the interest with which I shall surround the use of that first phonogram on its arrival here.
>
> In order that you may understand the importance of this, I may tell you that I am already arranging a list of the most distinguished people I know, many of whom I only know by reputation, but whom I shall not hesitate to

invite to *meet you* on an occasion which will be the talk of the whole reading and talking world. I shall give an "at home" for the purpose and shall issue cards, in these terms:

> To meet Prof. Edison,
> Non presentem, sed alloquentem!

Besides the duplicates of "Phonogram No. 1" which you send by Hamilton, send one or more by *mail*—in same and following steamers. In it ask me to use *only* the Phonograph in my future correspondence with you, and add— what a happy escape for both of us from the drudgery of the pen.

Gouraud also wrote to his brother-in-law, Rev. Dr. Horatio Nelson Powers, in Piermont-on-the-Hudson, New York, that he should approach Edison on the matter of inclusion of some words on this first phonogram appropriate to the inauguration of the phonograph in England. The result was the poem entitled "The Phonograph's Salutation."[6]

Gouraud planned that the phonograph should be heralded as the "Feature of the Evening" at a banquet to honor Sir John Pender, K.C.M.G. (and so forth), on April 23, 1888, but the first perfected phonograph did not arrive in time. In fact, it did not arrive until late June, when Gouraud himself made a trip to the United States and hand-carried it back to England, with an assistant, Harrold de Couvry Hamilton, in tow. Gouraud cautioned Edison not to exhibit or remark on his new invention prematurely, as subsequent patents in foreign countries required both translation and mailing, a procedure that could require nearly a month. He was concerned about the possible breakage and chipping of the fragile wax cylinders and suggested to Edison that he think about changing the format to a disc or rolling sheet phonogram.[7] By October 1, 1888, Edison had changed from a battery-powered to a treadle-powered machine with a harder wax cylinder, and he wrote to Gouraud:

> Don't be troubled in least about Edmunds blowing about engraving. Look close at paragraph in my 2nd English patent, where I state, wax may be recorded on directly, but as point clogs up prefer cover with foil under conditions old phono, that is true, used waxes too soft; graphophone wax was only got hard enough to prevent clogging by great amount experimenting.[8]

Gouraud gave a series of "at homes" or "kettle drums" to present the phonograph to society and political figures. He and his assistants, Hamilton and Charles

Rhenius Cruywagen Steytler, recorded the voices of a number of members of the British royal family and the nobility, as well as figures in the arts, the church, and the military.[9]

The first clue that Gouraud's style of promoting Edison's inventions was somewhat unusual came in 1880 when E. H. Johnson wrote to Edison:

> As Gouraud won't "lower" himself to the level of a "mere subordinate of the company" and speak to "an ungrateful dog," his curiosity to see the lamps has to be held in check until such time as the "dishonourable trickster" [Gouraud] whom [Edison] "took from the gutter of New York" and to whom he has "frequently loaned money" sees the error of his ways and recognizes the superior fitness for all things mortal of his Royal Highness, the Duke of Norwood.[10]

Samuel Insull, who was by this time employed in England for Edison interests, was known to call Gouraud the "illustrious Colonel" on occasion and reported to A. O. Tate, Edison's private secretary, that Gouraud was making a great deal of money by exhibiting the phonograph and pocketing the proceeds. Edison retaliated by asking Tate "to write Gouraud a strong letter about these advertising schemes. I don't propose to be Barnumized." John Vail was to write from London to Edison, "Gouraud is making a nice old advertisement *for himself* out of *your* phonograph." Even William H. Wiley, treasurer of the American Society of Mechanical Engineers, had his doubts:

> My dear Edison: Stanley discovered Livingston although I have always believed that Livingston not only did not care a —— about being discovered but would have actually have preferred not to have been discovered *at all.* Be that as it may, it seems from "Engineering" issue of Nov. 30 in the Report of the Society of Arts, that it was reserved for Gouraud to discover *you!* Not only this, but he seems also to have discovered in some way, the Phonograph. He also discovered my brother [O. S. Wiley], and if he is not stopped he will discover me.

According to Osgood S. Wiley, experimenter for Edison, there were queer rumors about Gouraud, exhibitions given for charity where the proceeds were scooped into his own pocket with the whole of London laughing at him. Gouraud refuted all claims to his conducting himself other than as a gentleman.[11]

Gouraud saw to it that heads of state and other prominent figures received working models of Edison's phonograph as gifts. Friedrich Krupp, the emperor of Japan, the king of Korea, Li Hung Chang, Tseng Kuo Chnan, President Diaz, Josef Hofmann, and Joseph Pulitzer all were recipients of the improved invention. J. Block recorded voices in eastern Europe and Russia, while Theodore Wangemann tapped German sources. Gouraud demonstrated the phonograph's capabilities to the British Association for the Advancement of Science meeting in Bath on September 6, 1888, the same meeting at which Henry Edmunds, then of W. T. Glover & Company in London, gave a demonstration of the Tainter graphophone. An ensuing battle erupted over patented rights to wax-incising recording methods.

The Edison Phonograph Company, Ltd., was first located at 181 Queen Victoria Street but later was moved to Northumberland House, Northumberland Avenue, London. Gouraud was its head, with J. Lewis Young as general manager. Down Queen Victoria Street at number eleven was the Graphophone Syndicate, Ltd., which received its certificate of incorporation on January 14, 1889. The graphophone was never exploited in Britain as it was in the United States, since the International Graphophone Company, formed in 1889 in West Virginia, had world rights to the Bell and Tainter patents. The governing officers of the International Graphophone Company convinced Edison to join forces with the Bell and Tainter interests through joint overseas patents. The outcome was the formation of the Edison United Phonograph Company of Newark, New Jersey.

Incorporated in 1890, the Edison United Phonograph Company had as its officers Thomas Edison, George Gouraud, and Jesse Seligman. Stephen Moriarty was appointed European representative. The Edison Phonograph Works in Orange was to manufacture the phonographs and cylinders for the Edison United Phonograph Company.

Following the formation of the Edison United Phonograph Company in the United States, the Edison Phonograph Company in London was re-formed as the Edison United Phonograph Company, a London branch of the parent company. The domain of the London company, managed by Gouraud, Moriarty, and Theodore Seligman, took in Central and South America, Europe, Asia, Africa, and Australasia. Moriarty was often at odds with his employer, Thomas Edison, probably because he had been associated with the graphophone interests prior to the formation of the Edison United Phonograph Company, Ltd.

The commercialization of the phonograph in Britain had not yet occurred, for it was almost impossible for anyone to obtain a machine. Although the first commercial catalog of phonograph records had already been published in the United States, no recordings were being made overseas for public sale.[12] Moriarty contended that the phonograph was strictly a commercial machine, should be used for dictating and business reasons, and would never be truly successful as entertainment.

By 1892 word had filtered back to Edison that Gouraud was not proving a good businessman in the selling of phonographs. Through the continued insistence of Moriarty, Jesse Seligman negotiated Gouraud's final resignation, though he continued to hold stock within the company.[13]

By October 30, 1892, Edison had transferred manufacturing rights in Great Britain to a new British company, Edison Bell Phonograph Corporation, Ltd., for one quarter of the stock and cash that Edison United would receive. Edison Bell Phonograph, at Bartholomew House, Bartholomew Lane, London, was formed on November 30, 1892. Edison, as a stockholder in Edison United Phonograph, had a continued interest in the Bell-Tainter patents in Britain; in the United States those same patents would continue to irk him time and again in the coming years. Members of the Edison Bell board were Moriarty, Jesse Seligman, Edward J. Coates, F. Faithfull Begg, D. Johnstone Smith, and William Alexander Smith. The company now had a monopoly on the Edison phonograph and the Bell-Tainter graphophone, along with any further improvements made by Edison, Alexander Graham Bell, Chichester Bell, or Charles Sumner Tainter. The only machine not reckoned with was the gramophone, due to be marketed by the Gramophone Company at Maiden Lane, near Charing Cross, London.[14] By December 1896 Stephen Moriarty had purchased Edison's shares in Edison United Phonograph, and thus ended all existing contracts between Thomas Edison, the Edison Phonograph Works, and the Edison United Phonograph Company. In August 1895 Edison United Phonograph entered into an agreement with Ludwig Stollwerck of the Gebrüder Stollwerck Company of Cologne, Germany, to sell phonographs and graphophones throughout the German empire.

With the increased popularity of gramophone records, it became apparent that the Edison Bell enterprises should sell machines and records, rather than lease them. Early in 1898 the Edison Bell Phonograph Corporation reorganized under Moriarty's direction to become the Edison Bell Consolidated Phonograph Company. Headquarters were established at 39 Charing Cross Road, London, with James Edward Hough appointed as general sales manager. Hough's Edisonia,

Ltd., founded June 15, 1897, became the manufacturing company for the new Edison Bell company.

The expiration in 1900 of the Bell-Tainter patent for recording by cutting into wax meant that the Gramophone Company, Ltd., could now record onto blank wax disc masters; by December the company became the Gramophone and Typewriter, Ltd.[15] Another reorganization at Edison Bell Consolidated Phonograph Company cleared the way for Edison machines and records to come into Britain free of the former Edison Bell company's control.

J. Lewis Young and E. Sinclair in 1902 began negotiations to establish a company called the National Phonograph Company, Ltd. On July 24, 1902, the company listed Sir George Croydon Marks as managing director and Young and Sinclair as his codirectors, with offices at 55–56 Chancery Lane, London. By January 1904 the company had moved to 25 Clerkenwell Road, with James White as managing director, Charles C. Squire as assistant manager, and Marks as chair of the directors.[16] The Recording Department, although housed in the same building, was neither administered nor controlled by the London company, since it was an outpost of the Recording Department at Orange, with William A. Hayes in charge.[17] Edison Bell Consolidated Phonograph and National Phonograph, Ltd., were now the reigning enterprises in the overseas recording business. National Phonograph, Ltd., had exclusive rights to the use of the Edison signature trademark and was the sole distributor in Britain for Edison phonographs. As a result, Edison Bell, Pathé Frères (London), Ltd.,[18] and Columbia Phonograph, newly removed from Paris, were to provide the main competition in Britain for the Edison phonograph.

By August 1907 a new factory was established by National Phonograph, Ltd., at Willesden Junction in northwest London. This year also was the last for Columbia cylinder records in Britain. Chief competition for the Edison product was to come from the Edison Bell Gold Moulded record and the Sterling record of the Russell Hunting Record Company, Ltd.[19]

By 1913 the cylinder business was rapidly declining as the disc's popularity rose. The Edison interests, now consolidated into a new company, Thomas A. Edison, Ltd.,[20] received instructions from Orange to close up and dispose of the Willesden factory and offices and to move all operations to the old premises at Clerkenwell Road.

Ten years later Edison Diamond Discs were being advertised in Great Britain, as in the United States, with tone tests, the first of which was held May 2, 1923, at St. George's Hall in Liverpool. The performance by soprano Helen Davis, accompanied by her husband, pianist and composer Victor Young, was as convincing as similar tone tests given by Davis and Young in the United States. The audience believed in the completeness of the recording, finding it an accurate "re-creation."

Electrical recording on Edison discs began in 1927, but none of these lateral-cut electrical recordings ever was advertised to the British consumer. To play an Edison disc record, whether acoustically or electrically recorded, required an Edison disc phonograph, a phenomenon peculiar to the Edison trademark. The Edison Company's hurriedly concocted scheme to produce electrical disc recordings in order to combat declining sales went unnoticed in Great Britain, and it was not long before word was received from the United States that the company had closed down its recording business as of October 30, 1929.

CHAPTER 13

Discs Versus Cylinders

PERHAPS THE most difficult fact of phonograph history for the layperson to accept is that the recording method that involved the more serious technical compromises was the one destined to win. The explanation lies in economics, for in a commercial venture the first concern is for profits rather than for technical perfection.

The technical superiority of the large concert cylinders over standard-diameter cylinders as compared with the discs illustrates this point. The principle behind the use of a large-diameter cylinder was that higher overtones could be recorded with greater facility and fidelity. Cylinder rotation, as compared to disc rotation, created an optimum surface speed for both recording and reproduction. Edison believed that the essential superiority of the cylinder over the disc lay in this inherent ability to record at a constant surface speed. He also felt that this advantage and the corresponding reproduction advantages would offset any conveniences offered by the discs in handling, filing, and space economy. Edison's confidence in the technical superiority of the cylinder over the disc meant that his company continued to develop the cylinder method long after most others had forsaken it. His attitude thus was responsible in large part for the belated development of an Edison disc instrument.

The cumbersome, fragile, five-inch-diameter concert-sized cylinders exaggerated the disadvantages of cylinders as compared with discs. The smaller-diameter cylinders were housed in cartons somewhat larger in diameter than the cylinder, so as to leave an air space all around. Concert cylinder cartons were of the same design, but larger—six inches in diameter and five inches high. In only an inch more of space, fifty of the comparatively unbreakable Berliner discs could be stacked. The cost of these large cylinders was another unfavorable factor. Each had to be an original recording, as no successful molding method was ever developed for them, although some were undoubtedly duplicated by transcribing. The original $5.00 cost decreased to $2.50, which would buy five of the seven-inch discs. Edison was well aware of these facts and devoted his attention to a method of transferring the improved quality and increased volume of the larger cylinders to the more convenient and inexpensive standard-size cylinders.

Around the turn of the century the revolutions per minute of all standard cylinders were increased from 120 to 160. Columbia introduced a line of XP high-speed cylinders, whose only drawback was that playing time was reduced conversely to the increase in speed, for the number of grooves to the inch remained 100. In 1897 Edison cylinder records were made at a speed of 90 rpm; in 1898 this became 120, and in 1899, 140, where the speed remained until the method of duplication changed to the molded process in 1902. Then it became 160 rpm, the last change in speed for cylinder records. The Edison disc was recorded at 80 rpm, 150 threads to the inch, 50 threads less than the Blue Amberol record. The master recording machine was tuned to the tone of A, or 435 vibrations. All Edison discs had a front margin of $\frac{21}{32}$ of an inch, and a space in the center of 4 inches where the label could be surmounted. The master blank had a shaved surface of $10\frac{1}{2}$ inches, a depth of $\frac{5}{8}$ of an inch, and a bottom diameter of $10\frac{3}{4}$ inches. The 12-inch blank had a shaved surface of $12\frac{7}{16}$ inches in diameter, a thickness of $\frac{5}{8}$ of an inch, and a bottom diameter of $12\frac{1}{2}$ inches. On both the cylinder record, 200 threads to the inch, and the disc record, 150 threads to the inch, a recording stylus .008 of an inch in diameter was used. Recording limit on 10-inch blanks was $2\frac{21}{32}$ inches, and on the 12-inch blank, $3\frac{11}{16}$ inches.

The cylinder method from the first was more scientific than that of the disc. The groove speed beneath the stylus of a standard ten-inch disc diminishes by more than 50 percent in traveling from the outermost turns of the groove spiral to the innermost.

After 1903 Victor abandoned the seven-inch record size, recording the same popular selections on eight-, ten-, and twelve-inch discs. The matrix of the earlier seven-inch discs was prefixed with the letter *A*, the ten-inch with the letter *B*, and the twelve-inch *C*. Very likely *D* was reserved for the short-lived fourteen-inch Victor series. In any case the new eight-inch series matrix numbers were prefixed with *E*. With the larger discs the customer received proportionately longer playing time and usually somewhat better tone quality and durability.

At first the standard molded cylinder records sold for $.50 each. During this same competitive period the seven-inch discs sold for $.50. The new eight-inch discs were priced at $.35, the ten-inch popular music discs at $1, and the twelve-inch at $1.50. The same selection, recorded by the same artist or artists, bore the same matrix number with the appropriate prefix letter on each size. The same catalog number was used for the eight- and ten-inch records of the same selection, although not for the twelve-inch. Columbia discs were also made in seven- and ten-inch sizes, using the same catalog number for the same selection.

One of the most successful and continuous advertising campaigns of all times had its inception shortly after the formation of the Eldridge Johnson's Victor Talking Machine Company in October 1901. Johnson was a firm believer in the business potentials of national advertising and distribution. The campaign began with small ads placed regularly in the more popular U.S. magazines. At first this advertising was centered around the Victor Talking Machine's capability as a home entertainer and recordings of popular artists. Then the famous listening-dog trademark of "Little Nipper" began to make its appearance, identifying each ad as that of the Victor Company. (Johnson had also used the dog trademark earlier in ads for his Consolidated Talking Machine Company.)

Within a year Victor was announcing to the trade that it had 10,000 dealers and had sold $2 million worth of goods. When the first group of Victor's Imported Red Seal records was offered for sale in 1902, through arrangement with its European affiliate, Gramophone & Typewriter, Ltd., the astute Johnson realized that he had the right combination for building prestige and volume sales for his company. Among these first releases were records by famous French baritone Maurice Renaud, Mme. Kristmann of the St. Petersburg Opera, noted French basso Pol Plançon, soprano Ada Crossley, baritone Jean Delmas, Antonio Scotti, baritone Mattia Battistini, and tenor Enrico Caruso.

In 1903, full-page ads on the Imported Red Seal records, with pictures of the artists, were featured in *Harper's Weekly* and other popular magazines. Sales of these celebrity records at prices considerably higher than those of popular records were phenomenal. The success of this initial offering undoubtedly inspired the inauguration of the Victor Red Seal series in 1904. In the metropolitan areas, in particular, sales of Victor Talking Machines began to increase rapidly as a result of the availability of operatic and celebrity recordings. By 1906, when Edison belatedly began issuing his Grand Opera series on two-minute wax cylinders, it was too late.

Competition centered around the Victor interests and the American Grapho-phone Company. The ambitious American Graphophone executives, with inter-ests in both kinds of record, decided to institute a red seal series under the Columbia label. Two series of popular disc records, seven-inch diameter at fifty cents and ten-inch at one dollar each, were already being offered under the black-and-silver Columbia label. In 1903 Columbia announced a red label Grand Opera series. The first issue featured records by Marcella Sembrich, Anton Van Rooy, Ernestine Schumann-Heink, Suzanne Adams, Giuseppe Campanari, and Edouard DeReszke. Three titles were offered by DeReszke, the only commercial records ever to be made by this renowned singer. The Columbia Grand Opera Series was poorly recorded, and the venture was comparatively unsuccessful.

The merchandising policies of Victor and Columbia differed in many ways. Columbia for a number of years adhered to its established cylinder business, opening its own branch salesrooms and warehouses. Victor appointed already well-established commercial houses as jobbers and distributors. As early as mid-1903 Victor had secured three times as many outlets as Columbia. Several jobbers carried both Edison and Victor merchandise.

The chief battleground for a time would be the markets rather than courts of law. Eldridge Johnson, with his characteristic sagacity and good business sense, placed an ad using the entire back cover of the April 1904 *Saturday Evening Post* to announce Victor's exclusive contract to record the voice of Enrico Caruso. Fully aware of the superiority of their goods, the Victor executives entered the latest Victor Talking Machines and records into the premium awards competition of the 1904 St. Louis Exposition. Columbia Phonograph did likewise, and both com-panies profited greatly from this exposure. A hot controversy developed between the leading talking-machine companies over awards made at the exposition.[1]

Victor and Columbia advertisements in *Talking Machine World* reflected a com-plete difference of opinion as to which had won the grand prize. Victor had a large ad claiming, "Victor wins the Grand Prize, highest possible award over all talking machines at the Exposition." Columbia's ad read, "The Graphophone and Columbia Records win highest honors—Double Grand Prize, three gold medals." Columbia's ad claimed that the Victor ad was based only on the *recom-mendation* of an inferior jury empowered to make recommendations, whereas final award decisions were in the hands of two superior juries. Eventually Columbia sued both the exposition authorities and the Victor company. When Columbia won the case, it had the opportunity to create a new celebrity label, the famous banner label, carrying the awards won.

A succession of new machines followed the St. Louis Exposition, some with very promising potential, but few with the proper financial or patent environments to survive. One new company named Talk-O-Phone began the production of a lateral disc machine and records in March 1904 and within a year claimed to have sold over 25,000 machines. Even the music-box manufacturers began to eye the talking-machine field: the Regina Company of Rahway, New Jersey, makers of a high-quality disc-type music box, the Reginaphone, a combination music box and disc-type phonograph. The Talk-O-Phone Company produced records on a large scale, which naturally brought it into court with companies holding key patents.

Many inventors worked on improvements for cylinders. John C. Dunton of Grand Rapids, Michigan, invented the Multiphone, which would hold and play automatically twenty-four standard cylinders. Dunton said a model would be made that would take cylinders up to twenty-five inches in length, for reproducing entire lectures or operas. A company was organized, and a considerable number of Multiphones were made and sold as coin-in-the-slot machines. Another new machine and record was introduced in England called the Neophone. A strawboard disc with a surface coating of celluloid, the record was the first hill-and-dale type disc commercially produced; a sapphire stylus was used for reproduction. It was patented in England, Austria, Italy, Russia, and Germany by Dr. Michaelis, and its manufacture assumed quite large proportions.

The original wire recorder, the Telegraphone, had been invented by Valdemar Poulsen, a Danish scientist, in 1898. On it, a previous recording could be erased simply by recording over it. There was no means of amplification, so the playback was through telephone earphones and its potential seemed to be in its use as a business machine. During the early 1900s Poulsen and his associates conducted considerable research in the United States with funds raised by stock subscription. Poulsen also developed a method of recording magnetically on iron discs $4\frac{1}{2}$ inches in diameter, about $\frac{1}{20}$ of an inch in thickness. Few were sold, for as far as is known none were sufficiently well developed to be marketed.

One of the more fascinating devices to be launched in this creative period was the Auxetophone invented by C. A. Parsons, of London. This machine employed a compressed-air amplifier based on the principle of the Aerophone, which

Edison had invented some years earlier to amplify the voice for out-of-doors communication. In the Auxetophone, a stream of compressed air was modulated by a valve actuated by the reproducing stylus. The rights to the Parsons patent were bought by Gramophone & Typewriter, Ltd., and the instruments were placed on the market. Capable of great volume, they were not of much use in the home because of a hissing sound. They were offered for sale in the United States by the Victor Talking Machine Company, but, even at the modest price of $500, not many were sold.

A machine developed to produce even greater volume was invented by Daniel Higham of Boston, based on the principle of a friction valve. Rights were bought by American Graphophone, and a machine was marketed in August 1905 as the Twentieth Century Graphophone, a cylinder machine with a larger than usual diaphragm to which amplified vibrations were delivered by means of a variable tension device involving a cord running over an amber wheel. The length of the mandrel was also extended to six inches to permit increased playing time. Some models, made to play concert size cylinders, were soon discontinued. The advertisements claimed that the Twentieth Century Grand would produce sixteen times the volume of the standard machines. Whether the claim was true or not, the machine was not as simple and foolproof an amplifying device as the Edison floating-weight principle, which was a type of mechanical advantage amplifier. By mounting a stylus bar with arms of unequal length upon the side of the floating weight toward the record, more pressure could be exerted upon the record and greater amplitude given to diaphragm movement. The amount of amplification depended on wear limitations.[2]

In the United States the purchase of improvements conceived by independent inventors was the exception rather than the rule. The course of development in the field was fairly well controlled by the big-three companies, Victor, Columbia, and Edison. Abroad, the situation was not so well defined. By 1905 cylinder machines manufactured in Germany and Switzerland were offered for sale in the United States. Bettini, Ltd., a New York company that had purchased the business created by pioneer recorder Gianni Bettini, introduced a disc machine called Hymnophone, made in Germany. Hymnophones had a tone arm carrying the reproducer, with a swivel joint connecting the tone arm to a horn emerging from the front under the turntable. Other machines exported to the United States from included the Clarion and Denham. The Germans also made miniature machines and post-card records for sale as novelties. Machines with aluminum horns and an all-glass horn were also exported from Europe. Means to deal with these sporadic efforts to invade the home market were evidently adequate, for the incursions seldom lasted long.

Victor, as early as 1904, was making twelve-inch records as well as a little-known series of fourteen-inch discs; these carried only popular music and were very bulky, weighing better than a pound apiece, which tended to nullify the advantage of most discs over the equally cumbersome concert-size cylinders. They met with little success and are now rare, as they were supplied only on order for about a year and then dropped. In Europe, some of the Gramophone affiliates and Fonotipia (see chapters 14 and 17) produced celebrity records on discs almost as large as Victor's fourteen-inch discs, though not as heavy. Pathé later sold vertical-cut discs of this diameter in the United States, and, of course, radio transcriptions have been made on discs up to twenty inches in diameter.

When the assets of the Universal Talking Machine Company were acquired by Eldridge Johnson for the Victor Talking Machine Company, Universal became a subsidiary of Victor, but Johnson kept the advertising of the two companies distinct, and the general public did not know who owned Universal. In June 1905 the first advertisement for Zonophone records appeared under the corporate name of the Universal Talking Machine Company and also announced four models of Zonophone talking machines, with tapered tone arms, ranging from $27.50 to $55. Johnson had invented the tapered tone arm to relieve the weight and inertia of the entire horn assembly. As horns had become larger and heavier, counterbalancing them failed, as the outer groove wall of the record spiral still had to work against the inertia of the horn sound-box assembly in order to propel it across the record. Slight eccentricities in the centering of the records not only resulted in frightful wear but produced distressing effects in reproduction.

Johnson's tapered tone arm was to become the focus of patent conflicts with other disc talking machines. The concept of the tone arm as a portion of the amplifying horn and not just as a sound conduction tube was original with Johnson.

Other manufacturers, some with experience in the cylinder field, attempted to get into the disc business. Leeds & Catlin, for example, had been almost continuously in the courts, having been attacked for various infringements by each of the big three. Despite innumerable setbacks, Leeds & Catlin persisted and in 1905 had large plants in Middletown, Connecticut, and in New York City.

A trend toward increased complexity as a result of competitive inventiveness has always been a feature of U.S. industrial development. During the early 1900s attempts to combine the advantages of one type of instrument with those of another resulted in the combination graphophone invented by Thomas H. Mac-Donald: two mandrels, one that would telescope within the other, enabled the playing of both standard- and concert-size cylinders on the same machine. Some of the later Twentieth Century Graphophones such as the Peerless also played two types of cylinders, the standard and the six-inch cylinders. It remained for an Englishman to invent a combination cylinder and disc machine, the Deuxphone, which was on the market for a short time.

While there was much activity in the cylinder field in England and in the United States, elsewhere the disc was already in the ascendancy. In Germany in 1904 the Beka Company announced the first double discs of the industry, thus multiplying by two the former advantage of the disc in handling and storage. A seemingly reactionary note in the United States at about the same time was the announcement by Rosenfeld, a New York manufacturer of automatic entertainment devices, of an illustrated song machine with ear tubes for use in the penny arcades.

There was a new wave of interest in the cultural uses of the phonograph, both cylinder and disc. Williams College adopted the phonograph for language instruction in 1905, although the International Correspondence Schools had used the Edison phonograph for language courses as early as 1897, and the eminent educator Rosenthal even before that. Cornet technique was taught by phonograph at an institute in Chicago.

Henry Seymour was the first person to demonstrate the Edison disc in England, before a gathering at Claremont Hall in London in 1913. Enthusiastic about the new disc, he later wrote in an article for *Sound Wave* that it had next to no surface noise, played nearly twice as long as other records of the same size, and displayed a remarkable refinement in tone. In the same 1922 article comparing Edison cylinders and Edison discs, Seymour reported that postwar disc recordings were decidedly inferior to disc recordings made before World War I. Cylinder and disc had the same type of track, a hill-and-dale configuration, yet the same sounds recorded on a cylinder revolving at 160 times per minute were different, when recorded with the same recorder, than on a ten-inch disc rotating at just half that speed. In two respects was the disc superior to the cylinder, and that was in its broader tone and slightly increased volume. The sibilant sounds were not nearly as pronounced and overtones were lacking, as in the best cylinders. Each had a quality that the other lacked.[3]

Nearly all the publicity of the early days came from direct advertising, demonstrations at fairs, phonograph concerts, and talking-machine parties. The three major companies competed hotly for business, and a price war was the result. In December 1905 Victor announced for the popular series the following price reductions: seven-inch records reduced from $.50 to $.35, ten-inch records reduced from $1 to $.60, and twelve-inch records reduced from $1.50 to $1. Columbia met the cuts the same day, and Leeds & Catlin reduced the prices of their Imperial records. Columbia also now offered double disc records for $1. Zonophone, now a Victor affiliate, announced a temporary price reduction "until a policy decision had been reached."

Although American Graphophone had the best lawyers, Victor began to prove it had the best businessmen. At the close of 1906 Columbia and American Graphophone had been in business seventeen years and had acquired an earned surplus of something less than $1.25 million. Victor had been in business but five years and had already almost $3 million in its cash and surplus account. Edison phonograph and record sales for 1906 were over $6 million. These facts naturally whetted the interest of other entrepreneurs.

The January 1906 issue of *Talking Machine World* carried a full-page advertisement by the Talk-O-Phone Company featuring a new mechanical-feed disc phonograph. Up to this time all cylinder machines had been mechanical-feed instruments; that is, the reproducer or sound box was carried across the record by a feed screw. In disc machines produced commercially, the reproducer was carried across the record by the sound groove of the record. In the ad for this new mechanical-feed disc machine, attention was directed to "the Fearful Grating Sound" produced by machines where the sound box was propelled by the record groove. This feature of lateral disc record practice was one of the basic claims of Berliner patents, so it was quickly averred by Victor that the Talk-O-Phone device was merely a pretext to avoid the Victor-owned patent. Victor sued the company and on April 25, 1906, was granted a decision. Litigation was finally closed in 1909, and the Talk-O-Phone and records were withdrawn from sale. For a considerable time these records carried the announcement, "Warning, for Use with Machines Equipped with Mechanical Feed Only," although the records were of the conventional lateral disc type, playable on any of the standard instruments.

The patent situation in the United States enabled the three leading companies to keep the recording field all but closed to independent inventors or opportunistic interlopers. Quite often, a carefully selected group of opinions culled from the many court cases would be brought to the attention of a prospective entrepreneur by legal counsel of one of the companies, with the result that the entrepreneur usually could be persuaded to sell out at a reasonable figure or agree to drop plans to enter the field in order to avoid almost certain prosecution. Many cases were begun and consent decrees obtained on just such a basis, especially by American Graphophone—all of which helped to present an even more convincing picture to the next victim. This procedure did not apply, however, to the relationships between the big three. The court records are filled with suits and appeals for decisions, but one looks in vain for evidence that the verdicts had any considerable monetary effect. The actual amount of money that changed hands between the three companies in any decade was infinitesimal. The purpose behind most of these suits was to garner publicity and ammunition to use on anyone who might have the temerity to try to break into phonograph or record manufacturing. The almost constant succession of suits served to notify prospective record or machine manufacturers that they would have to be prepared to spend a large share of their time and money in the courts should they persist, whether they had patents or not.

The advertising pages of *Talking Machine World* for February and March 1907 illustrate this point. The Victor Talking Machine Company had just sued the Duplex Phonograph Company of Kalamazoo, Michigan, then established for several years. Duplex made a two-horned monstrosity with a two-way reproducer between the horns and a good Duplex record that was achieving considerable sale and being used on other machines. By no coincidence, Edison's National Phonograph Company had notified jobbers that they were no longer permitted to carry other lines of talking-machine goods, calling attention to a long nonenforced clause in their contract to this effect. It seems that some of the Edison jobbers had been carrying the Duplex records.

Current publicity favored Edison and American Graphophone. Having no better way to put forth its case, Victor took a full page in *Talking Machine World* to detail for the trade the strength of its patent situation. The ad stressed the importance of its possession of the basic Berliner patent, 534,543, and summarized its position as being in full control of the industry:

1. That the Victor Co. controls the disc reproducing machine and disc record, where the reproducer is vibrated and propelled by the record.
2. That the Victor Co. controls this method of reproducing sound.

3. That the Victor Co. controls the disc records for use on these machines. The U. S. Courts have sustained this Berliner patent broadly (claims 5 & 35) in following decisions: Victor et al vs. American Graphophone Co., decision of U.S. Circuit Court S.D., New York, filed Sept. 28, 1905.

Victor et al vs. Leeds & Catlin Co., same court, April 26, 1906.

Victor et al vs. Talk-O-Phone Co., same court, April 26, 1906.

Victor et al vs. Leeds & Catlin Co., U.S. Circuit Court of Appeals, 2nd Circuit, Oct. 12, 1906.

Victor et al vs. Talk-O-Phone Co., U.S. Circuit Court of Appeals, 2nd Circuit, Oct. 12, 1906.

The U.S. Circuit Court for the Southern District of New York decision by Judge Lacombe filed Jan. 5, 1907, in contempt proceedings has held these claims of the Berliner patent include records as well as machines in the combination, and that a sale of such disc records for use in these disc machines was an infringement of the patent.

Then came one of the most astounding lines of the ad:

The Victor Co. hesitates at anything like bragging, but —the Victor Co. is on top. We have issued a license to the Universal Talking Machine Co. and to the American Graphophone Co.

This put the fat in the fire with a vengeance, and American Graphophone replied with four full pages in the next issue of *Talking Machine World* under the headline, "WHO'S WHO IN THE TALKING MACHINE INDUSTRY, WITH A FEW ILLUSTRATIONS BY U.S. JUDGES."

Thomas A. Edison was one of the first persons to recognize that an industry could be built upon the basic foundation which the Graphophone afforded, and the so-called Edison Phonograph IS A LICENSED GRAPHOPHONE, which would be of no commercial importance without the principles first given to the world with the invention of the Graphophone and which had lawful existence only when the Graphophone Co., after prolonged litigation granted the National Phonograph Co. the rights to use its patents.

Judge Shipman in the U.S. Circuit Court in New York, in American Graphophone Co. vs. Leeds, et al., referring to the earlier work of Mr. Edison, characterizes most of the descriptions as "confusedly vague" saying: "It is confessedly difficult to know the interpretation which the writer placed on some of the words which he uses."

"But," said Judge Shipman, "Bell and Tainter made an actual, living invention, and a court is not called upon to decipher an anticipation in the unfinished work and surmises of earlier students of the same subject"—87 Fed. 873.

A number of other court decisions are referred to in this four-page spread:

Judge Platt in the U. S. Circuit Court, Conn., in National Phonograph Co. vs. American Graphophone Co. said: "The Graphophonic art may be said to have fairly begun with the invention of Bell & Tainter, Letters Patent No. 341,214, dated May 4, 1886. This taught the public how to produce the commercial and transferrable sound record." 135 Fed. 809

Judge Grosscup in U. S. Court in Illinois, in American Graphophone Co. vs. Amet, said, "Bell and Tainter lay no claim to having conceived the idea of a mechanism whereby speech or sound could be recorded and reproduced. Much thought and experimentation, before their patents were completed, were expended upon the general conception of such an instrument. BUT THE FACT REMAINS THAT, PRIOR TO THEIR GRAPHOPHONE, THE CONCEPTION OF A PHONOGRAPH HAD NEVER BEEN MECHANICALLY WORKED OUT TO THE EXTENT OF MECHANICAL PERFECTION. THE GRAPHOPHONE, INDEED SEEMS TO HAVE TAKEN THE PLACE OF ALL PREVIOUS MECHANISMS, AND TO HAVE ADVANCED BY A VERY LARGE SPACE, THE ART OF RECORDING AND REPRODUCING SOUND."

The writer claimed for the graphophone the first spring motor, as used in the graphophone "Baby Grand." He also claimed that the first mechanical duplicating machine was invented by Thomas Macdonald, used for producing the first commercially duplicated cylinders. Other claims included:

The Graphophone Grand—created a sensation and was widely copied by Mr. Edison, who finally admitted the validity of the patent and became a licensee on payment of substantial royalty.

The moulded cylindrical record, invented by Macdonald, and sold in large quantities more than one year before a competitor put out its moulded records on the market. In the case of National Phonograph Co. vs. American Graphophone Co. already referred to before Judge Platt in Conn., the testimony showed conclusively that Edison, notwithstanding the oft-repeated claim that he is the inventor of the so-called Gold-Moulded record, had never up to that date, 1905, succeeded in making a practical and successful moulded sound record. By his own testimony it was proven that the records extensively advertised as his own are made by a process which was really the invention of two of his employees years after our process, invented by Macdonald, had been perfected.

Summing up was a list of claims with specific reference to the Victor ad of the month before:

1. The first disc talking machine was a Graphophone.
2. The first disc talking machine record was a Graphophone record.
3. Before Berliner conceived his uncommercial process of etching them, disc records had been made by others.
4. Long before our boastful competition were ever heard of we had licensed their predecessor, the National Gramophone Co., who admitted they were using Graphophone patents in order to make their product commercial, and who paid us substantial royalties up to the time of their dissolution.
5. The Victor Co. used our patented process to manufacture their records. They are licensed under our patents, and are absolutely dependent upon them in order to make a saleable record.

The advertisement closed with this modest statement: "IF ANY BRAGGING HAS BEEN INDULGED IN, THE U.S. CIRCUIT COURT JUDGES HAVE BEEN OUR MOUTHPIECES, AND WE ONLY HAVE TO QUOTE FROM A FEW DECISIONS TO USE THEM TO SUSTAIN EVERY CLAIM WE MAKE." Any of the big three could have made similar claims. By selecting the opinions from the right court cases they could prove anything they wished to anyone—except to each other.

In comparison with American Graphophone's reply, the Victor advertisement was a model of reserve and accuracy. Whether or not Victor had issued a license to the Universal Talking Machine Company was academic, as it was now a wholly owned subsidiary. The tables had now been turned since midsummer of 1900 when the National Gramophone Corporation had advertised that it, Universal

Talking Machine, American Graphophone, and Columbia "had made an agreement between themselves for legal protection and commercial advantage." From
the first, cross-licensing existed among the big three as a necessary result of the
defects in the U.S. patent system. The process had little financial significance,
although it permitted any one of them to put newcomers out of business at will.
Only in rare instances where court orders directed the payment of usually trivial
sums did money change hands among the big three. To all intents and purposes,
the cumulative result of all the patent litigation was to enforce the division of
the talking-machine world among the big three and to provide them with the
ammunition to drive off all others.

Thomas Edison, to whom more patents were issued than to any other person,
was well qualified to comment on the workings of the U.S. patent system:

> In England, when a case is finally decided it is settled for the entire coun-
try, while here it is not so. Here a patent having been once sustained, say,
in Boston, may have to be litigated all over again in New York, and again in
Philadelphia, and so on for all the Federal circuits. Furthermore, it seems
to me that scientific disputes should be decided by some court containing at
least one or two scientific men—men capable of comprehending the significance of an invention and the difficulties of its accomplishment,—if justice
is ever to be given an inventor. And I think also, that this court should have
the power to summon before it and examine any recognized expert in the
special art, who might be able to testify to facts for or against the patent,
instead of trying to gather the truth from the tedious essays of hired experts, whose depositions are really nothing but sworn arguments. The real
gist of patent suits is generally very simple, and I have no doubt that any
judge of fair intelligence, assisted by one or more scientific advisors, could
in a couple of days at the most examine all the necessary witnesses; hear all
the necessary arguments, and actually decide an ordinary patent suit in a
way that would more nearly be just, than can now be done at an expenditure
of a hundred times as much money and months and years of preparation.
And I have no doubt that the time taken by the court would be enormously
less, because if a judge attempts to read the bulky records, and briefs, that
work alone would require several days. Acting as judges, inventors would
not be very apt to correctly decide a complicated law point; and on the other

hand, it is hard to see how a lawyer can decide a complicated scientific point rightly. Some inventors complain of our Patent Office, but my own experience with the Patent Office is that the examiners are fair-minded and intelligent, and when they refuse a patent they are generally right; but I think the whole trouble lies with the system in vogue in the Federal Courts for trying patent cases, and in the fact, which cannot be disputed, that the Federal judges, with but few exceptions, do not understand complicated scientific questions. To secure uniformity in the several Federal circuits and correct errors, it has been proposed to establish a central court of patent appeals in Washington. This I believe in; but this court should also contain at least two scientific men, who would not be blind to the sophistry of paid experts. Men whose inventions would have created wealth of millions have been ruined and prevented from making any money whereby they could continue their careers as creators of wealth for the general good, just because the experts befuddled the judge by their misleading statements.[4]

Edison may have been inclined to tread lightly when it came to patent examiners. Indicative of his repressed feelings was a story in the August 1907 *Talking Machine World*, in which he was quoted as advising young inventors to keep their inventions secret and to manufacture without benefit of patents, in order to secure a return upon their efforts. The complex patent situation and the necessity of continually fighting innumerable and costly suits in defense of one's rights perhaps sufficiently explain Edison's delayed entrance into the disc field.

To sum up, the most important factors in the commercial conflicts between cylinders and discs were:

(1) The cylinder method was commercialized first because of its basic simplicity.

(2) The Edison patent application of 1878 covering important improvements to the phonograph, including a disc machine, was not acted on by the U.S. Patent Office.

(3) Bell & Tainter chose to adopt the Edison hill-and-dale cylinder method, rather than the disc.

(4) The ease of duplicating discs by molding or pressing gave the discs an advantage that offset cylinders' earlier commercialization.

(5) Discs could not be made everywhere.

(6) Discs were convenient to handle and store.

(7) Edison believed in the essential superiority of the cylinder with its uniform surface speed beneath the stylus.

Although musical cylinders were sold by Thomas A. Edison, Inc., until it retired from the field in 1929, the ultimate doom of the cylinder had been sounded with the announcement of the Edison Diamond Disc Phonograph in 1912.

CHAPTER 14

Internal-Horn Talking Machines and the Phonograph

DURING THE first decade of the twentieth century a number of inventors and entrepreneurs attempted to break into the burgeoning talking-machine industry. One of the most persistent was Loring L. Leeds, who even before the turn of the century manufactured cylinder records. Decrees handed down by the courts proclaimed him guilty of infringing patents owned by American Graphophone as early as 1896. Thus prevented from continuing profitably in the cylinder business, Leeds, together with Catlin, turned to the manufacture of disc records. Leeds and Catlin announced in the 1906 *Talking Machine World* a new disc talking machine, but by 1909 the upstart company had been forced into bankruptcy. At its demise, Edward F. Leeds was president and Henry Leeds, treasurer.

Other prominent entrepreneurs sought to invade the fast-developing disc market, among them Hawthorne and Sheble, American Record Company, Talk-O-Phone, Duplex, and International Record Company—all names to be found on early discs. When the Sonora Chime Company of New York City announced in the latter part of 1907 its intention to produce a talking machine, the Victor Talking Machine Company responded with an immediate suit on the basis of infringement of Berliner patent 534,543. Sonora replied that this Berliner patent was no longer in effect, as it was dependent on the expired Suess Canadian patent 41,901. Werner Suess had been an assistant to Emile Berliner at the time of his original Washington research and had assigned this and other patents to Berliner, which were subsequently transferred to Victor. The final result was that the courts refused an injunction to the plaintiff. The Sonora Chime Company became the Sonora Phonograph Company, a name familiar to the public for many years, along with its trademark, "Clear as a Bell." A few hill-and-dale records were produced with the Sonora label, and the company's machines were designed to play either lateral or hill-and-dale.

It was not until 1908 that the place of the phonograph in the home began to seem assured. Although the phonograph influenced the transformation of the nineteenth-century formal parlor into a room where visitors and friends might be entertained, designers of the early machines had little conception of how to enclose their machines to promote their parlor propriety.

The first successful invasion of the Victorian home by a functional machine was made by Elias Howe and Isaac Singer with their new sewing machine, and the redesign of the phonograph and the graphophone for the home market followed its lead. Such a pattern is easily explained in the case of the graphophone, which was made in the old Howe sewing machine factory in Bridgeport. Many of Howe's cabinetmakers and finishers stayed on when the factory was taken over by the American Graphophone Company, and the earlier business machines copied the sewing machine's foot treadle mechanism and table, as well as its materials and finishes—even the removable wooden cover.

Why Edison chose to follow virtually the same procedure for the Edison home phonograph with respect to materials, finishes, and design is less easily explained. It may be that the removable rounded top, attachable to the base by various latching devices, with a carrying handle at the top, was the simplest solution at the time. The early phonographs were for the most part recording machines, necessitating a design made for portability.

The initial awkwardness of the cylinder machine in homes was not obvious at first—it would take the altogether too obtrusive horn to produce a yearning for a more suitable parlor model. The advantages of the horn over ear tubes was so apparent that the more avid phonograph devotees soon were demanding bigger and better horns. Several companies sprang up to fill the demand for special horns, horn cranes, cabinets for records, and other accessories. Hawthorne & Sheble became one of the pioneers in the manufacture and sale of these items. Among other makers of patented types of horns was the Searchlight Horn Company. Horns were made of wood, brass, aluminum, and even glass. Although the Edison Gem, one of the cheapest phonographs to be marketed, came equipped with a short horn, most models were sold without horns until November 1907, when the National Phonograph Company announced one price for its first complete outfit of phonograph, large horn, and stand.

The cylinder market was different. Victor, from its founding in 1901, sold its talking machines as a complete unit. More important, the Victor machines from the beginning were not meant to be portable, since they were not equipped to make records. The Victor machines were designed to be placed somewhere in the home and left there. Victor also exhibited remarkable restraint in the plastering of florid decal scrolls across the front of its machines, compared with competitors who emblazoned "Edison Home Phonograph" and "Columbia Graphophone Grand" on their respective instruments.

The shape of horns progressed from an early conical form to one with an ever-expanding cross section from the reproducer end to a broad flare at the orifice. It was soon found more economical to build horns of this dimension by making the larger pieces out of sheet metal, brazed or soldered together, so that the horns were polygonal in cross-section, and the familiar morning-glory horn was born. In the final stages of development these morning-glory horns were gilded or hand-painted with flowers.

Quite possibly it was the Hymnophone, a German-built disc machine offered for sale in the United States in 1905, that gave Eldridge Johnson the idea of the completely internal horn machine. The Hymnophone's horn was attached in back of the machine and under the turntable and motor so that only its bell protruded in front. Johnson may also have been inspired by the storage cabinets sold for records for both cylinder- and disc-type machines that also served as tables for the machines. By 1906 sales of these cabinets had reached large proportions. The British Auxetophone, a compressed-air amplified talking machine marketed in the United States by Victor, came enclosed in a massive cabinet and sold at the modest price of $500. Perhaps this machine prompted Johnson to build standard machines with the horn enclosed.

In 1906 Victor announced the Victrola, a machine with an internal horn and record storage space. Johnson had already overcome the main obstacle to building an internal-horn disc machine with his ball-bearing, swivel-pointed tone arm, incorporating a gooseneck join for turning back the reproducer for changing the needles. This tone arm was already in use on open-horn machines, so Johnson only needed to turn its back end down instead of up. Designing a horn to fit in limited cabinet space was harder. Johnson mounted the redesigned tone arm on a cast-iron section of horn at the bend, with the remaining part of the horn made of wood. He had to sacrifice the bell, or outermost part of the flare, which adversely affected tone reproduction. Actually, the open-horn Victor Model VI of 1906 or any of the larger open-horn machines made by Victor were better reproducing instruments than any of the internal-horn Victrolas made right up to the period of electrical recording. Even the Victor school machines used an open horn until 1925; for these, articulation, tone range, volume, and quality were the requirements, rather than style.

In the United States the concept of the Victrola as a piece of furniture thus took hold, and tone quality became secondary. In 1907 a new company formed to take advantage of the trend: the Schroeder Hornless Phonograph Manufacturing Company, which advertised in *Talking Machine World*. In England, however, even long after the inception of electrical methods, custom-built open-horn gramophones were produced by at least two prominent makers.

That U.S. music dealers preferred the Victrola over other instruments influenced the trend. Favorable trade-ins could be arranged on the old open-horn machines, making them obsolete. Although technically the Victrola represented a step backward, stylistically and financially, it was a tremendous success. By the end of 1906 Victor had an earned surplus of $6 million, and Columbia Phonograph Company, not quite $2.5 million.

Earlier that year, Guglielmo Marconi, the inventor of wireless telegraphy, paid a visit to the American Graphophone plant at Bridgeport. Shortly thereafter, it was announced that Marconi had been retained as a consulting physicist. Upon his departure for England he stated that he intended to make a thorough study of sound recording and reproducing techniques. The American Graphophone–Columbia Phonograph alliance was in need of expert help, and that help was to be Marconi. Victor was running away with the disc business; introduction of the Victrola had brought Columbia graphophone sales almost to a standstill. Edison had the lion's share of the cylinder business, despite the introduction of the Twentieth Century Graphophone machine. Marconi either did a phenomenally quick job of research or had the idea in mind before approaching American Graphophone, for the first announcement of the new Columbia Marconi Velvet-Tone records was made in July 1906. These thin, flexible, laminated records, with a paper core and a plastic surface, were pressed by American Graphophone from standard stampers at a slight advance in price. They were manufactured in both single- and double-faced records, carrying the same catalog numbers as the regular editions. Marconi's method probably influenced the eventual adoption of the laminated process for the standard Columbia discs, which had an inflexible core of coarser materials between two layers of paper, coated with a surface of finer shellac and other ingredients. In later years the name "Velvet-Tone" was used by Columbia and successor companies for records made for the so-called ten-cent store trade.

Columbia became more and more concerned with the astounding success of the Victor Red Seal series of celebrity recordings, which had caught both Columbia and Edison with little to offer in competition. Eldridge Johnson and his director of repertoire, Calvin Childs, from the first instituted a firm policy of signing great artists on exclusive, long-term contracts whenever possible. Even as early as 1907, Columbia had trouble finding operatic stars to make a respectable showing against Victor's all-star aggregation: Enrico Caruso, Antonio Scotti, Marcella Sembrich, Nellie Melba, Johanna Gadski, Louise Homer, Ernestine Schumann-Heink, Pol Plançon, Marcel Journet, and many other famous performers. Moreover, by placing what was then a colossal advertising budget behind the exploitation of these well-known names, Victor further inflated their reputations. In a desperate attempt to compete, Columbia signed the famous Wagnerian soprano Lillian Nordica to an exclusive contract. Nordica was by this time considerably past her prime, but so were several of the artists of the Victor company. Although thousands of the Nordica records were ultimately sold, they were poorly recorded, and the net result was no increase in public esteem for American Graphophone's products. Perhaps nothing could have stemmed the Victor tide, whose early high-water mark had been set when Johnson secured Caruso, the greatest salesman Victor ever had and well worth the millions paid him. Caruso records were exported all over the world by means of masters delivered to the several affiliated European companies.

Columbia, now frantic, introduced records by Alessandro Bonci, an Italian tenor brought to New York in 1907 by Manhattan Opera impressario Oscar Hammerstein to offset Caruso at the Metropolitan. Columbia announced a list of no fewer than forty-six titles by Bonci, including three fourteen-inch discs. Few people experienced in the industry then or since would consider it sound judgment to issue at one time so many records by an artist whose public appeal was untested. These records were recorded in Europe by the Societé de Fonotipia. Bonci later made records at the American Graphophone studio, but their quality was inferior, both artistically and tonally.

Columbia's approach with Bonci contrasts with Victor's to Nellie Melba, who first recorded in Europe for Gramophone & Typewriter, Ltd. Victor first issued pressings made from imported masters, providing them with a special mauve label bearing the caption "Victor Melba Record." Priced at five dollars, these were packaged in a special container with a glassine window on one side the size of the label, so that as the record was withdrawn, a picture of the famous diva appeared in the opening. As soon as Victor could arrange to secure Melba's signature on an exclusive contract, work was begun on re-recording. Victor then offered a special trade-in offer of new Melba records for the old—the new, better Melba records were priced at three dollars, minus the special packaging. The Victor men were shrewd students of sales psychology.

Victor was responsible for another thorn in the side of American Graphophone: the new Zonophone open-horn talking machines and records made by Universal Talking Machine, a subsidiary of Victor, were selling well and at prices intentionally competitive with Columbia's disc line. The Zonophone machines incorporated the Johnson tapered tone arm and were superior in reproduction to the Columbia machines and lower in price than the Victor. Zonophone issued the first records in the United States by the great Tetrazzini in January 1908, recorded in Europe by the International Zonophone Company on nine-inch discs. Tetrazzini had also been recorded in Europe by Gramophone & Typewriter, Ltd., and Victor issued some of these on twelve-inch discs in March, announcing the acquisition of this artist on an exclusive basis. Shortly after Tetrazzini came to the United States, these records pressed from English masters were replaced by domestically recorded discs, following Victor's now-familiar pattern.

Columbia's choice of Bonci to balance Caruso was to no avail. To American ears, Caruso was the ideal Italian tenor. No erudite discussion of Bonci's alleged superior mastery of the art of bel canto would serve to equate him with Caruso in the eyes (or ears) of U.S. opera lovers. Nor did the announcement the same year by Columbia that it was offering the U.S. public the choicest of the Fonotipia and Odeon recordings by famous European artists shake the power of the Victor lineup. The initial U.S. market for operatic recordings had been created largely by Victor advertising, based on a canny appreciation of the prestige of Caruso and the Metropolitan Opera Company. Victor easily met the challenge of the Columbia-Fonotipia series by instituting as a regular feature of its catalog selected records by "Famous European Artists," pressed from masters supplied by its European affiliates.

On the cylinder front, the picture was also shifting. The Indestructible Record Company, having secured the Lambert and other celluloid record patents, acquired a large factory in Albany, New York, in 1907 and opened a recording laboratory in Brooklyn. The company was amply financed, with production confined to the manufacture of high-quality popular cylinders at low prices. From the viewpoint of the cylinder machine manufacturers, this operation was parasitical. After the reorganization of the cylinder industry following the Lippincott debacle, it had concentrated on developing the home phonograph market. With the perfection of molding methods, control of the record market was back in the hands of the parent companies, National Phonograph and American Graphophone, who competed for the larger share of the record business. When Indestructible appeared on the scene, the two had come to expect greater profits from their record sales than from machines, so that, as the upstart company began flooding the market with high quality, unbreakable records, even the normally imperturbable Edison began to take notice.

Edison's announcement of the first four-minute wax Amberol records in September 1908 might seem to have been his answer to the Indestructible challenge. But these new cylinders, with double the playing time of the old, were molded of the same fragile, metallic soap compounds as the standard two-minute cylinders, and required adapter kits for existing Edison phonographs. These kits contained a gear reducer, a reproducer, and a set of ten specially recorded demonstration records selling as a unit for $5 to $8.50, depending on the model to be equipped. Obviously, no profit was made on these kits, but by the end of a year, thousands of the older Edison phonographs had been equipped to play the new (200 grooves per inch) longer-playing records. When the records were fresh and new, the reproduction from the new cylinders of longer playing time was excellent. As with any standard wax cylinders, however, they were fragile and easily damaged. The finer grooves were subject to more wear. Groove sidewall breakdown caused annoying repeating of sound.

Despite technical difficulties, National Phonograph pushed ahead. The Edison Grand Opera Series initiated in 1906 in the standard two-minute records had titles embossed in light blue on the edge of the cylinder and sold for seventy-five cents each. This series was extended into the new four-minute Amberol records with prices up to two dollars. Within the next year or so many fine operatic selections were recorded by first-rank singers such as sopranos Blanche Arral and Bessie Abbot, and tenors Leo Slezak and Riccardo Martin. The difficulty was that these records were not durable enough for the cost involved; consequently, they did not receive wide circulation. Edison distributed complimentary machines and cylinder records to key entrepreneurs and close friends such as J. Wesley Allison of Morrisburg, Ontario, to stimulate business. To plague Edison further, another manufacturer of cylinders entered the competition in 1908: the Cleveland Record Company, incorporated with a capital of $300,000 with the object of supplying principally the mail-order market developed by Henry B. Babson and other distributors.

Probably the last company to enter the field of cylinder machine manufacture was the United Talking Machine Company, which announced the Echo-Phone. In December 1908, Regina, the music-box manufacturer, announced the Regina Hexaphone, an automatic coin-machine phonograph offering a choice of six cylinders.

The year 1909 was an eventful one in the history of the phonograph. Columbia gave up the production of cylinder machines and records and made a deal with the Indestructible Record Company to market records under the Columbia label. With this move Columbia was able to put out four-minute cylinder records in competition with those of Edison manufacture. National Phonograph in July notified all dealers and jobbers that henceforth they were not permitted to carry other makes of cylinder records or machines, in accordance with the clause in their contracts to that effect. National sued another company engaging in the manufacture of cylinder records, Donnelly and Fahey, on the basis of the Edison-owned Aylesworth patent for duplicating records. In Europe, cylinders were losing the battle to discs, and National Phonograph announced that it was closing its European branches and would confine all future recording activities to the United States.

The switch from cylinders to discs in the United States became more and more evident. The Multiphone Company, manufacturers of coin machines offering a choice of twenty-four cylinders, went bankrupt, and Gabel's Automatic Entertainer was introduced, offering a choice of twenty-four discs. The machine somewhat resembled the Multiphone in that it had a large horn protruding from the top.

Some of the attempts to compete with Johnson's internal-horn Victrola were quite ludicrous. One such attempt was the Orchestraphone, which had a large squarish horn protruding over the top like a kitchen wall cabinet, with doors. American Graphophone in 1907 came out with the Symphony Grand Graphophone, which had the general appearance of one of the upright pianos of the time, with little discernible design derived from its function. John Herzog, a cabinet manufacturer, advertised a line of tall cabinets with folding doors to house various standard open-horn disc and cylinder machines. The cabinets had a shelf for

holding the machine, with a grilled aperture above through which the horn could
be heard but not seen. Under the machine shelf were shelves or racks for holding
records. The Star Company made an internal-horn talking machine as early as
1908, but for the most part it was not until 1910 that other manufacturers began
to catch up with Johnson's Victrola and produce their own "olas."[1]

But the greatest financial success of the Victor Talking Machine Company
was yet to come, founded on three factors: first, Victor's monopoly of the leading Metropolitan stars, and of the leading concert and stage celebrities; second,
the smartest advertising staff assembled up to that time; third, possession of the
Johnson tapered tone-arm patent. Although the Victrola tone reproduction suffered when the horn was squeezed down, the tapered tone arm as an integral part
of the total tone-passage design assisted in developing properly the middle- and
upper-register response. Thus, for example, the introduction of the Columbia
Grafonola was delayed until 1911 because the Johnson patent prevented the use
of a tone arm of expanding cross-section, and its tubular tone arm reduced the
Grafonola's reproduction quality.

The style trend established through the power of Victor advertising forced
other companies to abandon external-horn machines. Only two technical functions were served by the internal-horn Victrolas: to transform what had been
considered a talking machine into a musical instrument more compatible with
the home environment and to provide a storage place for records. The machines
nevertheless became objects of conspicuous consumption. So popular was the
name "Victrola" that the word replaced "phonograph" and "talking machine" in
popular use as the generic name for record-playing machines.

As late as 1920, the Victor Talking Machine Company secured an injunction
against the Brunswick-Balke-Collender Company for infringement of Johnson's
patents on the tapered tone arm and the internal-horn talking machine. A sub
rosa interference proceeding had been pending before the U.S. patent examiners to determine whether John B. Browning or Johnson was the true inventor of
these features, the case being brought into court by Brunswick, who had bought
the Browning patents. On April 4, 1921, the Court of Appeals of the District of
Columbia not only held that Browning was the prior inventor of the enclosed-
horn talking machine with doors, but also that the evidence overwhelmingly indicated that Johnson had derived both this idea and the important tapered tone-arm
concept from Browning.

A prominent exhibit in the case was a sketch and description of Browning's machine penciled on the back of a printed dance program dated May 3, 1897. The sketch bore Browning's signature and was witnessed by two women who presumably had been at the dance. Evidence was also introduced showing that Browning had subsequently submitted other drawings and a crude model of his instrument to Johnson and that Browning had later been employed by the Victor Talking Machine Company. The sketch dated May 3, 1897, unmistakably shows the tapered tone arm, horizontal louvers, and sound-controlling doors—all features of the internal-horn Victrolas from their introduction in 1906 to the advent of the Orthophonic Victrola in 1925.

The fact nevertheless remains that the Victrola established a style trend that sprang not from the machine's technical excellence but from the power of Victor advertising and prestige. The other companies as a result were forced to abandon external-horn machines. In the naming of the Columbia "Grafonolas" and the Edison "Amberolas" is to be found the sincerest tribute to the accomplishments of Eldridge R. Johnson.

CHAPTER 15 ━━

The Edison Diamond Disc
Phonograph

OVER THE YEARS before 1910, rumors circulated from time to time in trade circles that Thomas Edison was contemplating the manufacture of a disc machine and records. In a patent applied for December 24, 1877, Edison wrote: "It is obvious that many forms of mechanism may be used to give motion to the material to be indented. For instance, a revolving plate may have a volute spiral etc." In an important British patent, 1644, dated April 24, 1878, Edison wrote: "The phonogram may be in the form of a disc, a sheet, an endless belt, a cylinder, a roller, or a belt, or strip, and the marks are to be either in straight lines, spiral, zig-zag or in any other convenient form." [1]

A popular misconception is that Edison was limited by his patents to the use of tinfoil. Not only does the British patent prove otherwise, but a caveat Edison filed in the U.S. Patent Office on March 8, 1878, stated that "the material for recording upon may be various metallic foils or sheets, such as tin-foils of various compositions, iron, copper, brass, lead, tin, cadmium, zinc; also, paper and various absorbent materials may be used and coated with paraffine and other hard hydro-carbons, waxes, gums, lacs, and these may be used to record on directly, or they may have a metallic surface." Moreover, in a later patent that had been granted, Edison claimed "a graphic sound record on a disc-like or cylindrical blank formed of a sinuous groove of substantially uniform depth and width, as distinguished from a phonograph wherein these dimensions of a record groove are not uniform." [2]

Although Edison built an experimental spring-motor disc phonograph in 1878 and included a completely designed disc machine in his British patent of that same year, for many years he was convinced that the technical superiority of the cylinder as a moving surface would ultimately result in public preference for it. The cylinder format insured a constant speed beneath the recording and repro- ducing styli. By 1907, however, some of Edison's business associates had begun to lose confidence in the eventual supremacy of cylinders. The spectular gains made by Victor had not gone unnoticed. Edison often intimated that someone else making money was not a sufficient reason for making a change. So it was with considerable trepidation that his advisers began to urge action to meet the competition. A persuasive argument was the fragility and short playing time of the standard Edison cylinders.

To compete with the longer playing time of the larger discs ($3\frac{1}{2}$ minutes for the twelve-inch disc as against 2 minutes for the standard cylinder then in use), Edison introduced the Amberol record with 200 grooves per inch, which would play for 4 minutes. The patent application on this record was filed January 3, 1907, and the first records were issued in 1908. Not much time was lost in tooling up for producing feed mechanism attachments for existing Edison machines.

The new Amberol cylinders were molded from a somewhat harder metallic soap compound than had been used for the standard two-minute cylinders. Being harder, they were more brittle, and with the unit area pressure from the stylus greatly increased, these records were more easily cut in playing, or otherwise damaged. As the Indestructible Record Company was now introducing a spe- cial heavier reproducer for use on the Edison machine in conjunction with its celluloid Indestructible records, the shortcomings of the fragile waxlike Edison cylinders became even more obvious.

The year 1909 was decisive for Edison and his associates. The Amberol cylin- ders were fragile and easily damaged, and the Victrola and discs were sweeping the country. Especially in urban stores and homes, the open-horn phonographs and talking machines were being rapidly supplanted by Victrolas. Edison was by now aware of the need for drastic action.

By 1910, some of Edison's associates were so concerned by the competitive situation that they decided to initiate a secret project in experimental disc record- ing, hoping to convert Edison if the results were promising. The experiments were hardly under way when Edison discovered them. Instead of opposing the project, he enthusiastically endorsed it and, to the dismay of some, assumed full leadership. He expanded the objectives to include a search for better materials for the manufacture of cylinder records. As a result, experimentation emphasized adapting the already highly perfected hill-and-dale method of recording to the flat surface, rather than resorting to the lateral recording method.

Progress in the new experimental project came first in improved recording techniques. Heretofore, the damping of the glass diaphragms in the recording heads had been accomplished with rubber rings. It was discovered that a viscous substance could be used in damping, with the edges of the diaphragm floating in this semifluid. The improvement in quality was so spectacular that it was decided to start recording immediately with this cutter on disc masters. Wax blanks for recording purposes could easily be made in cylinder or disc form, and a recording lathe could be set up for either type of recording.

Early in 1910, Edison's recording expert, Thomas Graf, and an assistant, Bocchi, were sent to Europe to make cylinder and disc masters. The same recorder, made a bit heavier, was used for the discs. The same wax was used for both cylinders and discs, with test playbacks using the same lightweight reproducer. These facts explain, according to an interview with Will Hayes,[3] veteran Edison recording expert, why the vaults of Edison National Historic Site contained scores of unprocessed twelve-inch disc wax masters by famous European artists like Giuseppe Kaschmann, as well as a number of others that were converted to test pressings only after a lapse of several years; none were made available to the public.[4]

Technical difficulties prevented the successful processing of the twelve-inch discs for a number of years; not until 1927 were twelve-inch Edison discs sold to the public, and then only in the form of an Edison forty-minute long-playing record. (This 450-groove long-playing record was a dubbed record, made from existing ten-inch commercial recordings.) After the 1921 introduction of the high-speed process and the abandonment of gold sputtering (in which gold was vaporized in a vacuum and deposited on wax masters to facilitate further electroplating), twelve-inch sampler discs were made for circulation to dealers only.

Cutting records with the new viscous-damped recording heads had two important effects. First, the increased breadth and volume now incised into the records made it imperative that an improved material be found for molding the four-minute cylinders, for the metallic wax compound was not standing up well in use. Second, the variation in surface speed beneath the stylus in reproducing required a new and harder surfacing material for the contemplated discs.

Some of the two-minute Indestructible celluloid cylinders then in use on

Regina Hexaphones and other early jukeboxes were highly durable. Earlier attempts to use celluloid in discs had proved unsuccessful. Two celluloid-faced discs still exist at Edison National Historic Site, showing that Edison contemplated the use of celluloid not only for cylinders but also for discs. Beginning in 1904 in England celluloid was used in making the Neophone disc, some with twenty-inch diameters. In Europe Pathé at this time was producing vertical-cut discs pressed in a shellac composition differing but little from the lateral disc Victor records. Pathé discs were played by a sapphire ball stylus of rather large diameter, so the grooves were shallow and wide; consequently, there was less playing time for a given diameter than with the conventional lateral disc. To offset this disadvantage, Pathé records were regularly issued in diameters up to fourteen inches. The sapphire ball had a tendency to bounce out of the groove, since a permanently flat plane was difficult to come by. This would send the tone arm and sound box skittering across the record, alarming listeners. (In spite of such problems, the anticipated invasion of Pathé-Frères was later undoubtedly an important factor in Edison's decision to enter the disc market.)

To avoid similar difficulties, Edison decided to use a stylus of smaller diameter, to impose more weight on the record, and to use precision-ground diamond styli. The tip diameter was to be about .0075 mil. The maximum depth of groove was determined by the minimum land to be left between the grooves. In this way cutting and playback styli of the same diameter could be used for both the 200-groove-per-inch cylinders and the 150-groove-per-inch discs. The greater weight of the stylus assembly imposed a considerably greater unit-area pressure on the discs than on the cylinders.

Experiments with various surfaces for the cylinder records resulted in the adoption of a brilliant blue celluloid outer layer around a rigid supporting core of plaster of Paris. Later, royal purple came to designate the celebrity and grand opera series. The reacting surface of this new celluloid composition was smooth and hard. Even though several white celluloid-laminated experimental discs have been preserved in the holdings of Edison National Historic Site, celluloid was deemed too soft as the sole material for the new discs. They needed a rigid, non-warping core to provide an absolutely plane surface to which the recording action and tracking force would be perpendicular. Such an inner core was developed by compressing under great pressure a mixture of wood flour, lampblack, phenol resin, and hexamethylene tetramine.[5] For the surface, Aylesworth and his associates developed a phenolic resin varnish that he named Condensite.

That Edison during these years still considered the cylinder record the ideal surface is indicated by his choosing it for the Kinetophone, the first theater talking-picture sound machine, introduced in 1912. For it he used 5½-inch-diameter cylinders 8 inches long—really giant-sized Blue Amberol cylinders—with a corresponding core of plaster of Paris.

Perfecting molding mechanisms for the new disc records required considerable time and much experimentation. The first experimental disc machines for playing the new disc records evolved directly from the improved Amberola cylinder machines developed for playing the Blue Amberol cylinders. The improved cylinder reproducer employed a laminated diaphragm made of some twenty layers of rice paper impregnated with shellac, with a stiffening cork disc on the side toward the woven silk cord that connected it to the stylus lever. The new disc reproducer was of similar design, with a slightly larger diaphragm and a heavier floating weight. A stock Herzog cabinet, such as was sold to the trade for concealing the overhead-horn cylinder and disc machines, was equipped with a spring-driven disc turntable and an overhead horn made of sheet iron. The tone arm was propelled across the record by a feed-screw device. As in the internal-horn table model Amberolas introduced about this time, sound reproduction suffered from air leaks in the slip joints of the tone-arm assembly, just as it had in the the lateral disc talking machines.

Edison solved this problem in his Concert model cylinder phonograph, made both with external and internal horns. This machine was equipped with a built-in gearshift to enable the playing of both the two- and four-minute wax records and a combination reproducer with a turnover stylus assembly for playing the two types, operated by turning a button at the front. The internal-horn machine was named the Concert Amberola and sold for $200. In the bottom of the well-built cabinet were four drawers for records.

Unquestionably, up to and during this period of heavy experimentation, Edison's National Phonograph Company had lost ground rapidly to disc competition, a circumstance for which Edison has often been held personally responsible by critics. Many basic U.S. patents were about to expire, and consequently a European invasion loomed. The decline of the cylinder industry in England had resulted in Russell Hunting's appointment as director of all recording activities for the French firm of Pathé-Frères, which had recording laboratories in the principal European countries, manufacturing both cylinders and discs. Hunting's success at Pathé-Frères culminated in a decision to attempt a conquest of

the U.S. market, and Hunting was sent to New York in 1910 to outfit a factory and recording laboratory preparatory to launching Pathé disc machines and
records. For a time, the records were made much like the Pathé discs in Europe;
that is, center start, with the groove beginning at the label and spiralling outward.
There were good technical reasons for a center start. One was that centrifugal
force naturally tends to throw a gliding weight resting upon a revolving horizontal surface outward; hence, the center-start records offered less resistance to the
passage of the sapphire ball. Another reason was that the tendency to throw the
reproducing ball out of the groove was lessened with center-start records. Believing in the technical superiority of the vertical method, Hunting and his men
were canny in designing the Pathé machines with a universal tone arm, so that
they might be used to play either lateral records or the new Pathé discs. The example had now been set for other companies entering the field during the next
decade, such as the Aeolian and the Brunswick-Balke-Collender companies.

Acoustically, the Pathé machines were unable to demonstrate the superiority of
the Pathé recordings. With the tapered tone-arm patents firmly held by Eldridge
Johnson of the Victor Talking Machine Company, the design of the tone-arm
system of the new Pathé machine suffered in precisely the same way as did that
of the Grafonola. In other words, Victor's superior internal tone passage system
served to offset any superiority inherent in the Pathé record. The entry of Pathé
into the fray, however, stirred conjecture that Edison might enter the disc field.

As soon as the ghost of the Lippincott debacle was laid to rest in 1908, the
Edison laboratories began a company reorganization. Up to this time most of the
phonographic patents in use by National Phonograph were held by Edison himself. In 1910 all of the manufacturing enterprises controlled by Edison organized
as separate corporations, such as the National Phonograph, were dissolved and
brought into one corporation, Thomas A. Edison, Inc. The phonograph business was continued as the Phonograph Division, the dictating machine business,
as the Ediphone Division, with other divisions created for the storage battery,
cement manufacturing, and so on.

Before this reorganization, a patent-holding corporation, New Jersey Patents
Company, pooled the patents of Edison and his associates. Patents issued to J. P.
Ott in 1909 were assigned to this company, along with a 1910 patent issued to
W. F. Messer, who had been granted a celluloid cylinder patent in 1902. This
earlier Messer patent supplied the basis for both the Lambert and the Inde-

structible Record Company operations, with this patent date appearing on all the cylinders of the latter company.

In 1910 and 1911 more phonographic improvements were patented by Walter Miller and E. L. Aiken, both Edison associates. Steve Porter, a recording comedian, even invented a laterally recorded disc of constantly varying depth to compensate for needle wear. Porter assigned half interest to Walter Miller, indicating that both were toying with the idea of a lateral disc record at that time. That Edison had no intention of abandoning cylinders seems proven by the fact that, until after the Edison Diamond Disc phonograph was actually produced in 1912, the larger number of his patented improvements were on cylinder records or devices. Apart from Pathé-Frères, Edison was the only manufacturer of both cylinder machines and records left in the world.

In 1912, there was a veritable flood of phonographic patents issued to Edison associates. Among the most notable were those issued in the name of Jonas Aylesworth, such as "Forming Phenolic Condensation Products," "Fusable Phenolic Resin and Forming Same," "Electrotyping," and "Phonograph Record Molding Apparatus." One or two patents on talking machines were issued to Frank L. Dyer, Edison's attorney and personal biographer.[6] Other inventors who at this time assigned patents to either the New Jersey Patent Company or to Thomas A. Edison, Inc., included Leslie A. Brown, Bedford, Indiana; Charles P. Carter, Kingston, New York; Herbert L. Dyke, Charles L. Hubbard, and Newman H. Holland, East Orange, New Jersey; Frank D. Lewis, Elizabeth, New Jersey; Alexander N. Pierman, Newark, New Jersey; and Charles Schiffl, Peter Weber, and Albert F. Wurth, all of the Edison staff. Theodore Edison, son of the inventor, disclosed that the diamonds were mounted to the shanks by electroplating with nickel, an element that plates under tension.[7]

In 1912 Edison received nine patents on phonographic devices, some of which were on essentials of the forthcoming Edison disc phonograph. In 1910 and 1911 he had received ten other phonographic patents, mostly applicable to cylinder machines and records. In 1912 Edison also sought every possible creative use of concrete through his newly developed concrete business. Phonograph cabinets (for both the cylinder and disc machine), refrigerators, furniture, fireplaces, stairways, bathtubs, and prefabricated houses all were being made out of Edison cement. Models of the concrete phonograph cabinets were placed on exhibit in Pittsburgh at the national cement show and in Chicago at the furniture exhibition.

The public reaction was reflected in an article in *Furniture World:* "Making furniture out of concrete is not a proposition to lay before a furniture manufacturer, because it will make him laugh. I can't imagine building real furniture out of concrete. In the first place, it is extremely heavy."[8] Edison was undaunted by all the criticism. Production got under way in Building no. 28 at the Edison complex in Orange and West Orange, New Jersey, to build 300 concrete "Edison Moulded Cabinets" of a design that could not be duplicated in wood, such as statuary or bas-relief.[9] The entire operation was accomplished in ten steps: cleaning molds, greasing, filling, pouring, troweling, knocking out, seasoning, cementing, trimming, and painting. Each cabinet required a set of nine mold forms for casting. The grill was made of stamped metal by the Yale and Towne Manufacturing Company, and the frame and drawers were made by C. Wollersen, New York. These concrete cabinets proved to be fragile in shipping, for invariably they arrived at their destination damaged. No mention is made in the documents at Edison National Historic Site of when the concrete furniture project was finally discontinued.

Wooden phonograph cabinets made by the Edison Company showed efficiency in using up existing materials. Those that had been originally designed for the large-cylinder Amberola phonograph were now used for enclosing the air-tight horn reproducer assembly disc mechanisms. Even the space below the mechanism, which formerly held four sliding drawers for cylinder storage, was now rearranged to accommodate two drawers for the vertical filing of the ten-inch Edison discs. Under contract to the Edison Phonograph Works to produce cabinets were the Diamond Furniture Company, Jamestown, New York, and the premier furniture manufacturing company of the day, the White Furniture Company of Mebane, North Carolina.[10]

During the height of the development period, fate again dealt Edison a powerful blow. On December 9, 1914, a fire broke out in the motion picture film plant at the Edison Works, destroying six brick and wood buildings as well as the flammable contents of seven reinforced concrete structures. Although in his usual indomitable fashion Edison ordered reconstruction begun immediately, much valuable material was irretrievably lost. Many priceless master records were destroyed, both cylinder and disc, along with a great deal of experimental apparatus. Production machinery and supplies of raw materials were also lost, hastening the effects of the war shortages already beginning to hamper the industry. The British blockade of Germany cut off machine tools and essential chemicals from the

United States, then quite dependent upon German manufacture. As the British required all of their own limited production of phenol, the supply sources for the United States were entirely cut off, for no phenol was produced commercially in the Western hemisphere. Large quantities were already required for the production of the new Edison disc records. By this time, Thomas A. Edison, Inc., was reputedly the largest consumer of phenol in the United States. Another import int chemical used in the manufacture of the Edison discs was paraphen lenediamii ., imported from Germany.

Faced with a stoppage in record production, Edison contacted various U.S. chemical manufacturers to see if they would synthesize phenol. The most favorable reports were that it would take from six to nine months to deliver. Undaunted, Edison set to work to study all existing formulas and methods of manufacture, eventually perfecting a new process of his own. Within eighteen days after the building of a new plant was begun, half a ton of phenol per day was being produced right at West Orange, enough to supply the disc record needs. Within a month the plant was turning out a ton per day and selling the surplus to other hard-hit manufacturers.

By 1915 it was variously estimated that from $2 million to $3 million had been spent in the development of the Edison disc phonograph, aside from the i sses incurred from the fire and the shortage of phenol. This is not to say that all of Edison's decisions were wise ones in the light of the knowledge we now have. For instance, he decided that the labels of the new disc records should not carry the name of the artist. It is true that the record sleeves did sometimes divulge this information, but after Edison had paid large sums to record first-rank operatic stars (including Alessandro Bonci, Lucrezia Bori, Aino Ackte, and Emmy Destinn), it is difficult to understand why their names should have been omitted from the discs. The early labels contained the Edison trademark, a photo of Edison, the title of the selection, and the composer engraved into the glossy black surface of the record itself by means of a half-tone electrotype. As a result, the early Edison label was difficult to read. It is anyone's guess which killed the most sales—the monotonous description of the arias given on the reverse sides of most of the celebrity records by elocutionist Harry E. Humphrey, or the unreadable labels with incomplete information. To make matters even more confusing, especially to the clerks at the music counters, the catalog numbers were stamped in three places around the edge of the record. Often one had to look at all three to find a number that was completely legible.

At this time all of the Victor Red Seal records were single sided and had a maximum playing time of about 3½ minutes. With hindsight, it is easy to see that it would have paid to capitalize on the longer playing time of the Edison discs, and to place a musical selection on each side, a move that would have more than offset the double thickness of the Edison discs, which provided the absolutely plane surface necessary for reproduction.

The ten-inch Edison discs weighed ten ounces as against an average of perhaps eight ounces for the twelve-inch Victor record of that same period. The Columbia records were laminated—in that sense similar to the Edison discs—and were stronger than the Victor records, although thicker. These were errors of manufacturing judgment and selling technique rather than technical faults as far as reproduction of sound was concerned. Regardless of these initial mistakes, the intense striving to produce a more perfect reproducing instrument went on.

Just how successful were the Edison research activities was revealed publicly on October 21, 1915, through an event having a rather remote connection with the Panama-Pacific Exposition in San Francisco. The exposition authorities had named October 21 Edison Day, for it was the thirty-sixth anniversary of Edison's first successful incandescent lamp. Thomas Alva and Mina Edison were guests of the exposition for the occasion.

Meanwhile, in the library of the Edison laboratory at West Orange, New Jersey, another distinguished group of visitors gathered to witness the first demonstration of the new Official Laboratory Model Edison phonograph. The beautiful operatic soprano Anna Case, who had recently scored a great success at the Metropolitan, sang for the assembled guests so that they could compare her singing with her recorded voice as reproduced on the New Edison instrument. Her first selection was the aria "Depuis le Jour" from Charpentier's "Louise." To the amazement of all, they were unable to detect any difference between the voice of the singer and that coming from the phonograph. Christine Miller, a contralto, offered the audience a similar comparison, singing "Ah, Mio Son" from "Prophete." The result was the same; the audience found it impossible to distinguish between the voice of the singer and the phonographic reproduction. The recorded voice of Anna Case was carried to Edison at the Panama-Pacific Exposition in San Francisco by long-distance telephone. When interviewed some time later about this first audacious tone test, Case said, "Everybody, including myself, was astonished to find that it was impossible to distinguish between my own voice, and Mr. Edison's re-creation of it." [11]

The following year on April 28, Marie Rappold, dramatic soprano of the Metropolitan, sang before an audience of 2,500 in Carnegie Hall in New York to demonstrate the precision of voice reproduction attainable with the new Edison phonograph. Eminent music critics expressed their amazement, among them the critic for the *New York Tribune,* who wrote, "Edison snares the soul of music." The critic of the *New York Globe* described the instrument as "the phonograph with a soul." [12]

Within the next year or two, hundreds of similar tone tests were conducted in scores of cities in the United States and Canada, in which a number of vocal and instrumental artists participated.[13] In these tone tests, the artist played or sang in unison with the phonographic reproduction, from time to time either pausing to permit the phonograph to carry on alone or singing or playing in obligato to the recorded melody. Thus, a most critical and direct comparison could be made of the timbre and nuances of the voice and the reproduction of it. In a dramatic climax during the latter part of the program, the stage would be darkened, ostensibly so that the auditors could guess as to when the artist was singing and when only the record was playing. Suddenly the lights would come on, revealing an empty stage. Invariably, members of the audience gave an involuntary collective gasp as they realized that they had been utterly unable to tell when the artist had ceased performing.

Music critics from leading newspapers were uniformly generous with their praise of Edison's accomplishment: "Just how true and faithful is this Re-creation of the human voice was best illustrated when Miss Christine Miller sang a duet with herself, it being impossible to distinguish between the singer's living voice and its Re-creation by the instrument that bears the stamp of Edison's genius" (*Boston Herald*). "Unless one watched the singer's lips it was quite impossible to determine from the quality of tone whether Mr. [Thomas] Chalmers [of the Boston Opera Company] was singing or whether he was not, the tone of the re-creation being exactly like his own living voice in every shade of tonal color" (*Pittsburgh Leader*). Of a London, Ontario, tone test by tenor Hardy Williamson: "The most sensitive ear could not detect the slightest difference between the tone of the singer and the tone of the mechanical device. Both were equally liquid, flexible, and vibrant" (*London Advertiser*).[14]

Understandably, there were skeptics. During one of the later tone-test recitals given by Anna Case, Roy T. Burke of the Edison staff sat in a box with one of New York's best known advertising writers, also a well-known artist. When Case was about to sing her first number with the New Edison, the artist said, "I'll show you that I can detect a difference. I'll sit down on the floor, so that I cannot see the stage, then when Miss Case stops and the phonograph sings alone, I'll press your foot; when Miss Case starts to sing in unison with the instrument, I'll press your foot again." Case stopped singing, and the phonograph continued alone, but no signal came. Case resumed singing with the phonograph, but again no signal. Twice she sang with the instrument, twice it sang alone, but never did a signal come. Upon completion of the song, the artist arose and said, "She sang with it all the time, you can't fool me." Even though the others in the box assured him he was wrong, he steadfastly refused to believe it.[15]

For the most part, however, the critics and general public were unanimous enough in their approval to worry competitors in the talking machine industry. For many years there had been a virtual truce between the Victor Talking Machine Company and the Edison interests, and the products of both companies had been handled in several territories by the same jobbers. As long as Edison adhered to cylinders and Johnson to discs, there was little inclination on either side to stir up costly hostilities. But as the Edison disc aroused popular interest, R. H. Macy in New York began dumping Victrolas and Victor records on the market at cut prices. Other dealers followed suit. To plug the break in the price dike Victor sued Straus, owner of Macy's, on the basis of the price agreement embodied in the sales contract. At first the case against Straus was dismissed, but Victor won upon appeal. During this litigation other Victor dealers became frightened and, though not many dared to cut prices, refrained from buying except on a hand-to-mouth basis. This action accounts for the comparative scarcity of certain Victor records issued during this period.

The situation was unprecedented for Eldridge Johnson. To meet it the Victor Talking Machine Company sued Thomas A. Edison, Inc., for infringement of its Johnson patents 814,786 and 1,060,550. The former was the famous tapered tone-arm patent with a total of forty-two claims, and the other a late patent upon an idea that had been used earlier on open-horn machines. The Edison method involved swinging the entire reproducer-horn assembly from a single pivot, however, the reproducer being carried across the record by a feed-screw device, which permitted an air-tight tone passage from diaphragm to outer periphery of the horn. The feed screw was inherent to Edison technology from the first; the groove had never been used to propel a tone arm across the record. Nothing even remotely resembled the Johnson patents in fundamental concept. Unquestionably the sole purpose of the suit was to bolster the wavering morale of Victor jobbers and dealers. On appeal, the Edison disc phonograph was found not to infringe these patents.

CHAPTER 16 ⟶

Tone-Test Reverberations
and the Vertical-Cut Bandwagon

THAT THE laboratory model of the Edison phonograph could successfully withstand repeated public tone-test comparisons with live vocal and instrumental performances using stock phonographs and records is a stunning fact, yet the phenomenon should not be taken out of context. Comparison performance was in its infancy in the first quarter of the twentieth century; to the public's ear, live performance and recorded performance were one and the same. Still, contemporary newspapers from coast to coast touted the Edison phonographic recording as most nearly like the actual performance, and it was.

In striving toward the goal of precise reproduction of the human voice, it was found that the more sensitive the recording diaphragm was, the better the captured reproduction. The better record processing and reproduction methods became at registering sound, the more room resonance or reflected sound affected the overall rendition. And the more reflected sound infringed on the directly recorded voice, the less the reproduced sound from the phonograph sounded like the singer.

Consequently, it became necessary to employ a dead studio for making tone-test records—records that would be used to directly compare voice and instrument. Then the sounds issuing from the phonograph would be the close-up sounds as they issued from the singer's mouth, or as heard from a few feet away from the violinist—not as heard in a concert hall. When an artist performed in a tone test, the recorded vocal or instrumental sounds were not surrounded by the sound pattern reflections of another room or auditorium.

The industry's reaction to the sensational Edison tone tests was a rush for the vertical-cut bandwagon. The Aeolian Company, then a principal manufacturer of pianos and pipe organs, came out with a line of phonographs and vertical-cut shellac records. The cut of the grooves of the new Aeolian disc was precisely that of the Edison disc, with the same number of threads per inch, 150. The Aeolian-Vocalion machine, as it was named, was equipped with a universal tone arm, so that both lateral- and vertical-cut discs could be played by changing the reproducer stylus and the position of the reproducer. In England, where these machines and records were also manufactured, the Edison idea of a descriptive narrative on the reverse side appeared for a time. Within a year or so, however, these hill-and-dale records were replaced with laterally recorded discs.

Henry Burr, a popular recording tenor who made records for all of the companies, apparently was equally impressed with the results obtainable by the new Edison methods. He organized a recording company of his own called Par-O-Ket, whose records had the same groove cut and number of threads per inch as the Edison discs. The Par-O-Ket records were only eight inches in diameter, although Par-O-Ket did make a ten-inch disc of the same type under another label. The Par-O-Ket and the Aeolian-Vocalion records could be played on the Edison Diamond Disc machines by putting two discs on at the same time to raise the playing surface to the requisite height. The difficulty lay in the shellac base records, which were not hard enough to stand up under the action of the Edison reproducer. At this time it would have been a wise move on the part of the Edison executives to license their complete process, including the harder condensite record-surfacing material. Their failure to do so was an important factor in the triumph of the more easily adaptable lateral disc.

Another company to jump on the vertical-cut bandwagon, Starr Piano of Richmond, Indiana, in 1918 brought out a line of hill-and-dale discs again with the Edison cut and named them the Gennett Art-Tone series. As with the Aeolian-Vocalion vertical-cut records, these were shortly replaced with lateral recordings as a result of factors such as poor design and excessive inertia of the sound-box and tone-arm assemblies. The lack of sufficient compliance in the diaphragm stylus assembly was another contributing factor.

One of the best-known recording experts of the era was Victor H. Emerson, an early employee of Edison and later of the United States Phonograph Company. He and his brothers, also ex-employees, had left after a dispute over some missing cylinders around 1900 and were immediately hired by American Graphophone. Greatly impressed with the technical success of the new Edison process, Emerson set to work to find a way to circumvent the patents involved. He came up with the idea of a record that was universally adaptable, rather than a machine that would play either type of record. To accomplish this, he designed a cutter that would record on a bias, producing a record groove that was partially vertical and partially lateral. It could be reproduced on Edison machines designed to play only one type of vertical disc, or on the Victor or Columbia machines designed to play only laterally recorded discs. Emerson had developed the first forty-five–degree cutter. The fallacy in his idea lay in his record's tendency to play even less well on the Edison phonograph than the other shellac discs with the requisite 150 grooves per inch. The bias cut reduced the vertical bearing surface by half.

Emerson resigned from his position with American Graphophone and founded the Emerson Phonograph Company. Although American Graphophone indicated its displeasure by bringing suit against him almost immediately, his unique concept of a universal record served to protect him from the legal clutches of his former employer. He ventured into some interesting areas, though some might be considered a bit unethical, among them a low-priced series of seven-inch discs to be played with a sapphire ball. Some were dubbed from Pathé records made by great artists and are now considered great rarities. The voice of Enrico Caruso as recorded originally upon cylinders by the Anglo-Italian Commerce Company was one example, although the label did not carry his name.

The introduction of vertical-cut discs and machines by Pathé and Edison gave independent inventors and entrepreneurs the opportunity they had been seeking. The new phonographs were universal, accommodating the Pathé sapphire-ball records, the Edison-cut records, and lateral discs. There were even several instruments designed to play all types of records, including Pathé, Aeolian-Vocalion, Emerson, and Gennett. The superiority of the hill-and-dale record had been proved by the Edison tone tests, as attempts by others to use it confirmed.

Events in world history as well as economics seemed to move against the sanguine Edison enterprise. Less than a week before the first memorable tone test, Edison was summoned to Washington, D.C., to head the Naval Consulting Board. The threat of unrestricted submarine warfare was very real; war-created material shortages impeded production everywhere. During the World War I years, the Edison disc records became inordinately noisy and inferior to the prewar product.

Failure to license the process and failure to set up an adequate advertising budget were probably the two most important reasons why the Edison Company eventually swung away from the vertical-cut discs. As illustration, consider the following: the first time around, the sensational tone tests made the headlines everywhere, but repeat performances at least as successful seldom drew the same attention from the newspapers, partly because the novelty had worn off but perhaps more the result of the influence of the newspapers' largest advertisers—Edison's competitors, particularly Victor and Columbia. Edison spent large sums for tone tests but not for newspaper advertising. Advertising managers of some newspapers, through subtle hinting, were able to persuade their music critics to stay away from tone tests.

Furthermore, the opposition's sales forces suggested to prospective purchasers that the Edison tone tests were faked, that the singers simulated the reproduced voices, that the violinists imitated the recorded violin tones. To meet this turn of events, Edison officials encouraged popular vaudeville artists to use the phonograph in connection with their acts. Numerous comparisons were given on the Keith and other circuits by singers, Hawaiian guitarists, banjoists, and marimba and xylophone players. The impossibility of mimicking these instruments was quite obvious to the audience, as there is no control over the quality after the string has been plucked or the hammer used. To anyone who heard the magic of the banjo of Joe Roberts or the xylophone of Signor Friscoe perfectly reproduced by a stock laboratory model Edison phonograph from the stage, there was no question it was a true performance.

Apart from its uncanny accuracy in reproducing solo voices and instruments or small ensembles, the Edison phonograph had some serious faults. One was surface noise, particularly between 1917 and 1920, years when public acceptance was most critical. Another was the comparative "deafness" of the Edison dead studio recording technique. Although essential to the reproduction of an instrument or voice alone, this method limited the size of orchestras that could be recorded satisfactorily. Edison believed that one should be able to hear each individual instrument in the band or orchestra. Before the successful development of microphonic recording and broadcasting, it was not nearly so obvious that, in recording large groups, to satisfy the ear it would be necessary to record some of the reflected sound, or room resonance, along with the source sounds.

By 1918 Edison was able to record thirty-five–piece orchestras, with each instrument individually registered. As the number of instruments increased, the proportional volume of each decreased; those farthest from the recording horn were diminished the most. As the average volume of individual instruments diminished, the abominable surface noise became more obvious. Edison made a futile attempt to solve this problem by constructing a huge recording horn of solid brass two blocks long (125 feet). This horn was eventually dismantled for scrap metal in World War II.

In 1919 an article that was to have far-reaching repercussions appeared in the *Proceedings of the American Physical Society*. It was written by A. G. Webster and entitled "Acoustical Impedance and the Theory of Horns and the Phonograph." Webster outlined the functions of a logarithmic horn and suggested corresponding relationships in electrical circuits, originating a considerable amount of the phraseology subsequently employed in theories and ideas later developed by others, such as that of "impedance" in an acoustical system, which could be balanced by a corresponding "electrical impedance" in an electrical circuit. Undoubtedly as a result of this basic concept, a number of inventors began to research the possibilities of electrical recording. Hanna and Slepian in 1924 published "The Function and Design of Horns for Loud Speakers," but it was the work of J. P. Maxfield and H. C. Harrison that resulted in the introduction of the Western Electric system of recording and the Orthophonic Victrola and Viva-Tonal Columbia Phonograph in 1925. They summarized the results of their work in "Methods of High Quality Recording and Reproduction of Sound Based on Telephone Research," published in the *Transactions of the American Institute of Electrical Engineers* in 1926.

The Victor Orthophonic's radio timbre startled the public; people liked it. It created a demand for volume and a deeper resonance, which the Edison Company tried to meet by putting out the Dance Reproducer, a special-order reproducer that was "blasty" on certain records—an idea that did not go over well.[1]

A few remaining developments in the acoustic period precede the commercial introduction of electrically recorded records. One involves the Brunswick-Balke-Collender Company, well-known manufacturer of billiard and bowling equipment. Rumors claimed that Edison cabinets had been supplied by this company. A disagreement occurred, supposedly over certain standards of manufacture. At any rate, a large shipment of cabinets intended for Edison use was refused, and the Brunswick executives decided to make a talking machine of their own using the cabinets. In 1920 both the Brunswick phonograph and the Brunswick record were introduced. The phonograph featured a universal tone arm, but the records were conventional lateral-cut shellac discs. Deluxe models employed what the Brunswick advertisements termed the Ultona reproducer, which was the best device provided by a competitor for playing Edison discs, equipped with a permanent diamond point with an independent stylus-diaphragm assembly and an ingenious sliding weight for providing the proper pressure upon the disc, whether it be lateral or vertical. In comparison with other lateral discs, the Brunswick records were well recorded, brilliant in the higher register, and smoothly surfaced. The Brunswick records of pianist Leopold Godowsky, among others, were considered sensationally good at the time.

Perhaps this was the basis for the decision of the Edison executives to secure Sergei Rachmaninoff for a series of Edison records. On the first recordings, issued in 1920, noisy surfaces detracted considerably from the excellent fidelity and volume. There is no question that the Edison men tried to persuade Rachmaninoff to agree to a tone-test appearance. He evidently refused, so the Edison advertising writers did what they thought was the next best thing. They had Rachmaninoff pose for a picture at a piano with a jury behind a screen in a privately conducted tone test. An advertisement featuring this picture appeared in *Etude* for December 1920 and other national magazines. The picture was captioned, "Hear Rachmaninoff on the New Edison," and the ad copy read: "Now you can make a straightforward comparison and find out which is the best phonograph. Rachmaninoff himself, the great Russian pianist, gives you this opportunity. He has made recordings for one of the standard talking machines. We are very glad he has done so. For now you can compare." As Rachmaninoff was also recording for Victor at this time, the implications of the ad were obvious. At any rate, Rachmaninoff made no more Edison records thereafter.

It was not Edison's intention to feature artists or sell records by using the artist's name. Instead, the Edison Company relied entirely upon the tune and the quality of the voices.[2] Edison wrote in 1911 to Thomas Graf:

Since my return I have taken up the direction of the musical end of the new disc, because we have no head to the musical end of our recording department, and our selection of people, arrangement of voices, selection of instruments to accompany, has always been left to a man who I do not think is equal to the duty. We use bands when they should be orchestras. We keep instruments in our orchestra which hurt the whole by beating and interfering with the other instruments. We accompany a singer with a loud strident blast. Our men play out of time. We have a flute that on high notes gives a piercing abnormal sound like machinery that wants oiling, because the man has had this defective flute for years. None of the men we have can recognize a good from a bad opera singer; they think if they sing at the Metropolitan Opera House they are fine. They select and record opera which is merely recitative, without tune or connection when put on the phonograph. They do not realize that a song which, with the aid of the environment of the stage and scenery might be good, is dead and of no value on the phonograph. The phonograph exaggerates the tremolo which is present in nearly every voice. It also misses some of the weaker overtones which give beauty to the voice. I propose to depend upon the *quality of the records* and not on the reputation of the singers. There are, of course, many people who will buy a distorted, ill-recorded and scratchy record if the singer has a great reputation, but there are infinitely more who will buy for the beauty of the record. These are lovers of good music and are the only constant and continuous buyers of records.

I see Hammerstein in London has started his Opera House and has great success. He starts out with [the] announcement that he will use no stars in the Opera World and will put on new talent. He is a genius and a fine musician himself. Doubtless you can manage to get some test records from his talent and send them over.[3]

On March 22, 1915, however, Edison finally consented to having the name of the talent appear on the disc record plate label—but only on new label plates, not on those already produced.[4]

In spite of his detailed musical criticism, Edison was so deaf that he had to use an ear trumpet right up against the phonograph horn itself to hear any semblance of the recording.[5] He wrote of his condition to the *Tully Times* in Tully, New York, in 1908: "I am so deaf I can't hear a single word in a theatre, although on the front row, and nothing at the table, yet I don't mind it much. In fact I don't think it would help my nerves or give me much pleasure to have my hearing restored. Now everything is quiet, and my nerves are perfect, and I am satisfied."[6]

In 1922, Columbia introduced a new silent surface record developed by its affiliate, English Columbia, undoubtedly a factor in the Victor decision to double all of the Red Seal series and to withdraw from the market thousands of their rather noisy surfaced single discs that had been piling up in warehouses and on the shelves of dealers since before the war. Unsold record-return allowances had been a policy of all companies, but these allowances were insufficient. So Victor for the first time in its history permitted dealers to sell at reduced prices—half price—all single-faced Red Seal records.

By 1924 Edison credited the great depression in the phonograph, piano, and motion picture business "to a slowing-down in retail trade and manufacturing, the selling of Ford cars for $265 on a $5 a week installment plan, the radio, and Mah Jong, the sales of which were enormous. Three of these things will change, but one will continue, and that will be the Ford machine, because that produces more real pleasure than any other thing and also provides for desirable transportation." [7] England's public did not welcome the radio with the gusto shown in the United States, in part perhaps because of the lack of competition, as there were no commercially sponsored programs. Consequently, the gramophone did not seem to be threatened in England with the serious inroads that early became apparent across the Atlantic. Immediately following the war, great strides were made by English recorders in improving the quality of acoustical lateral disc recordings and in developing better sound boxes and horns. In 1922 a machine was placed upon the market in England called the World, which operated on the principle of a constant speed beneath the point that had been covered in the original Bell-Tainter patents of 1886, allowing the production of records with a playing time of several minutes. Reports were that the reproduction quality was excellent, but by this time the preponderance of machines and records in England had been standardized as lateral, and lack of artists and other considerations prevented the success that the idea merited. As with a number of other industry developments through the years, this was an example of the correct principle introduced at the wrong time, or under the wrong auspices.

Another factor of vital importance to the successful merchandising of phonographs, particularly in the United States, was the design of the cabinets. The increasingly rapid shift in interior decorating trends meant that style played a large part in the building and crash of phonographic dynasties. The largest upswing in Victor fortunes began after the introduction of the internal-horn Victrola in 1906, whose design represented not an improvement in reproduction but an endeavor to adapt the form of the machine to the home environment—that is, it was largely a stylistic development.

Eldridge R. Johnson was canny in envisioning the Victrola as a musical instrument and styling it in a manner acceptable in the best of homes. For Johnson, the Victrola was a unique musical instrument, rather than a reproducing machine, and should have a unique format expressing its function, like that of a harp, cello, or piano. Purchasers of Victrolas looked upon these instruments primarily as items of furniture—not being particularly concerned with the appropriateness of the design in a philosophic sense. This differing viewpoint eventually resulted in the loss of whole-hearted public acceptance of the machine—an acceptance that a few short years before had made *victrola* the generic term for "talking machine." For Victor advertising writers, it was embarrassing that the redundant phrase the "Victor Victrola" had to be used in later years to denote their product.

Having established the trend and set the pace for so many years, the executives and directors of the Victor organization not surprisingly grew somewhat overconfident and insensitive to changes in public taste. Edison was the first competitor to take a step along the path that would result in the eventual overthrow of what might be termed the "ola" style cycle. In 1916 it was decided that the new line of Edison instruments should be considered neither as machines, the prior Edison concept, nor as musical instruments, the Johnson concept, but as furniture housing a sound reproducing instrument. The function was not to be concealed, and the foremost cabinet designers would supply a sufficiently wide number of styles so as to fit properly into any home environment. At that time it would have been impossible for any smart furniture designer to have bucked the trend toward the so-called period styling in home furniture design. Cabinets designed by Elsie de Wolfe for Edison came in various woods and finishes in designs founded on furniture motifs of the famous eclectic designers of the late Renaissance. Among these were the original line of upright cabinet models called the Chippendale, William and Mary, Sheraton, and Jacobean. The careful styling of these cabinets promoted acceptance by those who rebelled against the nontraditional conventionalism of Victor cabinet styling.

In 1918 articles began to appear in popular publications making note of the failure of phonograph manufacturers to keep pace with new trends in interior decoration. A fad developed for taking the functioning mechanism out of the manufacturer's cabinet and installing it in a special cabinet. The changeover evolved into quite a profitable business for small furniture factories making special deluxe period model cabinets for the trade. Other companies, such as Cheney and Sonora, were soon putting out models with custom-built cabinets at high prices. This trend led to the famous DeLuxe handmade Sonora phonograph with all-wood tone arms and tone chambers. Some of these Sonoras sold for as much as $1,500. When Brunswick-Balke-Collender entered the field in 1920, it also put out a line of period models and custom-built cabinets for the higher-priced units. Sonora was one of the first regular manufacturers to market the so-called console models, which were horizontal rather than vertical. The Edison Company soon had companion console models patterned after their upright period models. Only Victor resisted the trend toward the consideration of the phonograph primarily as a piece of furniture or as a console.

In 1923, when the console craze reached its height, Victor sales dropped 20 percent. Victor representatives and jobbers all over the country were astounded to find Victor dealers extremely resentful that Victor was not preparing to meet the strong consumer demand. Especially in metropolitan areas, dealers felt obligated in self-defense to take on competing lines rather than to sell Victor models exclusively. Many of these dealers, freed from Victor loyalty, never again went back to an exclusive basis. The situation finally forced Victor's directors into action, and they persuaded Johnson that a line of console models had become essential, although Johnson insisted on adhering to the styles and curvatures that had become so thoroughly identified with Victor design. The new console Victrola from the modern design point of view was a success, but a failure from the standpoint of the housewife who wished to use the console as a table when not in use as a Victrola. The new models had curved top surfaces on either end, with the conventional Victor lift top rising yet higher in the center. These models were promptly labeled "humpbacks" by some irate dealers.

Highlights of the experience of the industry leaders provide a financial picture of the final days of the acoustic phonographic industry. In 1915, Victor's assets were about $21 million, with about $14 million surplus, of which half was cash. That year, Edward Easton, president of American Graphophone, died leaving an estate of about $1 million. The assets of Columbia Graphophone were then about $14 million, with about $2 million surplus. By 1917 American Graphophone's assets had grown to $19 million, still with a surplus of about $2 million. Meanwhile, Victor's assets leaped to $33 million with a surplus of $23 million, of which $5 million was cash. Edison's total phonograph and record sales in 1917 was something over $9 million but jumped to $22 million by 1921, its largest year.

Phonograph stocks were not listed on the New York Stock Exchange until 1919, when a New York financier bought control of American Graphophone stock. He changed the capitalization from 150,000 shares of $100 par value to 1,500,000 of no-par value and had this new stock listed on the exchange. The list price moved steadily upward until it was quoted at $65 per share. On that basis the new capitalization was over $90 million, although the actual assets of the company were less than a third of that figure.

To create an income picture corresponding to this inflated capitalization, production and sales promotion were expanded. The product was not sufficiently improved to create the requisite demand, however, and much merchandise remained unsold. The situation was observed by the investing public, and the price per share dropped to below $5. The financier who started this cycle of activities retired with a handsome profit on his initial investment, but the oldest company in the phonograph industry was ruined. The bankers kept it going for a year or two, but in 1923, receivers were appointed.

Victor in the meantime had purchased a half interest in the English Gramophone Company in 1921 for $9 million. That year Victor sales exceeded $51 million, topping 1920 sales of more than $50 million. Years before, Eldridge Johnson had sold the controlling interest in English Gramophone for $50 million.

In its first twenty years, the Victor Company earned assets of $43 million, of which $31 million was surplus and undivided profits. In 1922 $30 million was distributed by means of a six-for-one stock dividend. That year Victor's net operating income was over $7 million. The next year, however, Victor's gross sales dropped by $10 million to approximately $37 million. Meanwhile, radio sales were zooming to astronomical heights, more than offsetting the drop in sales of phonographs and records.

January 1, 1924, Victor gave its first broadcast party, with John McCormack and Lucrezia Bori. In more ways than one this event epitomized the victory of radio. Thomas A. Edison, Inc., continued to plug along, paying no attention to radio. The strange reluctance of Edison and his associates to interest themselves in the latter-day development of electronics in which they had played such a vital role in the telegraph and telephone days has never been satisfactorily explained.

CHAPTER 17

Motion Pictures
and Sound Recording

IN 1884 Thomas Edison began experiments with the stated objective of doing visually what his phonograph did aurally, and of combining both to produce motion pictures with sound. The experiments went forward at the Edison laboratory under the direction of Edison and William Kennedy Laurie Dickson, an expert amateur photographer who had come to Edison in 1883. A newly discovered letter from Dickson to Edison dated April 11, 1913, outlines the sequence of events and discoveries within the Edison compound:

Some early notes that may be of some use to Mr. Edison re: Moving Photog. Figure 1. Roads near Newark Edison Laboratory and Edison Lab. Newark Lamp Co., May, 1887.

A = Spot where Mr. Edison talked to me of his Ore Milling, & what he wanted me to experiment on. (End of Ap. 1887).

B = Dickson's Ore Milling Bench—for experiments on Magnetic Ore Separator.

C = Photo Darkroom to develop plates I took pyromagnetic generator (E) on stove, etc.

As I spent much of my spare time in acquiring the art of photography, photographing the various apparatus or completed Edison inventions, using (C) for my dark room, Mr. Edison thought I might be able to carry out a new scheme he had in mind of combining his phonograph with photography, which he described fully to me at his desk (D).

Mr. Edison said that this photo phono work would be entrusted to me to experiment on as soon as we got into his new Laboratory at Orange then in process of completion. I was to select two rooms, one for the Ore Milling & the other for Kinetophono work.

Mr. Edison further explained that it was his dream to be able to synchronize his phonograph with a large number of pinpoint photos, taken together & reproduced so as to give the effect of sight & sound, or "talking pictures."

I was one of the first to move into the Orange Laboratory. Mr. Edison gave me choice of top floor end room for ore milling & Room 5 on the floor below for moving picture work. Work proceeded rapidly. Mr. Edison brot [sic] several visitors to Room 5, showing the micro photos & explaining what he was aiming at. Among the number there was a certain Mr. Russell dubbed "Edison's Private Detective."

Mr. Edison told him in a few words what he hoped to accomplish:
Figure 2. Drawing of Photo and Phono Mandrels joined in unison.
This interview was impressed on my memory, because a tired workman, having taken refuge behind a reflecting screen, left a pair of boots in full view, which Mr. Edison characteristically ignored. (Dated between May & June, 1887).

Towards the end of '87 a night watchman broke into Room 5 in the early hours carrying a light & completely ruining my photo emulsion (which had taken 3 weeks to prepare) for the drum or cylinder micro combine.

Mr. Edison, having heard of the disaster from the watchman (whom I had thoroughly cussed at the time) came in next morning with John Ott & asked for further particulars. (End of 1887).

[Samuel] Insull was also told of this invention & brought to Room 5. His memory or evidence may be useful (End of 1887). Then came a long year of work.

This now brings us to an important episode. In the early part of 1888 Mr. Edison called me into the Library where I learned that several reporters, etc. were expected next day to get "copy" re Phono-Kineto combine. It was therefore up to us to make as good a show as possible.

I anticipated in the demonstration what Mr. Edison expected to do. I fixed the Colts arc lamp projecting lantern in the gallery facing the clock, draped the clock with a sheet, & collecting everything I had done or made in that line, produced a workable bluff, though, an honest exhibition of Mr. Edison's ambition. We both talked a great deal to these gentlemen when they arrived & I think this show secured the first important newspaper items you are looking for.

Work continued & various modifications were made, then Mr. Edison went abroad, & I saw him off, and when standing on the steamer as it moved out, he raised his hands to his eyes, imitating viewing lenses of the Kinetoscope, having previously on the wharf given me his final instructions.

Immediately on his return Mr. Edison came to the New Studio in the grounds to see how I had carried out his instructions while he was absent & seemed well pleased. A week or two later Mr. Edison brot [sic] Saml Insull & two other gentlemen & they saw a short projection by the aid of the Zeis micro outfit & arc light, etc.

Figure 3. Sketch of Interior of Photo Studio.

There is much good evidence of priority of invention still I think, to be dug out. Ask Mr. Edison if he can trace the date of the Brooklyn Technical Institute Exhibition of the first rough wood cased model of the Kinetoscope (single perforation) that I made for him. There was a lecturer re this & afterwards I let the audience file passed [sic] the constantly running Kineto. Don't forget my early article (illustrated) in the Century Magazine date, June . . . I hope this data may be of some help & may lead to fresh evidence by referring to some of the parties mentioned herein. There must be a date in the Orange Laboratory when these early reporters appeared on the scene as the work had really only just commenced & I expect this is what Mr. Edison remembers.

If there is anything more I can do, write me. I may think of something else. With kind rem. to Mr. Edison, I remain

      Yours Sincerely,

      W. K. L. Dickson.[1]

On October 6, 1889, Edison received a demonstration of the new motion pictures after a trip abroad.[2] The image was thrown on a four-foot-square screen by a projector using the film stock made to Edison's specifications by Eastman. The sound was supplied by synchronized wax-type cylinder recordings. Dickson described the scene, including his own role in it: "The crowning point of realism was attained on the occasion of Mr. Edison's return from the Paris Exposition in 1889, when Mr. Dickson himself stepped out on the screen, raised his hat, and

smiled, while uttering the words of greeting: 'Good morning, Mr. Edison, glad to
see you back. I hope you are satisfied with the kineto-phonograph' "[3] Edison re-
called the event differently: "I recall the fact that the moment I got back I went to
see the kinetoscope where they had worked it up to reproduce the films taken on
the kinetograph, and that they had it practically perfect, but there was no screen
as Mr. Dickson says."[4]

A letter Edison wrote to the *Pittsburgh Press,* published September 20, 1896,
should dispel any lingering doubts as to the breadth of his concept of the possibilities of motion pictures:

> In the year of 1887 the idea occurred to me that it was possible to devise
> an instrument which should do for the eye what the phonograph does for
> the ear, and that by a combination of the two all motion and sound could
> be recorded and reproduced simultaneously. This idea, the germ of which
> came from the little toy called the Zoetrope, and the work of Muybridge,
> Marie [Marey] and others has now been accomplished, so that every change
> of facial expression can be recorded and reproduced life size. The kineto-
> scope is only a small model illustrating the present stage of progress, but
> with each month new possibilities are brought into view. I believe that in
> coming years, by my own work and that of Dickson, Muybridge, Marie, and
> others who will doubtless enter the field that grand opera can be given at
> the Metropolitan Opera House at New York without any material change
> from the original, and with artists and musicians long since dead.

In 1891, Edison applied for patents on the Kinetograph camera and the
Kinetoscope viewing apparatus. "The phonograph and the kinetoscope were run
together so that you could put the tubes to your ears and look into the peephole
and see the motion and hear the sound," Edison explained on January 30, 1900.[5]

In his typical style Edison trumpeted to the public through the *Phonoscope* that
the combined powers of the kinetoscope and the phonograph would soon make
it possible for people to sit in a New York theater and enjoy a London play. "The
phonographs would be operated by electricity, being connected on the same circuit that works the kinetoscope, thus making the timing of a player's motion and
his voice correspond perfectly. Not only is the plan feasible, but it is my original idea, long before the kinetoscope had been invented. There are two things
that have to be overcome, and these are the metallic character of the tone of

the phonographs, and the change of its timbre to that of the human voice, so that all the beautiful modulations of the singers and actors can be exactly reproduced, and the second is the synchronization of the phonographs with the kinetoscopic reproduction."[6] In Paris at this time, Reynard had opened the Theatre Optique, using films with hand-drawn pictures, progenitor of our modern cartoon pictures. Before the Kinetograph, however, no motion picture camera of any description existed.

The first ten of Edison's peephole kinetoscopes were shipped April 6, 1894, to Holland Brothers, 1155 Broadway, New York City,[7] and on April 14, 1894, the first machines went into operation, using a continuous fifty-foot spool of film. Later in the year they were introduced in London and Paris, where they were the principal incentive to his competitors, for Edison had failed to apply for foreign patents. From this time forward, there was not a day when motion pictures were not shown somewhere in the world.

In 1895, successful projection of motion pictures on a screen was achieved in Paris by Louis and August Lumière with a machine they called the Cinematograph, in England by Robert W. Paul with the Bioscope, and in the United States by Thomas Armat, C. Francis Jenkins, the Lathams, and others. Edison at first sold the films and the Kinetoscopes outright. His attitude toward projection was that showing pictures to large audiences would quickly kill the usefulness of the films. (Without the theater experience now familiar to all of us, it is hard to understand that this was a perfectly rational approach, yet Edison has been ridiculed in more than a few accounts on the movies because of it.) His agents advised him that the public wanted projection equipment and would certainly obtain it from unlicensed sources if he did not supply it.

The result was that on April 23, 1896, the first gala showing of Edison pictures was made in Koster & Bial's Music Hall, Herald Square, New York City. An Armat-designed projector was used, built by Edison. Befitting the importance of the occasion, the affair was a formal dress function—to the probable disgust of Edison, who disdained formality, but who nevertheless was seated in a box. The projection was superintended by Armat. As prelude to this first motion picture premiere, six acts of vaudeville were presented by Albert Bial, manager of the theater, but the motion pictures stole the show. Twelve of the fifty-foot skits standard for the Kinetoscopes were shown, among them "Sea Waves," "Umbrella Dance," "The Barber Shop," "A Boxing Bout," "Venice, Showing Gondoliers," and "Kaiser Wilhelm Reviewing His Troops." The shadow stage was ready, the novelty of picture in motion sufficed for the moment, but the development of a film art was yet to come.

In spite of spending much on experiments, attorney's fees, and patents, Edison found his patents infringed and circumvented on all sides. By his own error, he failed to have his basic motion picture devices patented in Europe. Hence others were able to take out European patents on similar devices and even to market certain products in the United States. Busy with development work, Edison was too occupied to spend time in long, drawn-out court cases against the many outright infringements by those who now publicly and ostentatiously claimed credit for the invention of motion pictures. The commercially successful Peephole Kinetoscope with its sound mechanism lasted only through the spring of 1895.[8] An eyewitness description of the performance of the phonograph in conjunction with the continuous loop of film appeared in 1895:

> We saw the conductor wave from the podium and spread both his arms to give the signal for the instruments to begin playing. The music immediately began playing softly. Through this unusual experience one senses the imperfection of the apparatus. The phonograph can accompany fairly well at a distance the movements of the ballet dancer, or a conductor, but the synchronization of music and motion is still not perfected.[9]

Edison resumed work on his projecting Kinetoscope, independent of the Armat device, which was called the Vitascope.

In 1897 George W. Brown claimed the invention of a device for synchronizing the projector and the phonograph. Three years later, Léon Gaumont received a patent on a sync motor method. Others who confined their attention to screen projectors were much more numerous, as there was a ready-made market awaiting. These included many names later familiar in the industry: Owen A. Eames of Boston, Edison Hill Amet of Chicago, W. C. Hughes, H. B. and Jack Warner, Gossart, Perret & Lacroix, Sulle & Mazo, Gauthier, Messager, Baxter and Wray.

In 1903 Eugene Lauste invented and demonstrated a method of producing sound from film by means of photographed sound waves, accomplished by projecting light through the film onto a selenium cell. (That light affected the conductivity of selenium had been known for many years; in fact, Alexander Graham Bell invented a method of projecting sound by means of this principle over a beam of light, which he called the Photophone.) Meanwhile the Edison enterprise was establishing a commercial foundation for the development of a new medium of art expression, entertainment, and education. In this same year the first film exchange was opened by Miles Brothers, San Francisco exhibitors. Films at this time were sold outright to the exhibitors, so this move represented a more economic use of films and marked the beginning of the end of the tent-show or barnstorming period, in which an exhibitor traveled with one set of films until they were worn out. This was much the same basis on which the tinfoil phonograph was launched—traveling exhibitors. Also in 1903 "The Great Train Robbery" was produced by the Edison Company—the first movie to tell a complete story.

The improvement in the content of films led to the development of the motion picture theater. Davis and Harris, Pittsburgh demonstrators, redesigned an empty shed that they had been using on the usual temporary basis into a permanent, luxurious showplace that they named the Nickelodeon. It was the prototype of today's picture theaters. Within two years 5,000 such permanent motion picture theaters had sprung up all over the country.

In 1906 Lee DeForest combined Lauste's sound-on-film principle with the photoelectric cell and experimented with amplification by means of his new three-element vacuum tube. Also of future importance in the exploitation of talking pictures, but purely incidental at the time, was the establishment by the four Warner brothers of their first motion picture theater, the Cascade, in a converted store in New Castle, Pennsylvania.

By 1907 all the get-rich-quick opportunists of the country were trying to get into the act. Edison and the other licensed producers could not keep up with the mounting demand for films, and illegitimate producers materialized right and left. With no legal way to secure motion picture cameras or film in the United States, where the incontestably basic Edison patents were presumably in effect, most of the more careful entrepreneurs bought European-made copies of the Edison camera—others, with everything to gain and nothing to lose, went right ahead and made their own. To illustrate just how flagrant the activity was, consider that the first successful motion picture film had been made to Edison's specifications by George Eastman. It was Edison who determined the width of the film (35 mm.), and designed the four notches per frame for the ratchet feed device—both of which are standard yet today. In fact, a large box of punchings from film found in the chemical storeroom at West Orange proves that the sprocket holes were punched at the Edison Laboratory. All of Edison's early competitors were dependent upon Edison films in the development of projectors and cameras. Another dodge that avoided paying for copies of Edison films was the production of bootleg film used for copying, or "duping," the original films, thus removing the profit from their production.

This situation led to the formation of the Motion Picture Patents Corporation (MPPC) in 1908, at first intended to embrace only those companies considered to possess legitimate, operable patents—Edison, Biograph, and Vitagraph. Later others who wanted to operate on a legitimate basis were added, and the roster was increased to include Essanay, Selig, Lubin, and Kalem in the United States and Melies and Pathé in France. One reason some foreign companies found it desirable to come into the fold, even though the basic Edison inventions had not received foreign patents, was that Edison had improved the shutter mechanism and other important elements considerably while perfecting his projection Kinetoscope.

In 1910 the MPPC established a nationwide film exchange, the General Film Company, to act as sole distributors for the member producers. General Film acquired fifty-seven of the fifty-eight existing distributing exchanges. The sole standout was owned by William Fox, the powerful and independent producer and owner of a chain of theaters, who was now in a position to buck what he called "the trust." In 1911, in order to assist in bringing order out of the chaos that had prevailed before the formation of the Motion Picture Patents Corporation, George Eastman, a friend of Edison, gave Jules Brulatour the exclusive distributorship of all cinematograph positive film stock to be produced by the Eastman Kodak Company. Brulatour then proceeded to acquire all of his legitimate competitors.[10]

In 1912, Fox brought suit against the MPPC for representing an illegal monopoly operating in restraint of trade in violation of the Sherman antitrust laws. Back of him, of course, were the thousand and one scoundrels who had been making a killing pirating patented devices, operating in most cases without patents or licenses of any kind. Some of the independents other than Fox were also powerful and clever, without Fox's strategic position as producer, distributor, and theater chain operator. One of these independents was Adolph Zukor, who, in the drought occasioned by the drying up of the supply of unlicensed films through the operation of the patents pool and Brulatour, imported a French-made picture starring Sarah Bernhardt, which was shown through independent theaters with great success. Encouraged, Zukor had the rather colossal nerve, in view of the circumstances, to attempt to secure the approval and backing of the legitimate members of the MPPC for an extension of his activities, a request that was refused. Zukor was determined to stay in the industry, however, and organized the Famous Players in Famous Plays Company, employing the best-known director in the industry outside of D. W. Griffith—Edwin S. Porter.

One of the important factors nurturing this outright flaunting of patent rights was the popular uprising against the "interests" and "trusts." The chief incitement of this popular wave of indignation came from the trust-busting activities of President Theodore Roosevelt. The elements allied with Fox were exceedingly active in engaging newspaper support and in spreading propaganda. As usual in these situations, the pioneer inventors were poor publicity men, and the net result was that the public was entirely unable to differentiate between the legitimate monopoly that is conferred upon inventors for a specified length of time by the granting of letters patent and the type of monopoly that is represented by financial interests gaining control of formerly competing manufacturers. By 1912 a number of other producers and distributors of motion pictures decided also to buck "the trust," emboldened by Fox's stand.

Whether in reaction to this situation or not, in 1913 Edison gave demonstrations in many U.S. cities of his latest talking picture device, the Kinetophone. The Kinetophone employed a 7½-inch-long celluloid cylinder record with a 4½-inch diameter, similar to the Blue Amberol record. A mechanical advantage amplifier was used to step up the volume, and synchronization was managed by a long pulley system connecting the projector in one end of the theater with the mandrel of the phonograph behind the screen at the other end. The mechanism was far from foolproof: the sound often got out of step with the pictures, film breaks were not spliced in the manner required, and the results, while at times hilariously funny, were disastrous to the enterprise.

Edison realized that in order to synchronize light and sound waves, it would be necessary to record voice and action simultaneously.[11] Experimental work went on in the West Orange Kinetophone tent out in the main laboratory yard, while actual filming took place at the Bronx Studio on Decatur Avenue in New York. Lighting was the greatest problem, for arc lighting cast hard shadows, and daylight alone was changeable throughout the day. At the Bronx Studio the executive offices cut off much valuable light, especially when most needed—for afternoon work in the winter season. The pitch of the skylight projected light not on the floor but on the wall, where it was improperly reflected.

Edison used film supplied by the Eastman Company. The Eastman negative emulsion was sensitive only to ultraviolet, violet, blue, and a small amount of blue-green. For green, yellow, orange, and red, it was absolutely insensitive, thus requiring considerable thought to be put into the pigments chosen for scenery and into the selection of costumes. Pigments had to be restricted to those that had the same value in arc light and in daylight, and that were as neutral in their translation into monotone as black and white. Red, orange, and yellow were expected to register in values of black or dark gray. Green registered as gray, while blue and violet as almost white. The Edison Company was using in 1913 a converted Pathé camera with a Voigtlander lens.

Actors were instructed to speak as distinctly as possible and louder than for ordinary acting and to face the recording horn, if possible. The stage was narrow, so that the recorder could be as close to the actors as possible and good lip movement could be seen. Apparent breadth was realized by the use of heavy furniture at the ends and of perspective angles in the settings. "Echoes become more disturbing the further the actors are from the horn, but canvas and carpets stop it," noted Edison. Marjorie Ellison, Laura Dean, Nellie Grant, Bob Lett, John Charles Thomas, Albert Farrington, and Thomas Chalmers were among those who made trials for Kinetoscope recording.

Loudness was critical in the playback of the Kinetoscope recording: the greater the friction, the louder the sound. Daniel Higham, an inventor in Bridgeport, Connecticut, held patents issued between 1901 and 1905 on Sound Reproducing Apparatus, the most important of which was a mechanical amplifier.[12] By dubbing a newly recorded Kinetoscope cylinder with a Higham amplifier, a much louder copy could be generated, a necessary step for theater sound reproduction. Although the original Higham patents were controlled by the Columbia Phonograph Company, negotiations with the Highmophone Company in 1913 gave the Edison Company license to use the Higham patents, upon the payment of a royalty.[13]

The phonograph, built on the Higham frictional principle, was operated by an electric motor and was located behind the screen. The governing device on this motor was supposed to keep the phonograph rotating at a constant speed, regardless of small variations in line voltage. Attached to the phonograph was a small pulley wheel, which drove a braided silk trout line over various ball-bearing pulleys to the Kinetoscope synchronizer. The synchronizer was a device that prevented the Kinetoscope operator from turning the handle faster than it should be turned. First the title was thrown on the screen, then there was a blank space of one second followed by the picture. The phonograph motor was operating, but not the cylinder, so that when the picture began, the clutch on the cylinder could be thrown, causing the phonograph to reproduce the sound at 120 rpm. The record was positioned by ensuring that a white mark on it started out on top; by placing one's finger in one of the holes in the end of the mandrel, one could rotate the cylinder slowly to the right until a loud, distinct knock (coconut clappers) was heard. This knock—$\frac{3}{32}$ from the white mark—was the starting point for the phonograph reproducer. Mounted on the side of the horn was a telephone transmitter connected to a headband outfit on the operator's head. The operator could then hear the phonograph, see the picture, and work the synchronizer to perfection.[14]

Synchronization was far from a sure thing, however. Most operators were ill-prepared to operate the equipment; film broke and had to be spliced. Rats developed a strong appetite for the fishline string; Edison suggested soaking the string in a solution of quinine. The National American Woman Suffrage Association complained that motion pictures of the leaders of the movement were made to appear grotesque and elongated, and for that reason they should be withdrawn. These drawbacks, coupled with the decision of the Federal Court ordering the dissolution of the Motion Picture Patents Corporation in 1915, marked the end of Edison's attempts to coordinate sound with pictures. He did, however, attempt to make a stereoscopic Kinetoscope Screen made up of a number of vertical flutings, of such configuration that everyone with two-eye vision would see two pictures running synchronously, producing a stereoscopic effect. In addition, Edison made two special disc records, serial nos. 3248–3249, of a mob scene for Klaw & Erlanger to be used for some New York production.[15]

The Edison Company made one more foray into matching sound with motion picture—Cinemusic, or Ediscope recording. Cinemusic was developed in the 1927–28 period by Theodore Edison. The idea was to have a machine that could run without attention for as long a time as possible and have a volume of sound approximating that of a small motion picture theatre organ or orchestra. Many problems arose in the actual performance of the machine, such as weakness in sound reproduction that resulted in extremely high electrical amplification, creating a certain amount of distortion. In spite of these problems, Theodore Edison felt that the quality of music produced would be an immeasurable improvement over the tin-pan pianos found in many of the small theaters.[16] The Cinemusic disc had 360 grooves per inch; in other words, one inch represented fifteen minutes' worth of recording. The disc played anywhere from 24 rpm to 30 rpm.[17]

In one known instance a Cinemusic disc was coupled with the Technicolor film "The Story of Cinderella." Curiously enough, one of the voices on an extant Cinemusic disc sounds amazingly like Ann Edison, wife of Theodore Edison.[18]

In 1915 Lee DeForest was demonstrating for Western Electric his Audion amplifier system. Theodore W. Case, of Auburn, New York, worked for a number of years on the idea of using a tiny mirror attached to a diaphragm vibrated by sound waves to register sound simultaneously with sight on the same film. The first of a long series of patents upon elements of this process was granted to him in 1919. It seems altogether too obvious now that this should have proven to be the ultimate method, but the synchronized record approach was the first to receive the enthusiastic acclaim of the public. Satisfactory and consistent results from sound on film proved to be a will-o'-the-wisp for a number of years. It was difficult for the developers of the process to get theaters to book the short specialties produced on an experimental basis, first because of the need to install special equipment, and second because of the unreliable quality of the sound.

The methods of presenting silent pictures with subtitles and musical scores played by orchestras and pipe organ had been developed to a point where this mutation and synthetic substitutions for normal sounds was completely accepted by most people when Lee DeForest became interested in the possibilities of the Case invention. He acquired the rights to the Case patents, including the Tellafide photoelectric cell, the heart of the projector unit that transforms the variations in light of the sound track into variable electric currents, which when amplified operated the loudspeakers located behind the screen. DeForest succeeded in making a considerable improvement in the quality of voice and music reproduction. He also had the idea of building up a library of short subjects that would not depend too much on release dates, so that a market might gradually be built up; as new outlets were provided with equipment, the existing material could be shown in areas where it had not been seen. Meanwhile, Case continued his research, and beginning in 1925 all Case patents were assigned to Case Research Laboratory, Auburn, New York.

By November 1925 DeForest had added to the Phonofilm Library sound pictures by the following groups and artists: Eddie Cantor; Weber & Fields; Sissle & Blake; Balieff and his Chauve-Souris; Raymond Hitchcock; Puck & White; the Ben Bernie, Ray Miller, and Paul Specht bands; Roy Smeck; Monroe Silver; Harry Hirshfield; opera singers Bernice DePasquale, Leon Rothier, and Mme. Marie Rappold; Anna Pavlova; Max Rosen; Roger Wolfe Kahn's band;

Chauncey M. Depew; and Frank Crane. Al Jolson was announced about this time as the latest new recruit of Phonofilm, and a publicity blurb stated that he was to receive a higher fee than he had ever earned in making phonograph records. There was no question that the Jolson name was magic. In 1929 he was to set the all-time high for copies of "Sonny Boy," which he had also recorded for Brunswick. The acquisition of the services of Jolson by DeForest seems to indicate that sound on film was receiving considerable acceptance at that time.

But, again, just as the expenditure of the efforts of many and the investment of millions of dollars seemed about to pay off, Bell Telephone became interested in the talking picture field. It was found that by certain relatively minor changes, the Western Electric system could be adapted to produce considerably better acoustical results than the existing sound-film technique. This was done by reducing the recording speed from 78 rpm to 33 ⅓ rpm, thus securing a longer playing time, further increased by using larger discs. Positive synchronization of record with projector was achieved by synchronous motors. Starting points of both film and record were marked to make absolute synchronization easily controlled. With the improvement of films as well as of film projection mechanisms, breakdowns were less frequent; duplicate prints took care of any emergency. A high-quality amplifier was provided, the same kind as used for the new recording process. Folded, re-entrant horns of the type developed by Harrison for the Orthophonic Victrola were used in back of the screen, with powerful dynamic-type driving units.

Nevertheless, the fallacy of the steel needle was perpetuated in this new film process, which was called the Vitaphone. The new discs were made up to twenty inches in diameter, and in order to reduce surface noise to a tolerable level with the high amplification necessary, abrasives in the surface material were eliminated, resulting in a much smoother but less durable surface. These records were provided with a space on the label to indicate the number of playings, which was strictly limited. It is interesting to note that these records were processed and pressed in the Victor plant. Warner Brothers, then in a critical financial condition, saw the possibilities of the new Western Electric process and decided to gamble everything on it, signing a contract on June 25, 1925. Stanley Watkins of Maxfield's Western Electric sound staff moved a crew and equipment into the old Brooklyn Vitagraph studio, owned by Warner Brothers. Here experimentation was carried on until most of the more obvious difficulties were ironed out.

For the debut of the new talking pictures a series of shorts were recorded by artists with names well known to record buyers. The exception was Anna

Case, who made a full-length feature motion picture in 1915, a phenomenon quite unknown to motion picture audiences. Artists making the new talking pictures included Giovanni Martinelli, violinists Mischa Elman and Efrem Zimbalist, pianist Harold Bauer, and soprano Marion Talley. These great artists were presented by Will S. Hays, arbiter of the film industry. The world premiere on February 19, 1927, was a gala occasion at Warner Brothers' New York theater, on Broadway between Fifty-first and Fifty-seond streets. Also shown was the latest Warner Brothers feature picture, "Don Juan," with John Barrymore, which was specially provided with a symphonic score on Vitaphone discs. On October 6, 1927, Warners presented the first full-length talking picture, "The Jazz Singer," featuring Al Jolson, the picture that sounded the death knell for silent pictures.

By this time William Fox had purchased the Movietone rights and was issuing travel and news pictures whose sound quality was nearly equal to that of the Vitaphone. The first of the Fox Movietone shorts was shown on June 21, 1927, at the Roxie, and the first all-Movietone newsreel was shown on October 28, with King George V, Crown Prince Edward, Marshal Foch, Raymond Poincaré, the Crown Prince of Sweden, David Lloyd George, and Ramsey MacDonald.

At first, talking pictures had only a few talking sequences, to permit movie audiences to become accustomed to the change. Techniques had to be perfected—the demands of the microphone suddenly immobilized what had been a very active visual medium. Motion had been an inherent requirement to sustain interest in silent films. Traveling booms for keeping the microphone over the principals had not yet been devised, nor had rapidly traveling sound trucks to keep up with outdoor action. There was considerable difficulty in solving the acoustic problems in many theaters, so that the sound was uniformly acceptable in definition and quality. During this transitional period many pictures already in production were equipped with "goat glands," as they were facetiously called in the industry—talking sequences—so that they might be advertised as "talking pictures."

William Fox was able to produce sound pictures by accepting a sublicense from Warner Brothers, who had an exclusive contract for the Western Electric process. Though hit hard by fall box office receipts, the other large producers demurred. "The Jazz Singer" had cost the record sum of $500,000 to produce but grossed $2.5 million.

When "The Jazz Singer" was released, there were only about 100 theaters wired for sound in the country. After the New York opening, bookings were arranged on a road-show basis, permitting time to install sound equipment in advance of each showing. Warner Brothers assumed the financial risk of the installations, to be repaid out of profits. The cost ran from $5,000 to $20,000 per theater depending on size and other variables. Warner Brothers bought the Stanley Company of America in the summer of 1928, getting 250 theaters and a third of First National Pictures. They then proceeded to buy control of the latter and so acquired an additional 500 theaters.

In order to overcome the objections of the other large producers to doing business through Warners, Western Electric and its parent company, AT&T, organized a new corporation, Electrical Research Products, Inc. (ERPI), to furnish engineering service and to license the use of equipment manufactured by Western Electric. To effect this program, the patent rights to Vitaphone and Movietone were recovered from Warner Brothers and Fox Film and pooled with other patents through ERPI. Now all the major producers expressed willingness to go ahead. The mammoth but profitable job of equipping the sound stages of Hollywood and thousands of theaters across the country began. By the end of 1929 over 4,000 theaters had received sound installations and $37 million had been taken in from the sale of equipment and services.

Only RCA was left on the outside; as a subsidiary of General Electric, it felt secure in its exclusive possession of the Photophone patents of the sound-on-film method.[19] Time was running out, however; virtually all the first-run theaters had been secured by either Paramount-Famous Players-Lasky, Loew's Inc. (MGM), and the large circuits affiliated with First National, now absorbed by Warner Brothers. Fox and Universal also gained outlets steadily, with Warners continuing its spectacular rise.

The Rockefeller-backed GE-RCA interests founded Radio-Keith-Orpheum, comprised of RCA, American Pathé, and the Keith-Albee-Orpheum theater chain, for the purpose of producing sound pictures. The Warner Brothers–ERPI–Western Electric–AT&T aggregation was a Morgan-financed operation. The financial importance of these alignments may be appreciated by considering that from a state of virtual insolvency in 1925, Warners' assets had expanded to $16 million by the close of 1928 and by the end of another year to $230 million.

Even with the stock market crash, the movie business held up. Wall Street financiers were amazed at what seemed to be a depression-proof industry. By 1933, however, attendance began to fall off in the theaters. The novelty of sound pictures had worn off, money was tighter than ever, savings had been dissipated, employment was at a new low. Even the magic spell of the flickering films failed to give solace. The result of the prolonged depression and the belated recession in the theater business was that in 1937 Paramount was bankrupt, RKO and Universal in receivership. Fox Film had to reorganize. The battle of the giants was over—the internal feud had been resolved with the Morgan-AT&T faction in complete control not only of the motion picture industry but of recording and communications by wire or through the air.

N O T E S

CHAPTER 1. BEFORE THE PHONOGRAPH

1. George Ebers, *Egypt,* vol. 2

2. National Phonograph Co., *The Phonograph and How To Use It* (West Orange, N.J.: National Phonograph Co., 1900). Faber's talking man had "flexible lips of rubber, and also a rubber tongue, ingeniously controlling vowels and consonants. In its throat is a tiny fan wheel, by which the letter 'r' is rolled. It has an ivory reed for vocal cords. Its mouth is an oval cavity, the size of which is regulated by sliding sections, rapidly operated from a keyboard. A tube is attac¹ ᵈ to its nose when it speaks French."

3. *Histoire Comique en Voyage dans la Lune,* translated by A. Lovell (1867; London: Doubleday & McClure, 1899).

As I opened the Box, I found within somewhat of Metal almost like to our Clocks, full of I know not what little Springs and imperceptible Engines. It was a Book, indeed, but a Strange and Wonderful Book, that had neither Leaves nor Letters. In fact, it was a Book made wholly for the Ears and not the Eyes. So that when any Body has a mind to read in it, he winds up the Machine with a great many little Springs; and he turns the Hand to the Chapter he desired to hear, and straight, as from the Mouth of Man, or a Musical Instrument, proceed all the distinct and different Sounds, which the Lunar Grandees make use of for expressing their Thoughts, instead of Language.

When I since reflected on the Miraculous Invention, I no longer wondered that the Young Men of that Country were more knowing at Sixteen or Eighteen years Old, than the Gray-Beards of our Climate; for knowing how to Read as soon as speak, they are never without Lectures, in their Chambers, their Walks, the Town, or Traveling; they may have in their Pockets, or at their Girdles, Thirty of these Books, where they need but wind up a Spring to hear a whole chapter, and so, more, if they have a mind to hear the Book quite through; living and dead, who entertain you with Living Voices. This Present employed me about an hour, and then hanging them to my Ears, like a pair of Pendants, I went to walking.

4. "Telegraphy," *U.S. Patent Office Gazette,* patent application filed by Alexander Graham Bell, February 14, 1876, granted March 7, 1876, 9:474; Theodore Achille Louis du Moncel, *The Telephone, the Microphone, and the Phonograph* (New York: Harper, 1879); George B. Prescott, *The Speaking Telephone, Talking Phonograph, and Other Novelties* (New York: Appleton, 1878) and *Bell's Electric Speaking Telephone: Its Invention, Construction, Application, Modification, and History* (New York: Appleton, 1884).

5. According to Edward McCurdy, *The Mind of Leonardo da Vinci* (New York: Dodd, Mead, 1928) and *The Notebooks of Leonardo da Vinci* (New York: Reynal & Hitchcock, 1938), Leonardo da Vinci was familiar with the acoustical properties of tubes and trumpets. The combination of the two in the design of a manufactured intercommunication system may have been the first a priori invention in the phonographic series.

6. John Tyndall, *Sound* (New York: Appleton, 1895).

7. Henry Seymour, *The Reproduction of Sound* (London: W. B. Tattersall, 1918); R. D. Darrell, *Sewanee Review* (January–March 1933); Roland Gelatt, *The Fabulous Phonograph* (Philadelphia: Lippincott, 1955).

CHAPTER 2. THE EDISON TINFOIL PHONOGRAPH

1. Alfred O. Tate, *Edison's Open Door* (New York: Dutton, 1938).

2. Patent on the loud-speaking telephone, embodying the electro-motograph principle, was sold by Thomas A. Edison on March 20, 1880, to the Western Union Telegraph Co. for $100,000.

3. Batchelor Collection, Edison National Historic Site (hereafter abbreviated as ENHS).

4. Document Collection, ENHS.

5. Deposition of Charles Batchelor, *American Graphophone Company vs. Edison Phonograph Works on letters patent nos. 341,214, 341,288,* U.S. Circuit Court, District of New Jersey, Equity no. 3500. See also Raymond R. Wile, "The Wonder of the Age: The Invention of the Phonograph," *Phonographs and Gramophones Symposium* (July 2, 1977): 13.

6. See Wile, "Wonder of the Age," 18.

7. Laboratory sheet, September 7, 1877, Document Collection, ENHS.

8. See Wile, "Wonder of the Age," 18.

9. Batchelor Diary, Document Collection, ENHS.

10. Document Collection, ENHS.

11. Telegram, Johnson to Painter, December 7, 1877, Document Collection, ENHS. Joseph Henry was secretary of the Smithsonian Institution; Benjamin F. Butler was a former Civil War general, later a member of Congress. See also Wile, "Wonder of the Age"; E. H. Johnson to Uriah H. Painter, December 8, 1877, Uriah H. Painter Papers, Historical Society of Pennsylvania. Uriah Hunt Painter was born in West Chester, Pa., in 1837, educated at Oberlin College, and at the age of twenty succeeded to his father's lumber business in West Chester, Pennsylvania. At the beginning of the Civil War he went to Washington, D.C., as the correspondent of the *Philadelphia Inquirer.* At the first battle of Bull Run he escaped capture by temporarily donning a surgeon's apron in the field hospital, afterward making his way to Washington. Foreseeing the

news of the Union disaster would not be permitted to pass the censor, Painter took a train to Philadelphia and his paper printed a full account of the battle 24 hours in advance of its competitors. After the battle of Chantilly he sent to Washington the information that Lee's army was about to invade Virginia. As no such reports had been received from army officers, Secretary Seward, considering it treasonable, insisted on his arrest. When the news was confirmed later by Lee crossing the Potomac, the correspondent was released. His relations with Lincoln and Stanton were close. After the war he remained in Washington as correspondent for the *Inquirer, New York Sun,* and *New York Tribune.* At one time Painter held the option for the Bell telephone patents which he endeavored to sell to Jay Gould for the Western Union Telegraph Company. Gould thought it would never amount to anything except as a toy and declined to purchase. The local Bell telephone company in Washington was organized by Painter. He died at Long Branch, New Jersey, on October 20, 1900. Batchelor Collection, ENHS.

12. Baltimore, Md., *Gazette,* April 20, 1878.

13. Document Collection, ENHS.

14. Wile, "Wonder of the Age," 31.

CHAPTER 3. THE NORTH AMERICAN PHONOGRAPH COMPANY AND THE BELL-TAINTER GRAPHOPHONE

1. In the ENHS patent files, a marginal note on U.S. Patent 382,419 reveals Edison's viewpoint:

Note, the broad application on duplications, filed Jan. 5, 1888, was abandoned. Edison's English patent No. 1644 of 1878 was acknowledged as covering a "part" of the invention. The application was abandoned apparently under the doctrine of Fuller v. Eagle Co., since the specification was the same as patent No. 484,582.

It is difficult to see now why this was done since patent 484,582 covers the specific vacuum process, and the broad application was comprehensive enough to include graphite, silver salts, and gold leaf chemically reduced. Possibly the doctrine of double patenting was not clearly understood.

2. Document Collection, ENHS.

3. U.S. patents granted May 4, 1886, applied for June 27, 1885, as follows: to Alexander G. Bell, Chichester A. Bell, and Charles Sumner Tainter

No. 341,212—Reproducing sounds from phonograph records No. 341,213—Transmitting and reproducing speech and other sounds by radiant energy

to Chichester Bell and Charles Sumner Tainter

No. 341,214—Recording and reproducing speech and other sounds
No. 341,287—Sounds, recording and reproducing
No. 341,288—Sound apparatus for recording and reproducing

4. George S. Bryan, *Edison: The Man and His Work* (New York: Knopf, 1926).

CHAPTER 4. THE LOCAL PHONOGRAPH COMPANIES

1. "Agreement for Exhibition in the State of Ohio between Ezra T. Gilliland and the Edison Speaking Phonograph Company," Uriah Hunt Painter Papers.

2. Letterhead on a letter, Louis Glass to A. O. Tate, June 19, 1888, *Thomas A. Edison vs. Ezra T. Gilliland and John C. Tomlinson*, U.S. Circuit Court, Southern District of New York, Equity no. 4652.

3. Testimony of George Tewksbury, *American Graphophone Company vs. Edison Phonograph Works*, U.S. Circuit Court, District of New Jersey, Equity no. 3500.

4. Ibid.

5. Raymond R. Wile, "Provisional Listing of the Local Phonograph Companies, 1890–1893," *Journal of the Association for Recorded Sound Collections* 3, nos. 2–3 (Fall 1971): 13–23.

6. "Metropolitan Phonograph Co. Preliminary Prospectus," *American Graphophone vs. Edison Phonograph Works*.

7. Metropolitan Phonograph Company, *Minute Book*, 6, Document Collection, ENHS.

8. Deposition of Edward D. Easton, *American Graphophone Co. vs. U.S. Phonograph Co., et al.*, Equity no. 3668, Document Collection, ENHS.

9. Metropolitan Phonograph Company, *Minute Book*, April 3, 1889, 91.

10. *Keller vs. Douglass vs. Magden vs. Gilliland and Tappan et al.*, U.S. Patent Office, Interference no. 15005, Document no. 53.

11. "North American Phonograph Co. Circular Letter No. ?" August 1, 1890, *New York Phonograph Co. vs. Thomas A. Edison, the Edison Phonograph Company, the Edison Phonograph Works and the National Phonograph Co.*, U.S. Circuit Court, Southern District of New York, Equity no. 7719.

12. Document Collection, ENHS.

13. *New York Times*, February 9, 1890, 2.

14. "Agreement," Automatic Phonograph Exhibition Company and New York Phonograph Company, February 27, 1890, Document Collection ENHS.

15. A. O. Tate to Louis Glass, March 13, 1890, Document Collection, ENHS.

16. Memorandum, Edison from ?, October 17, 1890, Document Collection, ENHS.

17. *American Graphophone vs. Edison Phonograph Works*.

18. *New York Phonograph vs. Edison et al.*

19. *Automatic Phonograph Exhibition Company vs. North American Phonograph Company*, U.S. Circuit Court, Southern District of New York, Equity no. 4989.

20. Virginia McRae, the *Phonogram*'s owner and manager, was guaranteed 5,000 subscribers by Thomas R. Lombard, who based his estimate on replies by the local phonograph companies to a circular sent out by North American. After the first issue, the companies canceled at least half the subscriptions. V. H. McRae to A. O. Tate, July 25, 1891.

21. National Phonograph Association, *Proceedings of the Second Annual Convention of Local Phonograph Companies of the U.S.*, New York, June 16–18, 1891.

22. *Columbia Phonograph Company vs. North American Phonograph Company, George E. Tewksbury, and Leonard Garfield Spencer,* Supreme Court of the District of Columbia, Equity no. 14580.

23. Minutes, North American Phonograph Company, July 14, 1892, 177, 218–19, Document Collection, ENHS.

24. "Mr. Edison at the Helm," *Phonogram* 2, nos. 7–8 (July–August 1892): 15; "Unification of Phonograph Interests," *Phonogram* 2, nos. 7–8 (July–August 1892): 152; A. O. Tate to Thomas Edison, July 29, 1892, Document Collection, ENHS.

25. Minutes, North American Phonograph Company, July 14, 1892, 231–32, 230, Document Collection, ENHS.

26. Edward D. Easton, "Report to the Board of Directors, 1895," *Report to the Stockholders, 1899,* American Graphophone Company, 1.

27. Ibid., 4–5.

28. *Edison United Phonograph Company vs. Edison Phonograph Works and North American Phonograph Company,* New Jersey, in chancery, Nov. 13, 1893, Document Collection, ENHS.

29. *Walter Cutting, Executor, et al. vs. the North American Phonograph Company,* New Jersey, in chancery, docket no. 6737, Document Collection, ENHS.

30. Ibid., Newark, N.J., Feb. 15, 1895. See also "The Wizard Explains," Jersey City *News,* April 29, 1895.

31. Circular letter, American Graphophone Company per E. D. Easton, October 31, 1894, *Cutting vs. North American Phonograph.*

32. *Report to the Stockholders, 1899,* 5–6.

33. Testimony of James L. Andem, *New York Phonograph vs. Edison.*

34. *Cutting, Exececutor, John R. Hardin, Receiver, vs. Edison Phonograph Works, et al.,* New Jersey, in chancery, 3; Final Decree, *New York Phonograph Company et al.,* 829–31.

35. Agreement, Thomas A. Edison and Charles A. Boston, December 26, 1895, Document Collection, ENHS.

36. "An indenture made this 18th day of February, 1896, between John R. Hardin . . . and the National Phonograph Co.," circular, John R. Hardin, Receiver, January 20, 1896, Document Collection ENHS.

37. To the Board of Directors of the National Phonograph Co. from Thomas A. Edison, January 28, 1896, memorandum, Document Collection, ENHS.

38. "Indenture made this 18th day of February 1896" details the specifics of the split.

39. *Cutting, Executor.*

40. Ibid.

41. Bill of complaint, *New York Phonograph vs. Edison;* bill of complaint, *New York Phonograph Co. vs. the American Graphophone Co. et al.* For the correspondence concerning the consent decree and the cross-licensing agreement between the Edison group and American Graphophone, November 19–December 7, 1896, see *National Phonograph Co. vs. American Graphophone Co. and Columbia Phonograph Co., General,* U.S. Circuit Court, District of Connecticut, Equity no. 1166, Document Collection, ENHS.

42. See *F. M. Prescott vs. Thomas A. Edison, William E. Gilmore, Charles E. Stevens, National Phonograph Company and T. J. Monks.* Part of the bill of complaint was reprinted in *Phonoscope* 3, no. 7 (July 1899): 12–13.

43. Minutes, New York Phonograph Company; *New York Phonograph Co. vs. Edison et al.*, 26–29, 66–67, 96–97, Document Collection, ENHS.

44. *The Edison Phonograph Co., a firm formed for doing business in the State of Ohio vs. Ilsen and Co.*, Supreme Court of Cincinnati, Ohio, 1899.

45. National Phonograph Association, *Fifth Annual Convention of the Local Phonograph Companies to be held at Cincinnati, September 25, 1900*, 1, 4, 5 passim, Document Collection ENHS.

46. Ibid, *Resolutions adopted, Cincinnati, O., September 25th, 1900, by the Fifth Annual Convention*, Document Collection, ENHS.

47. *New York Phonograph Co. vs. Edison et al.*, exhibit 1 on motion of New York Phonograph Company and James L. Andem for substitution of solicitors.

48. "Second affidavit of James L. Andem," *Thomas A. Edison et al. vs. New York Phonograph Co. et al.*, Supreme Court, County of Westchester, New York; Motion for injunction Pendente Lite and papers submitted in opposition and in reply, 190.

49. Ibid.

50. Ibid.; Frank L. Dyer to Thomas A. Edison, April 4, 1909, Document Collection, ENHS.

51. *Edison vs. New York Phonograph*, passim.

52. Edward D. Easton, President of Columbia Phonograph Co., to Secretary of State of West Virginia, June 16, 1913.

CHAPTER 5. THE EDISON TALKING DOLL PHONOGRAPH

1. Laboratory note sheet, written by Thomas Edison and witnessed by Charles Batchelor, J. Kruesi, James Adams, G. E. Carman, and M. N. Force, November 23, 1877, Document Collection, ENHS.

2. Raymond R. Wile, "The Fate of the Edison Phonograph Toy Manufacturing Company," unpublished manuscript, 1984–85.

3. "Agreement between Thomas A. Edison and Lowell C. Briggs and William W. Jacques," October 1, 1887, Document Collection, ENHS.

4. Wile, "Fate of the Edison Phonograph Toy."

5. Laboratory notebook, March 31, April 16, 1888, Batchelor Collection, ENHS.

6. Wile, "Fate of the Edison Phonograph Toy"; voucher, Thomas A. Edison from the Edison Phonograph Works, December 20, 1888, Document Collection, ENHS.

7. Document Collection, ENHS.

8. Wile, "Fate of the Edison Phonograph Toy."

9. In the course of conservation work on one of the Edison talking dolls at Edison National Historic Site, it was discovered that the doll did indeed have a 1 ¼-inch diameter hole in the top of the head under a mass of tangled red hair, and that many years earlier the original embroidered batiste dress had been stuffed into the cavity. The dress was rescued, washed, air dried,

and mended according to accepted conservation procedures, and the doll was dressed in its original batiste clothing. Artifact Collection, ENHS.

10. Document Collection, ENHS.

11. Wile, "Fate of the Edison Phonograph Toy."

12. Ibid.

13. Ibid.

CHAPTER 6. THE NEW GRAPHOPHONE

1. "Annual Report of the American Graphophone Company," New York, 1900, Document Collection, ENHS.

2. Raymond R. Wile, "The Background of the Entrance of the American Graphophone Company and the Columbia Phonograph Company into the Disc Record Business, 1897–1903," unpublished manuscript, 1984.

3. Ibid.

4. *New York Electrical Review*, Document Collection, ENHS.

5. Document Collection, ENHS.

6. The *Edison Phonograph News*, published for a time after 1893 by James L. Andem, was an Edison house organ devoted to the Edison phonograph and the interests of the local companies and operators. Andem also wrote an official service manual for the Edison phonograph. Document Collection, ENHS.

CHAPTER 7. THE BETTINI STORY

1. *U.S. Patent Gazette* 45, p. 895 (applied September 5, 1888; issued August 13, 1889). U.S. Patent Office.

2. "Recording and Reproducing Sounds," *U.S. Patent Gazette* 48, p. 921 (filed April 11, 1889; issued August 13, 1889). U.S. Patent Office.

3. Russell Hunting, "Trade Notes," *Phonoscope* (November 1896); "Voices from the Dead," *Phonoscope* (November 1896).

4. J. Mount Bleyer, "The Edison Phonograph and the Bettini Micro-Phonograph—The Principles Underlying Them and the Fulfillment of their Expectations," paper presented at the 43rd Annual Meeting of the American Medical Association, Detroit, June 1892. Bleyer also presented the paper at the American Electro-Therapeutical Association.

5. Batchelor Collection, ENHS.

6. Bettini to New York Phonograph Company, February 19, 1892.

7. A more promising find of Bettini cylinders near Syracuse, New York, in 1952 (some of them in a barn) included records by the Metropolitan tenor Thomas Salignac, Emilio de Gogorza, Frances Sayville, Dante del Papa, Giuseppe Campanari, and other opera artists, totaling twenty-two cylinders.

8. *Phonoscope* (August 1898).

9. Document Collection, ENHS.

10. *Phonoscope* (March 1898).

CHAPTER 8. THE CONCERT CYLINDERS

1. W. Gillett, *The Phonograph and How to Construct It* (London: Spon, 1892); James L. Andem, *A Practical Guide to the Use of the Edison Phonograph* (Cincinnati: Krehbiel, 1892), and C. W. Noyes, *Handbook of the Phonograph* (1901).

2. *U.S. Patent Gazette*, Sept. 23, 1879, patent no. 219,939, to A. Wilford Hall. "This invention consists in certain improvements in the phonograph which is the subject of letters patent No. 200,521, dated February 19, 1878 to Thomas A. Edison." The device described was a dual-cylinder recording machine that used both sides of the sound wave, one half being indented in the recording surface on the two opposed cylinders. A lever arm from the diaphragm had two styli at the other end that, when at rest, would just touch the recording surface of the two cylinders.

3. A letter from North American Phonograph to all local companies, May 12, 1890, stated price reductions on all musical cylinders. Band records were reduced to $1.00 each, vocal quartets to $1.20, and instrumental solos to 75 cents. There would also be a further reduction on cylinders that were not quite perfect, including those *not so loud*. Laboratory notebook, N-03-02-27.1 and 2, N-91-11-24, Document Collection, ENHS.

4. Fred W. Gaisberg, *The Music Goes Round* (New York: Macmillan, 1943).

5. Document Collection, ENHS.

6. Buffalo, N.Y., *Express,* June 8, 1902, Document Collection, ENHS.

7. *Phonoscope* (March 1898).

8. Document Collection, ENHS.

9. *U.S. Patent Gazette*, no. 484,583, issued Oct. 18, 1892, applied for May 27, 1890, jewelled point cutting tool, issued to Thomas A. Edison.

CHAPTER 9. THE CELLULOID CYLINDER AND MOLDING PATENTS

1. Folder 8, Legal Box 21, Document Collection, ENHS.

2. *Phonoscope* 1, no. 8 (July 1897).

3. "Unknown Soldiers in Edison's Service," *Daily Courier,* October 21, 1929, Document Collection, ENHS.

4. The extensive research accomplished by Edison and his associates in the chemistry of thermoplastic materials at this time marked the beginning of our modern synthetic thermosetting plastics industry. Leo Baekeland, working only a few miles away, came up with Bakelite, a phenolic resin plastic quite similar to the Condensite developed by Edison and his associates.

CHAPTER 10. THE COIN-SLOT PHONOGRAPH INDUSTRY

1. Document Collection, ENHS.

2. Announcement, North American Phonograph Company, reducing prices on band and orchestra records to $1.00 each, June 19, 1890, Document Collection, ENHS.

3. Gaisberg, *The Music Goes Round.*

4. Ibid.

5. *Phonoscope* 1, no. 2 (December 15, 1896).

6. W. L. Pace, Beaumont, Texas, to the Edison Company, November 30, 1927, Document Collection, ENHS.

7. Document Collection, ENHS.

1. V. K. Chew, *Talking Machines* (London: Her Majesty's Stationery Office, 1967).

2. Raymond R. Wile, "The Gramophone Becomes a Success in America, 1896–1898," unpublished manuscript, 1984.

3. Articles on Ferguson's Lightophone were published in the *New York World, New York Herald,* and other newspapers in June 1897.

4. *Proceedings of the Second Annual Convention of the National Association of Phonograph Companies,* 1891.

5. *American Bell Telephone Co. vs. National Telephone Manufacturing Company,* Circuit Court D., Massachusetts, June 27, 1901.

6. Document Collection, ENHS.

7. In 1897 Tewksbury had written *A Complete Manual of the Edison Phonograph,* for which Edison wrote the introduction, in which he refers to "friend Tewksbury's book."

8. This trademark was used in advertising for Johnson's Consolidated Talking Machine Company that appeared in nationally circulated magazines several months before the organization of the Victor Talking Machine Company.

1. Paul Tritton to Leah Burt, July 28, 1980. Tritton adds that Edmunds, writing so long after the event, makes the mistake of dating his visit to Menlo as November 1877, rather than early December, very probably the fifth or sixth.

2. Paul Tritton, "The Godfather of Rolls-Royce," *Journal of Rolls-Royce Motors, Ltd.* 2, no. 1: 4–5.

3. The London Stereoscopic Company was not a licensed company; instead, it had an indenture giving it full rights to the Edison tinfoil phonograph and any improvements thereto. An indenture in Great Britain is an agreement written out twice on one sheet of paper which is then torn into two, with each party keeping a copy, the torn edge proving the same agreement. Information supplied by Frank Andrews.

4. George Edward Gouraud was born in 1842 at Cataract House in Niagara Falls, N.Y. A highly decorated Civil War officer, he received the Congressional Medal of Honor and a brevet promotion to major for gallantry at Honey Hill. As Edison's representative in England, Gouraud capitalized on his military career by wearing the fatigue dress of the U.S. Cavalry with an abundance of corps badges on his breast, when it was to his advantage to do so. At Little Menlo, his home at the crest of Beulah Hill near the Crystal Palace in London, hung photographs of Fort Sumter, portraits of Washington, Grant, Lincoln, Robert E. Lee, and "Stonewall" Jackson—and Jefferson Davis, hung upside down. His war-stained accoutrements—the ears of the charger he rode at Ball's Bluff, the battered bugle of the First Squadron, and pistols belonging to

Major Ball Waring, the notorious duelist—hung on the terra-cotta wall among graphic sketches of Civil War incidents.

5. Agreement between Edison and Gouraud, 1879, Document Collection, ENHS.

6. George Gouraud to Edison, November 30, 1887, Document Collection, ENHS; Edison from Horatio Nelson Powers, January 5, 1888, Document Collection, ENHS.

7. January 28, 1888, March 23, 1888, Document Collection, ENHS.

8. The perfected phonograph could be worked by treadle or electricity, but clockwork was discarded on account of the noise ("The Phonograph and Graphophone," *South London Press*, November 1888). The Chinese objected to the treadle as being too laborious and to the battery motors on account of the battery solution exhausting too quickly, so the clockwork mechanism was considered to overcome their objections in 1890 (Everett Frazar to Edison, June 6, 1890, Document Collection, ENHS).

9. Document Collection, ENHS. Charles R. C. Steytler was born in 1864 and joined Gouraud's employ in June 1888. Among those recorded: Postmaster General Cecil Raikes; Edmund Yates; Sir Arthur Sullivan; barrister A. M. Broadley; Knowles, editor of the *Nineteenth Century;* the earl of Aberdeen; the earl of Meath; Lord Rowton; Sir John Fowler of the Forth Bridge; author Sir William Wilson Hunter; Sir Morell Mackenzie; Roland Protheroe; Trumpeter Lansey; Bishop Suter of New Zealand; the Prince (later Edward VII) and Princess of Wales; Lord Wolsley; Viscount Berry; Lord Onslow; General Boulanger; actress Mrs. Stirling; J. Hatton; Commyngs Carr; actor Mr. Odell, Mr. and Mrs. Bancroft; the director of the National Telephone Company, James Staats Forbes; earl of Cork; Joseph Wilson Swan; Lord and Lady Armstrong; Henry M. Stanley; F. E. Baines; William Booner; Deputy Halse; Mme. Patti; William Ewart Gladstone; Joseph Pulitzer; lord mayor of the City of London, James Whitehead; attorney general Sir Richard Webster; actor Sir Henry Irving; speaker of the House of Commons Arthur Peel; the Duke of Cambridge; poet Robert Browning; Cardinal Manning; Sir Isaac Pitman; Prince Napoleon; Phineas T. Barnum; Florence Nightingale; Constant Coquelin; William Gillette; explorers Fridjof Nansen and Cecil Rhodes; Joseph Chamberlain, writers Alphonse and Leon Daudet; and Alfred, Lord Tennyson. Richard Bebb, "An Evening of Wax Cylinders," presented at Princeton University, 1978.

10. E. H. Johnson to Edison, March 18, 1880, Document Collection, ENHS.

11. Samuel Insull to A. O. Tate, October 16, 1888; Edison's notations on a letter from Gouraud to Edison, March 3, 1888; John Vail to Edison, September 5, 1888; William H. Wiley to Edison, December 11, 1888; Gouraud to Edison, May 4, 1889, Document Collection, ENHS.

12. A. Theodore Wangemann, "The First Book of Phonograph Records, 1889, Edison Laboratory," Document Collection, ENHS.

13. Gouraud, although no longer associated with Edison, kept up appearances by underwriting some of the inventions of Horace Leonard Short and establishing a laboratory at Hove, near Brighton, England, called Little Menlo. In 1900 he announced the development of a new sound transmitter, the Gouraudphone, attributing the invention to Short. After three or four years, owing to financial difficulties, Gouraud had to close down the laboratory at Hove, and in 1904, residing at Niagara Cottage, 108 Marine Parade, Brighton, he ran for the Brighton Town

Council, arranging to have his election address delivered simultaneously at a hundred points throughout the town by means of Edison phonographs.

14. The Gramophone Company, Ltd., was incorporated on August 25, 1899, with an authorized capital of 150,000 pounds sterling. The chief shareholders were E. T. L. Williams, W. B. Owen, B. G. Royal, E. Berliner, Mrs. Owen, Mrs. Williams, E. Storey, H. E. Fullerton, H. Bendixson, and T. B. Brinbaum.

15. The Gramophone & Typewriter, Ltd., enterprise was incorporated on December 10, 1900, with an authorized capital of 600,000 pounds sterling with 2445 shareholders, the chief shareholders being E. T. L. Williams, Emile Berliner, H. S. Storey, Alice le Poer Williams, Jacob Berliner, Helena E. Fullerton, C. Englebert, J. Ashton, E. Storey, C. B. C. Storey, F. Chaplin, and W. H. Lever. Directors were E. T. L. Williams, E. Storey, T. B. Birnbawn, Romer Williams, and J. Berliner.

16. James White resigned in March 1906, at which time John Schermerhorn was appointed manager, followed in 1908 by Thomas Graf. Graf resigned in June 1911 because of ill health, whereupon Paul N. Cromelin became managing director.

17. Bill Hayes became an important figure in the music hall world, and through his efforts, recordings were obtained of Sarah Bernhardt and Harry Lauder.

18. Pathé Frères (London), Ltd., was incorporated on November 1, 1904, with authorized capital of £160,000; chief shareholders were J. Marsh, Messrs A. Soury & Co., A. Soury, E. A. Ivatts, E. P. Ivatts, F. Petit, J. T. Marsh, L. Brown, and A. C. Doyle. Directors were A. Soury and C. P. Ivatts, with registered offices at 14, Lamb's Conduit Street, London.

19. The Sterling Record Company, Ltd., incorporated December 17, 1904, changed its name to the Russell Hunting Record Co., Ltd., and issued fresh shares in 1905, with a nominal capital of £25,000 sterling. Chief shareholders were F. J. Duck, C. Stroh, W. Haif, L. S. Sterling, Russell Hunting, P. A. Smithurst, A. Rink, and A. K. Watts. Directors were C. Stroh, E. S. Perry, L. S. Sterling, Russell Hunting, and P. A. Smithurst with registered offices at 1 and 2, Buckelsbury St., Cheapside, London. The Sterling and Hunting, Ltd., was incorporated on August 27, 1906, with an authorized capital of £20,150 sterling, the chief shareholders being Russell Hunting Record Co., Ltd., now of 31, City Road, London, the International Talking Machine Co., Ltd., of Berlin, E. S. Perry, Russell Hunting, F. J. Duck, C. Stroh, A. Watts, and L. S. Sterling. Directors were E. S. Perry, Russell Hunting, L. S. Sterling, C. Stroh, and A. Watts, with offices at 81, City Road, London.

20. Beginning in August 1912, the National Phonograph and Edison Manufacturing Companies operated as different divisions within a new company, Thomas A. Edison, Ltd., following the lead of the U.S. parent company a year earlier.

CHAPTER 13. DISCS VERSUS CYLINDERS

1. *Talking Machine World* (January 1905).

2. In 1912 Edison purchased rights to the Higham amplifier for use with the Kinetophone (talking pictures).

3. Henry Seymour, "Edison Discs and Edison Cylinders," *Sound Wave* (October 1922).

4. Document Collection, ENHS.

CHAPTER 14. INTERNAL-HORN TALKING MACHINES AND THE PHONOGRAPH

1. Earlier Columbia had introduced a table model advertised as "the Hornless Graphophone."

CHAPTER 15. THE EDISON DIAMOND DISC PHONOGRAPH

1. Document Collection, ENHS.

2. Ibid.

3. Raymond Wile interview with Will Hayes, Document Collection, ENHS.

4. The Kaschmann recordings, along with many of the test pressings, are housed at the Henry Ford Museum, Greenfield Village, Dearborn, Michigan, where they were transferred in 1978.

5. Leah S. Burt, "Chemical Technology in the Edison Recording Industry," *Journal of the Audio Engineering Society* 25, nos. 10–11 (October–November 1977): 712–17.

6. Frank Lewis Dyer, Thomas Commerford Martin, and William Henry Meadowcroft, *Thomas Alva Edison, Inventor* (1908).

7. Will Hayes interview with Theodore Edison, 1958.

8. *Furniture World* 34, no. 873 (December 21, 1911).

9. Committee report, 1912, Document Collection, ENHS.

10. Hamilton Musk, assistant secretary, Edison Phonograph Works, to Carl Wilson, April 11, 1916, ENHS. The White Furniture Company finally closed its factory doors in Mebane in February 1993.

11. Document Collection, ENHS.

12. Ibid.

13. Among the more well known artists who permitted public comparisons to be made were sopranos Frieda Hempel, Claudio Muzio, Yvonne de Treville, and Alice Verlet; contraltos Carolina Lazzari, Merle Alcock, and Margarete Matzenauer; tenors Jacques Urlus, Karl Jorn, Giovanni Zenatello, and Guido Ciccolini; and bassos Henri Scott, Arthur Middleton, and Otto Goritz. Instrumentalists also played in direct comparison with their recordings on some occasions, including the noted violinists Albert Spaulding and Vasa Prihoda.

14. Document Collection, ENHS.

15. Document Collection, ENHS.

CHAPTER 16. TONE-TEST REVERBERATIONS
AND THE VERTICAL-CUT BANDWAGON

1. Memorandum, "Reviewing the Phonograph Situation," Art Walsh to Charles Edison, April 25, 1927, Document Collection, ENHS.

2. Handwritten note by Thomas A. Edison, May 11, 1912, Document Collection, ENHS.

3. Thomas Edison to Thomas Graf, November 20, 1911, Document Collection, ENHS.

4. C. H. Wilson to L. C. McChesney and Clarence Hayes, March 11, 1915, Document Collection, ENHS.

5. Interview with Mary Amirault, secretary from 1914 to the Music Committee, Musical Phonograph Division, February 9, 1988.

6. Handwritten note on letter from J. G. Watson to Thomas Edison, March 30, 1908, Document Collection, ENHS. Edison's favorite pieces of music were "I'll Take You Home Again, Kathleen," "Little Gray Home in the West," "Evening Star" from "Tannhauser," Beethoven's "Moonlight Sonata," and "Oh, That We Two Were Maying." Theodore M. Edison to Spencer Tracy, November 28, 1939, Document Collection, ENHS.

7. Thomas Edison to Mark Silverstone, April 8, 1924, Document Collection, ENHS.

CHAPTER 17. MOTION PICTURES AND SOUND RECORDING

1. Document Collection, ENHS; second part of letter to T. A. Edison from W. K. L. Dickson, 4 Denman Street, Piccadilly Circus, London, England, written through Wm. Meadowcroft, Edison's secretary, April 11, 1913, ENHS.

2. *Thomas A. Edison vs. American Mutoscope Company and Benjamin L. Keith,* Brief for Complainant, U.S. Circuit Court, Southern District of New York, Equity no. 6928.

3. Ibid.

4. *Motion Picture Patents Company vs. Chicago Film Exchange,* Equity no. 28,605. Pleadings and Proofs. Deposition of Thomas Alva Edison, 204, Document Collection, ENHS.

5. Ibid, 23.

6. *Phonoscope* 1, no. 6 (May 1897): 11.

7. Ibid., 239.

8. A. R. Phillips, Jr., "Talking Pictures, 1894," *American Phonograph Journal* 1, no. 3 (September 1978).

9. Ibid.

10. Federal Trade Commission Docket no. 977.

11. Bangor, Maine, *Commercial,* January 8, 1913.

12. U.S. Patent no. 678,566, D. Higham, "Phonic Apparatus," patented July 16, 1901; U.S. Patent no. 712,930, D. Higham, "Sound Reproduction Apparatus, patented November 4, 1902; U.S. Patent no. 783,750, D. Higham, "Phonic Apparatus," patented February 28, 1905.

13. F. L. Dyer to Thomas Edison, September 18, 20, October 7, 1912, Document Collection, ENHS.

14. *Instructions on Operating the Kinetophone, 1913,* June 24, 1924; A. E. Kennelly to Charles Edison, February 13, 1913, Document Collection, ENHS.

15. Handwritten memorandum, Miller Reese Hutchison to Thomas Edison, April 15, 1913; Mary Ware Dennett to Thomas Edison, April 12, 1913; Laboratory Notebook N-13-02-27; W. H. Miller to Dinwiddie, August 24, 1914, Document Collection, ENHS.

16. Theodore Edison to Thomas Edison, January 10, 1928, Document Collection, ENHS.

17. Interview with Theodore Edison, April 14, 1983.

18. "Cinderella," experimental recordings made January 25, 27, February 8, 1928, Artifact Collection, ENHS.

19. Federal Communications Commission, *Report on Investigation of Telephone Development in the U.S.*, H. Document 340, 1939.

B I B L I O G R A P H Y

"Accuracy in Talkie Equipment." *Scientific American* 143 (August 1930): 102–3.

Adamson, Peter. "Berliner Discs." *Phonographs and Gramophones Symposium* (July 2, 1977): 73–94.

Aeolian Co. *A New Musical Instrument of the Phonograph Type.* New York: Aeolian Co., 1915.

Alda, Frances. *Men, Women, and Tenors.* Boston: Houghton Mifflin, 1937.

"Amazing Story of the Talkies." *Popular Mechanics* 50 (December 1928): 938–45.

Andem, James L. *A Practical Guide to the Use of the Edison Phonograph.* Cincinnati: Krehbiel, 1892.

"Archive of Voices." *Living Age* 318 (September 15, 1923): 524–25.

August, G. J. "In Defense of Canned Music." *Music Quarterly* 17 (January 1931): 138–49.

"Auxetophone for Reinforcing Gramophone Sounds." *Scientific American* (May 13, 1905).

Balmain, C. "Improvements in Gramophones." *Gramophone* 1, no. 7 (December 1923).

Banning, Kendall. "Thomas A. Edison, Manufacturer of Carbolic Acid." *System* (November 1914).

Barnes, Everette K. *A Treatise on Practical Wax Recording.* Inglewood, Calif.: Universal Microphone Co., 1936.

Barnet, H. T. "Technical Notes." *Gramophone* (March 1924).

Barraud, Francis. "How Nipper Became World Famous." *Strand* (August 1916).

Bauer, Robert. *Historical Records.* London: Sidgewick & Jackson, 1947.

Bazzoni, C. B. "The Piezo-Electric Oscillograph." *Radio News* (August 1925).

Beard, George M. "Nature of the Newly Discovered Force." *Scientific American* 33 (December 25, 1875): 400.

———. "The Newly Discovered Force [Etheric]." *Archives of Electrology and Neurology* 2 (1875): 257–82.

Bebb, Richard. "An Evening of Wax Cylinders." Presentation given at Princeton University, 1978.

Begun, D. R. "Magnetic Recording." *Electronics* (September 1938).

Benson, A. L. "Edison's Dream of New Music." *Cosmopolitan* 54 (May 1913): 797–800.

Berliner, Emile. "The Development of the Talking Machine." *Journal of the Franklin Institute* 176 (May 21, 1913): 189–202.

———. "The Gramophone." *Journal of the Franklin Institute* (May 16, 1888).

Bernhardt, Sarah. *Memories of My Life*. New York: Appleton, 1923.

Bettini, G. "The Micro-Graphophone." *Scientific American* 15 (May 9, 1890): 281–82.

Bispham, David. *A Quaker Singer's Recollections*. New York: Macmillan, 1920.

Bond, A. R. "Talking Thread." *St. Nicholas* (May 1921): 647–48.

Bottone, Selimo Romeo. *Talking Machines and Records*. London: G. Pitman, 1904.

Briggs, G. A. *Sound Reproduction*. Bradford, England: Wharfedale Wireless Works, 1950.

Bruch, Walter. *Die Fernseh-Story*. Stuttgart, Germany: W. Keller, 1969.

"The Brussels Decision as to Musical Copyright—Compagnie Generale des Phonographs, Pathé-Frères and Sociéte Ullman v. Marcenet and Pascini." *Talking Machine News* (February 1, 1906).

Bryan, George S. *Edison: The Man and His Work*. New York: Knopf, 1926.

Bryson, H. Courtney. *The Gramophone Record*. London: Earnest Benn, 1935.

Burt, Leah S. "Chemical Technology in the Edison Recording Industry." *Journal of the Audio Engineering Society* 25, nos. 10–11 (October–November 1977): 712–17.

Butler, J. H. "Radio To Make Movies Talk." *Illustrated World* 37 (July 1922): 373–77.

Caldwell, Orestes H. "Demonstration of an Original 'Edison Effect' Tube in a Radio Broadcast on 60th Anniversary of Its Invention." *Radio Retailing* (1943).

Calvé, Emma. *My Life*. New York: Appleton, 1922.

Camp, M. E. "Talking Machine in the Home." *American Homes* 11, no. 7.

Campbell, A. G., and O. J. Zobel. "Electrical Recording." *Bell System Technical Journal* (1923).

"Canned Music: Processing the Phonograph Record." *Scientific American* (March 1923): 128–82.

Caruso, Dorothy. *Enrico Caruso: His Life and Death*. New York: Simon & Schuster, 1945.

"Celluloid for Phonograph Records." *Scientific American* 86 (March 15, 1902): 191.

Chew, V. K. *Talking Machines*. London: Her Majesty's Stationery Office, 1967.

Child, A. P. "Clay Needles for Talking Machine." *Scientific American* 123 (September 18, 1920): 275.

Clements, Henry B. *Gramophones and Phonographs: Their Construction, Management, and Repair*. London: Cassell, 1913.

Cochrane, Ira Lee. *The Phonograph Book*. New York: Rider-Long, 1917.

"Colored Films, Talking Movies and Television." *Literary Digest* (August 11, 1928): 98–99.

"Combined Mutoscope and Talking Machine." *Scientific American* 98 (April 25, 1908): 292.

"Combined Radio and Phonograph." *Literary Digest* 83 (October 25, 1924): 27.

"Commercial Graphophone for Recording Dictation." *Scientific American*, sup. 53:22151 (March 30, 1907).

Cowley, H. E. "The Manufacture of Gramophone Records." *Junior Institute of Engineers, Journal and Record of Transactions* 35 (1925): 391–411.

Crawford, R. "Profits and Pirates: Interview with Thomas A. Edison." *Saturday Evening Post* 203 (September 27, 1930): 3–5.

"Crede Experts—A Current Survey of Gramophone Progress by the Expert Committee." *Gramophone* (January–August 1926).

Culshaw, John. *Sergei Rachmaninoff.* London: D. Dobson, 1949.

Davis, W. "New Film Phonograph." *Science Monthly* 71, no. 10 (January 24, 1930).

Dawson, Peter. *Fifty Years of Song.* London: Hutchinson, 1952.

Dearle, D. A. *Plastic Moulding.* New York: Chemical Publishing Co., n.d.

deBoer, K. "Experiments with Stereophonic Records." *Phillips Technical Review* 5 (1940): 182–86.

deForest, Lee. "When Light Speaks: Recording and Reproducing Sounds by Means of Light Intensities." *Scientic American* 129 (August 1923): 94.

Dethlefson, Ronald. *Edison Blue Amberol Recordings, 1912–1914.* New York: APM Press, 1980.

DeTreville, Yvonne. "Making a Phonograph Record." *Musician* 21 (November 1916): 658.

Dickson, W. K. L., and Antonia Dickson. "Edison's Invention of the Kineto-phonograph." *Century* 206 (June 1894): 14.

———. *The Life and Inventions of Thomas Alva Edison.* New York: Crowell, 1895.

Dime, Eric A. "The Light Ray Phonograph." *Science and Invention* 8 (1920): 851, 924.

Dorian, Frank. "Reminiscences of the Columbia Cylinder Records." *Phonograph Monthly Review* (January 1930).

Dreher, Carl. "Phonograph Pick-Ups." *Radio Broadcast* 13 (September 1928): 268.

———. "Sound Motion Picture." *Radio Broadcast* 13 (October–November 1928): 352–53; 14 (May 1929): 32.

———. "What Are Plastics Made Of?" *Popular Science* (January 1944): 58.

Duerr, W. A. "Will Radio Replace the Phonograph?" *Radio Broadcast* 2 (November 1922): 52–54.

Du Moncel, Theodore Achille Louis. *The Telephone, the Microphone, and the Phonograph.* New York: Harper, 1879.

Dunlap, O. E. "Edison Glimpsed at Radio in 1875: Scintillating Sparks Led to Discovery of Etheric Force." *Scientific American* 135 (December 1926): 424.

Dyer, Frank Lewis, Thomas Commerford Martin, and William Henry Meadowcroft. *Edison: His Life and Inventions.* New York & London: Harper, 1909.

Eames, Emma. *Some Memories and Reflections.* New York & London: Appleton, 1927.

Edholm, C. L. "A New Type of Phonograph." *Scientific American* 115 (December 16, 1916): 553.

Edison, Thomas A. "The Phonograph and Its Future." *North American Review* (May–June 1878).

———. *The Phonograph and Its Future; and The Auriphone and Its Future.* Toronto: Rose-Belford Publishing Co., 1878.

Edison Phonograph Works. *Inventor's Handbook of the Phonograph.* Newark, N.J.: Ward & Tichenor, 1889.

"Edison's Forty Years of Litigation." *Literary Digest* 47 (September 13, 1913): 449.

"Edison's Gift to Humanity." *Literary Digest* (October 2, 1915).

"Edison's Kinetograph and Cosmical Telephone." *Scientific American* 64 (June 20, 1891): 393.

"Edison's Use of the Dark Box." *Scientific American* 34 (December 25, 1876): 33.

Edmunds, Henry. "Reminiscences of a Pioneer." *M & C Apprentices' Magazine* 7, no. 25 (April 2, 1923): 3–7.

"Electro-Mechanical Phonograph." *Scientific American* 90 (June 4, 1904): 438.

"The Evolution of the Vacuum Tube." *Experimenter* (December 1925): 23–26.

"Expiration of the Berliner Talking Machine Patent." *Scientific American* 106 (January 13, 1912): 52–53.

Farrar, Geraldine. *Such Sweet Compulsion.* New York: Greystone Press, 1938.

Fessenden, Helen M. *Fessenden, Builder of Tomorrows.* New York: Coward-McCann, 1940.

Fessenden, Reginald A. "Wireless Telegraph." *Radio News* (January–November 1925).

Fewkes, J. W. "Edison Phonograph in the Preservation of the Languages of the American Indians." *Scientific American* (May 2, 1980); (May 24, 1980).

"Fifteen to 100 Phonograph Records without a Stop." *Scientific American* 125 (October 1, 1921): 242.

"Films That Talk." *Literary Digest* 71 (December 3, 1921): 20–21.

Finck, Henry T. *Success in Music and How It Is Won.* New York: Scribners, 1909.

"First Public Exhibition of Edison's Kinetograph." *Scientific American* 68 (May 20, 1893): 310.

Foley, A. L., and W. H. Souder. "Photographing Sound: A Demonstration of Wave Motion." *Scientific American,* sup. 75 (1913): 108–11.

Frampton, J. R. "Sound Reproducing Machine Records and the Private Teacher: An Intensive Study in Interpretation." *Etude* 40 (August 1922): 520.

Frow, George L. "The Cylinder Phonograph in Great Britain." *Phonographs and Gramophones Symposium* (July 2, 1977): 49–56.

———. *The Edison Disc Phonographs and the Diamond Discs.* N.p.: Privately printed by George L. Frow, 1982.

———, and Albert F. Sefl. *The Edison Cylinder Phonographs, 1877–1929.* N.p.: Privately printed by George L. Frow, 1978.

"Full House at Steinway Hall—Report of Acoustic Gramophone Competition." *Gramophone* (July 1924).

Fyfe, H. C. "Telegraphone and the British Post-Office." *Scientific American* 83 (April 25, 1903): 317.

Gaisberg, Fred W. *The Music Goes Round.* New York: Macmillan, 1943.

Garbit, Frederick J. *The Phonograph and Its Inventor, Thomas Alva Edison.* Boston: Gunn, Bliss, 1878.

Gaydon, Harry A. *The Art and Science of the Gramophone.* London: Dunlop, 1926.

Geber, A., and R. Helybut. *Backstage at the Opera.* New York: Crowell, 1937.

Gelatt, Roland. *The Fabulous Phonograph.* Philadelphia: Lippincott, 1955.

"German Law of Copyright on Phonograph Records." *Scientific American* 86 (March 8, 1902): 15.

"G. H. Herrington's Method of Recording Sound Vibrations." *Scientific American* (January 9, 1902).

Gillett, W. *The Phonograph and How to Construct It.* London: E. & F. N. Spon, 1892.

Goldsmith, Francis H., and Geisel, Victor G. *Techniques of Recording*. Chicago: Gamble Hinged Music Co., 1939.

Goodchild, R. "On Fibre Needles." *Gramophone* (March 1924).

Gouraud, François. *Description of the Daguerreotype Process*. Boston: Dutton and Wentworth's Printing Co., 1840.

"The Gramophone." *Scientific American* 74 (May 16, 1896): 311.

Gramophone, Ltd. *Novice Corner: An Elementary Handbook of the Gramophone*. London: Gramophone, 1928.

Grau, Robert. "Actors by Proxy." *Independent* (July 17, 1913).

Hall, C. I. "Induction Disc Motors." *Scientific American* 123 (September 1921): 282.

Hamlin, George. "Making of Records." *Musician* 22 (July 1917): 542.

Hammer, W. J. "Transmitting Sound by Phonograph and Telephone 104 Miles, through 48 Physical Changes." *Electrical Experimenter* (September 1917).

Harris, S. "How Radio Developments Have Improved Recording and Reproducing." *Radio Broadcast* 12 (April 1928): 414–15.

Hayden, E. "Phonographs as Art Furniture." *International Studio* 78 (December 1923): 249–51.

Henderson, W. J. *The Art of Singing*. New York: Dial Press, 1938.

Henry, O. [pseud.]. "Phonograph and the Graft." *McClure's* 20 (February 1903): 428–34.

Hickman, C. M. "Sound Recording on Magnetic Tape." *Bell System Technical Journal* (April 1937): 165–77.

Homer, Sidney. *My Wife and I*. New York: Macmillan, 1939.

Hopkins, G. M. "Scientific Uses of the Phonograph." *Scientific American* 62: 155, 248; 63: 100.

Houston, Edwin J. "Notes on Phenomena in Incandescent Lamps [Edison Effect]." *American Insitute of Electrical Engineers* 1, no. 1 (1884): 8.

Hurst, P. G. *The Golden Age Recorded*. Henfield, England: P. G. Hurst, 1946.

Hutto, Edgar, Jr. "Emile Berliner, Eldridge Johnson, and the Victor Talking Machine Company." *Journal of the Audio Engineering Society* 25, nos. 10–11 (October–November 1977): 666–73.

"Improved Process of Duplicating Phonograph Records." *Scientific American* 86 (March 8, 1902): 175.

"Improving the Reproduction of Talking Machine Records." *Scientific American*, sup. 27, vol. 109 (September 27, 1913): 247.

"Improving the Tonal Quality of the Phonograph." *Scientific American* 118 (February 2, 1918): 121.

"Increasing the Power of a Talking Machine by Compressed Air." *Scientific American* 94 (December 29, 1906): 490.

Inghelbrecht, D. E. *The Conductor's World*. London & New York: P. Nevell, 1953.

Inglis, William. "Edison and the New Education." *Harper's Weekly* (November 4, 1911).

"Inscribing and Reproducing Diaphragm for Phonographs." *Scientific American*, sup. 50:20508 (July 7, 1900).

"An Interview with Edison." *Daily Graphic* (July 19, 1878).

"Investigations in Phenomena of the Phonograph." *Scientific American,* sup. 56:23025 (July 18, 1903).

Jehl, Francis. *Menlo Park Reminiscences.* 3 vols. Dearborn, Mich., 1936–41.

J. E. Hough, Ltd. *The Story of Edison-Bell to 1924.* London: J. E. Hough, Ltd., 1934.

Jewett, T. B. "Edison's Contributions to Science and Industry." *Science* 65 (January 5, 1932): 65–68.

Johnson, Edward H. "A Wonderful Invention." *Scientific American* 37 (November 17, 1877): 304.

——— . *The Telephone Handbook.* New York, 1877.

Jones, Francis Arthur. *Thomas Alva Edison—60 Years of an Inventor's Life.* New York: Crowell, 1907.

Kelley, E. S. "Library of Living Melody." *Outlook* 99 (September 30, 1911): 283–87.

Kesler, C. H. "Famous Radio Patent." *Radio Broadcast* 2 (January–March 1923): 207–11.

Klein, Herman. *Golden Age of Opera.* London: G. Routledge, 1933.

——— . "The Gramophone and the Singer." *Gramophone* (June 1924).

——— . *Great Women Singers of My Time.* London: G. Routledge, 1931.

——— . *Musicians and Mummers.* London: Cassell, 1925.

——— . *The Reign of Patti.* New York: Century, 1920.

——— . *Thirty Years of Musical Life in London.* London: Heinemann, 1903.

Kobbe, Gustav. *Opera Singers.* Boston: Oliver Ditson, 1913.

Koenigsberg, Allen. *Edison Cylinder Records, 1889–1912, with an Illustrated History of the Phonograph.* New York: Stellar Productions, 1969.

——— . *The Patent History of the Phonograph, 1877–1912.* New York: APM Press, 1991.

Kolodin, Irving. *The Metropolitan Opera.* New York: Oxford University Press, 1936.

Lahee, Henry C. *The Grand Opera Singers of Today.* Boston: Page, 1922.

Lane, C. E. "Nature of Sound Pitch." *Physical Review* 26 (1925): 401.

Lanier, Charles D. "New Phonograph." *Review of Reviews* 73 (January 1926): 99–100.

Larson, E. J. D. "Music and Speech on a Tape." *Technical World* 19 (April 1913): 270–71.

Lawton, Mary. *Schumann-Heink—The Last of the Titans.* New York: Macmillan, 1928.

Lehmann, Lilli. *My Path through Life.* New York: Putnam's, 1914.

Leiser, Clara. *Jean deReszke and the Great Days of Opera.* London: G. Howe, 1933.

Lescarboura, A. C. "Art of Canning Music." *Independent and Weekly Review* 105 (March 5, 1921): 241.

——— . "At the Other End of the Phonograph." *Scientific American* 119 (August 31, 1918): 164.

Lewkowitsch, J. I. *Chemical Technology and Analysis of Oils, Fats, and Waxes.* New York: Macmillan, 1922.

"The Life and Work of Lee DeForest." *Radio News* (October 1924).

Lillington, A. "Talking Machine." *Living Age* 254 (August 24, 1907): 486–89.

Little, F. B. "Phonograph Made from an Echo." *Illustrated World* 36 (January 1922): 697–98.

Lounsberry, J. R. "Making Permanent Records of Radio Programs." *Radio Broadcast* 5 (September 1924): 363–68.

Lucas, F. F. "Looking Through the Phonograph Record." *Scientific American* 1 (June 1920): 518–20.

Lyle, Watson. *Rachmaninoff: A Biography.* London: W. Reeves Booksellers, 1939.

Mackenzie, Compton. "The Gramophone: Its Past, Its Present, Its Future." *The Musical Association Proceedings* (1924–25).

Maclaurin, R. C. "Edison's Service for Science." *Science* (June 4, 1915).

Macomber, Frank S. "The Sound of Fame: Syracuse University Audio Archive and Edison Re-recording Laboratory." *Courier* 14, nos. 1–2 (1977).

"Magnetic Recording and Reproducing." *Bell Laboratories Record* (September 1937).

Maitland, J. F., and others. "Musical Taste in England and the Influence of the Gramophone." *Bookman* (London) 60 (April 1921): 38–41.

Maken, Neil. *Hand-Cranked Phonographs.* Huntington Beach, Calif.: Privately printed, 1993.

"Making Phonograph Music." *Current Literature* 33 (August 1902): 169–70.

Mallory, T. J. "Magnetic Recording." *Electronics* (January 1930): 30.

"Manufacture of Edison Phonograph Records." *Scientific American* 83 (December 22, 1900): 389–90.

Mapplebeck, J. "Canning Music the World Over." *Saturday Evening Post* 195 (June 23, 1923): 18.

Maranies, H. S. "A Day Has Nine Lives: The Story of the Phonograph." *Annals of the American Academy of Social and Political Science* (September 1937).

Marchesi, Blanche. *Singer's Pilgrimage.* London: G. Richards, 1923.

Marcoson, I. F. "Coming of the Talking Picture." *Munsey's* 48 (March 1913): 956–60.

Marks, G. C. "How the Phonograph Came into Existence." *Etude* 42 (January 1924): 59.

Maxfield, J. P. "Electrical Phonograph Recording." *Science Monthly* 21 (January 1926): 71–79.

———. "Electrical Research Applied to the Phonograph." *Scientific American* 134 (February 1926): 104–5.

———, and H. C. Harrison. "Methods of High Quality Recording and Reproduction of Sound Based on Telephone Research." *Transactions of the American Institute of Electrical Engineers* (February 1926).

Maxwell, Bennett. *The Incunabula of Recorded Sound: A Guide to Early Edison Non-Commercial Cylinder Recordings.* London: Privately printed by Bennett Maxwell, 1989.

Maxwell, J. "Britain's Talkies Come To." *Living Age* 340 (April 1931): 207–8.

McCormack, Lille. *I Hear You Calling Me.* Milwaukee: Bruce Publishing Co., 1949.

McCurdy, Edward. *The Mind of Leonardo da Vinci.* New York: Dodd, Mead, 1928.

———. *The Notebooks of Leonardo da Vinci.* New York: Reynal & Hitchcock, 1938.

McKendrick, John G. "Further Experiments with the Gramophone." *Nature* 81 (1909): 488–90.

———. "The Gramophone as a Phonautograph." *Nature* 80 (1909): 188–91.

———. *Waves of Sound and Speech as Revealed by the Phonograph.* London: Macmillan, 1897.

Meadowcroft, William H. "Story of the Phonograph." *St. Nicholas* 49 (May 1922): 692–99.

Melba, Nellie. *Melodies and Memories.* London: Butterworth, 1925.

Melville-Mason, Graham. "The Gramophone as Furniture." *Phonographs and Gramophones Symposium* (July 2, 1977): 117–38.

Meyer, K. H. *Natural and Synthetic High Polymers*. New York & London: Interscience Publishers, 1950.

Millard, Bailey. "Pictures That Talk." *Technical World* 19 (March 1913): 16–21.

———. "Thomas Alva Edison." *Technical World* (October 1914).

Millen, J. "Building an Electrical Phonograph; Combined Radio and Electrical Phonograph." *Radio Broadcast* 11 (June 1927): 86–89.

———. "Electrical Phonograph; Principles Involved in Electrical Recording and Reproduction, the New Panatrope and Electrola; Data for the Home Constructor." *Radio Broadcast* 11 (May 1927): 20–23.

Miller, Phillip L. "Ghosts for Sale, Mapleson Cylinders in the New York Public Library." *Opera News* 6, no. 8 (December 8, 1941): 22, 29.

Millikan, R. A. "Edison as a Scientist." *Science* 75 (January 15, 1932): 68–70.

"The Mirrophone." *Bell Laboratories Record* 20, no. 1 (September 1941): 2–5.

Mitchell, Ogilvie. *The Talking Machine Industry*. London: Sir I. Pitman, 1922.

"The Modern Gramophone: Realistic Reproduction by Means of Valve Amplifiers." *Wireless World and Radio Review* 22 (March 1928): 273, 276.

Moses, Montrose J. *The Life of Heinrich Conreid*. New York: Crowell, 1916.

"Motion Pictures That Talk, a New Method." *Scientific American* 135 (June 1927): 53–54.

"Moving and Talking Pictures." *Scientific American* 108 (January 18, 1913): 64.

"Mr. DeForest's Talking Film." *Literary Digest* 74 (September 16, 1922): 28–29.

"Mr. Hoxie's Talking Film." *Literary Digest* 75 (December 9, 1922): 26–27.

"The Multiphone." *Scientific American* 86 (April 1, 1899): 197.

"Multiplex Phonograph with Five Cylinders." *Scientific American* 75 (November 28, 1896): 393.

"Multiplex Telegraphone." *Scientific American*, sup. 53:22151 (June 28, 1902).

"Museum of Sounds." *Scientific American* 134 (March 1926): 185–86.

National Phonograph Association. *Proceedings of Annual Conventions*. N.p.: National Phonograph Association, 1890, 1891, 1892, 1893.

National Phonograph Co. *The Phonograph and How to Use It*. West Orange, N.J.: National Phonograph Co., 1900.

Nernst, W., and R. von Lieben. "A New Phonographic Principle." *Electrician* (London) 47 (1901): 260–62.

"New Alliance: Phonograph and Radio." *Literary Digest* 92 (February 19, 1927): 21–22.

"New Mechanical Phonograph." *Science Monthly* 22 (March 1926): 264–71.

Newnes. "Storing Speech and Music." *Practical Mechanics* (April 1938).

"New Permanent Phonograph Record." *Scientific American* 84 (March 9, 1901): 147.

"New Phonograph." *Scientific American* 100 (April 24, 1909): 318.

"New Phonograph." *Scientific American* 106 (April 27, 1912): 382.

"New Telegraphone." *Scientific American* 89 (October 3, 1903): 237–38.

"The Papa of the Phonograph: An Afternoon with Edison." *Daily Graphic* (April 2, 1878).

"Paper-Weight, Unbreakable Phonograph Records." *Scientific American* 142 (April 1930): 307–8.

Parsons, Herbert R. "Phonofilms." *Gramophone* (March 1927).

Peck, A. P. "Giving a Voice to Motion Pictures." *Scientific American* 136 (June 1927): 378–79.

——— . "Sounds Recorded on Movie Film." *Scientific American* 137 (September 1927): 284–86.

Pengelly, Joe. "The Electrical Reproduction of Cylinders." *Phonographs and Gramophones Symposium* (July 2, 1977): 57–60.

Phillips, A. R., Jr. "Talking Pictures, 1894." *American Phonograph Journal* 1, no. 3 (September 1978).

Phillips, W. P. "Edison, Bogardus, and Carbolic Acid." *Electrical Review and Western Electrician* (November 14, 1914).

"Phonograph." *Scientific American* 75 (July 25, 1896): 65–66.

"Phonograph Appliance for Visible Record." *Scientific American* 100 (May 8, 1909): 354.

"Phonograph as a Decorative Element in the House." *Country Life* 33 (March 1918): 108–10.

"Phonograph Built Like An Ear." *Literary Digest* (September 9, 1922).

"Phonograph Improvements; G. H. Herrington's Method of Recording Sound Vibrations." *Scientific American* 66 (June 9, 1892): 20.

"Phonograph Needles of Bamboo." *Scientific American* 121 (July 5, 1919): 6.

"Phonograph Sound-Box with a Silk Diaphragm." *Scientific American* 120 (February 1, 1919): 103.

"Phonograph without Tone-Arm, Sound-Box, and Horn." *Scientific American* 120 (March 29, 1919): 322.

Piazze, T. E. "Automatic Record Changers." *Radio Broadcast* 16 (April 1930): 310–12.

"Pictures That Talk." *Scientific American* 128 (January 1923): 19.

Pierce, J. A., and F. V. Hunt. *On Distortion in Sound Reproduction from Phonograph Records.* Cambridge, Mass.: Harvard University Graduate School of Engineering Publications, 1938.

Plates [pseud.]. *Plastics in Industry.* New York: Chemical Publishing Co., 1941.

Plush, S. M. "Edison's Carbon Button Transmitter and the Speaking Phonograph." *Journal of the Franklin Institute* (April 1878).

Pollak, Hans. "Archives in Sound—An Account of the Work of the Phonogram Archives in Vienna." *Gramophone* (April 1925).

"The Polyphone: Novel Attachment for Phonographs." *Scientific American* 81 (August 12, 1899): 100.

Poulsen, V. "Telegraphone." *Scientific American,* sup. 50:20616 (August 25, 1900); sup. 51:20944 (January 19, 1901).

——— . "Telegraphone, Description." *Popular Science* 59 (August 1901): 413.

"Poulsen Magneto-Telephonograph." *English Mechanic* 19 (August 1900): 757–58.

"Poulsen's Telegraphone." *Scientific American* 83 (September 22, 1900): 178, 181.

Prescott, George B. *Bell's Electric Speaking Telephone: Its Invention, Construction, Application, Modification, and History.* New York: Appleton, 1884.

——— . *The Speaking Telephone, Electric Light, and Other Recent Electrical Inventions.* New York: Appleton, 1879.

——— . *The Speaking Telephone, Talking Phonograph, and Other Novelties.* New York: Appleton, 1878.

"Preserving Grand Opera Records for Future Generations." *Scientific American* 99 (July 25, 1908): 62.

"Principles of the Telephone Applied to the Phonograph." *Science Monthly* 21 (December 1925): 667–68.

Proudfoot, Christopher. "The Development of the Acoustic Gramophone in the United Kingdom." *Phonographs and Gramophones Symposium* (July 2, 1977): 61–72.

Rayleigh, John William Strutt. *The Theory of Sound.* London: Macmillan, 1877–78.

"Recording for Re-broadcasting in Germany." *Wireless World* (March 31, 1938).

"Recording Sound on Motion Picture Film." *Scientific American* 117 (December 22, 1917): 473.

"Records on Paper Tape from Mike or Phone." *Radio and Television* (March 1939).

Reddie, Lowell N. "The Gramophone and the Mechanical Recording and Reproduction of Musical Sounds." *Journal of the Society of Arts* 56 (1908): 637–38.

Reed, P. H. "Music in the Modern Home." *Woman's Home Companion* 55 (November 1928): 17.

Reissig, C. C. "Synchronization of Action and Sound in Talking Movies." *Bulletin of the Pan American Union* 63: 139–41.

Rhodes, H. E. "Phonograph-Radio Amplifiers." *Radio Broadcast* 14 (December 1928): 88–90.

Rider, John Francis. *Automatic Record Changers and Recorders.* New York: John F. Rider Publications, 1941.

Rinhart, Floyd, and Marion Rinhart. *The American Daguerreotype.* Athens: University of Georgia Press, 1981.

Rogers, W. *The Gramophone Handbook: A Practical Guide for Gramophone Owners, etc., with Foreword by Compton Mackenzie.* London: Sir I. Pitman, 1931.

Ronald, Sir Landon. *Myself and Others.* London: S. Low, Marston & Co., 1931.

Ross, Richardson. "Relationship between Stimulus, Intensity, and Loudness." *General Psychology* (1930): 288.

Rothermel Corporation, Ltd. "A Technical Treatise on the Application of Rochelle Salt Crystals to High Fidelity Sound Reproducers." *Piezo-Electricity* (1934).

"Rousselot's Apparatus for Inscribing Speech." *Scientific American* 67 (September 3, 1892): 151–52.

Schauffler, R. H. "Canned Music: The Phonograph Fan." *Collier's* 67 (April 23, 1921): 10–11.

———. "Mission of Mechanized Music." *Century* 89 (December 1914): 293–98.

Schor, George. "Galvano Plastic Reproduction from Metal Moulds." *Metal Industry* (September 1938).

"Science Again Comes to the Aid of Music." *Musician* 30 (November 1925): 9.

Scripture, E. W. "Graphics of the Voice." *Independent and Weekly Review* 63 (October 24, 1907): 969–76.

Seymour, Henry. "Edison Discs and Edison Cylinders." *Sound Wave* (October 1922).

———. *The Reproduction of Sound.* London: W. B. Tattersall, 1918.

Sharp, Clayton H. "The Edison Effect and Its Modern Applications." *Journal of the American Institute of Electrical Engineers* 41 (January 1922): 68–78.

———. "First Milestone in the Electronic Era." *Electronic Industries* (September 1943): 214.

Sherwood, Mabel R. "Industrial History of Bridgeport." *Bridgeport Life* (December 22, 1934–August 14, 1937).

Simonds, William Adams. *Edison: His Life, His Works, His Genius.* Indianapolis & New York: Bobbs-Merrill, 1934.

Skerrett, R. G. "A Phonograph That Is Always at Its Best." *Scientific American* 124 (February 26, 1921): 171.

Slezak, Leo. *Song of Motley.* London: W. Hodge & Co., 1938.

Slosson, E. E. "Talking Motion Picture." *Science Monthly* 24 (March 1927): 286–88.

"Sound Pictures." *Bell System Technical Journal* 8 (January 1929): 159–208.

"Sound Recorded on Steel Tape." *Radio Craft* (April 1942).

"Sound Recording on Magnetic Materials." *Radio Craft* (March 1936).

"The Speaking Phonograph." *Frank Leslie's Illustrated Newspaper*, March 30, 1878; April 10, 1878.

Sperling, L. H. "Jonas W. Aylesworth: Leif Erikson of Interpenetrating Polymer Networks." *Polymer News* 12 (1987): 332–34.

Stanley, Douglas, and J. P. Maxfield. *The Voice: Its Production and Reproduction.* New York: Pitman Publishing Corp., 1933.

"The Steel Tape Recorder." *Practical and Amateur Wireless* (July 2, 1938).

"Stereophonic Sound Film System." *Transactions of the Society of Motion Picture Engineers* 38: 331–426.

Stirling, W. "Gaumont Speaking Kinematograph Films." *Scientific American*, sup. 73:395 (June 22, 1912).

Stout, W. B. "How To Make a Gramophone." *Scientific American* 84 (February 23, 1901): 115.

"Synchronized Reproduction of Sound and Scene." *Bell Laboratories Record* (November 1928).

"T. A. Edison's Electro-Chemical Loud-Speaking Telephone." *Scientific American* (July 28, 1877).

"Talking Machines." *Outlook* 103 (March 8, 1913): 517.

"Talking Motion Pictures." *Scientific American* 175 (September 1926): 209.

"Talking Movies." *Radio Broadcast* 2 (December 1922): 95–96.

"The Talking Phonograph." *Scientific American* 37 (December 22, 1877): 384.

"Talking Thread." *Scientific American* 128 (January 1923): 25.

Tate, Alfred O. *Edison's Open Door.* New York: Dutton, 1938.

Taylor, J. B. "Microscopic Study of the Phonograph." *Scientific American* 117 (November 13, 1915): 428–29.

Taylor, Jocelyn Pierson. *Grosvenor Porter Lowrey.* N.p.: Privately printed by Jocelyn Pierson Kennedy Taylor, 1978.

Taylor, Sedley. *Sound and Music.* London & New York: Macmillan, 1883.

"Telemicro-Phonograph." *Scientific American*, sup.73:10 (January 6, 1912).

"Telephone with a Memory—Poulsen's Magneto Phonograph." *Literary Digest* 101 (May 18, 1929): 21.

Tetrazzini, Luisa. *My Life of Song.* London: Cassell, 1921.

Tewksbury, George E. *A Complete Manual of the Edison Phonograph with Introduction by Thomas A. Edison.* Newark, N.J.: United States Phonograph Co., 1897.

"Thirty-Seven Hours of Sound on a Single 16-mm. Reel." *Radio Craft* (May 1938).

Thompson, Oscar. *The American Singer.* New York: Dial Press, 1937.

"Time-Controlled Phonograph." *Scientific American* 96 (April 6, 1907): 289.

"Toy Phonograph." *Scientific American* 76 (April 10, 1897): 230.

Tritton, Paul. "The Godfather of Rolls-Royce." *Journal of Rolls-Royce Motors, Ltd.* 2, no. 1 (1981); no. 2 (1981).

———. *The Lost Voice of Queen Victoria: The Search for the First Royal Recording.* London: Academy Books, 1991.

Tyndall, John. *Sound.* New York: Appleton, 1895.

U.S. Library of Congress Music Division. *Checklist of Recorded Songs in the English Language in the Archives of American Folksong to July 1940.* Washington, D.C.: U.S. Government Printing Office, 1942.

Viall, Ethan. "Making Edison Phonographs." *American Machinist* 36 (1911): 486–827.

———. "Making Victor Talking Machines, etc." *American Machinist* 37 (August 29, 1912): 347–52, 726.

Wade, H. T. "The Transophone and the Telescribe." *Scientific American* (September 12, 1914).

Wagnalls, Mabel. *Stars of the Opera.* New York: Funk & Wagnalls, 1907.

Walsh, G. E. "With Edison in His Laboratory." *Independent* (September 4, 1913).

Watkins, D. E. "Apparatus for Recording Speeches." *Quarterly Journal of Speech Education* 10 (June 1924): 253–58.

Webster, A. G. "Acoustical Impedance and the Theory of Horns and the Phonograph." *American Physical Society* (May 1919).

———. *Theory of Electricity and Magnetism.* New York & London: Macmillan, 1897.

Wegefarth, W. D. "Talking Machine as a Public Educator." *Lippincott's* 86 (May 1911): 628–30.

Welch, Walter L. *Charles Batchelor: Edison's Chief Partner.* Syracuse: Syracuse University Press, 1972.

———. "Edison and His Contributions to the Record Industry." *Journal of the Audio Engineering Society* 25, nos. 10–11 (October–November 1977): 660–65.

———. "Preservation and Restoration of Authenticity in Sound Recordings." *Library Trends* 21, no. 1 (July 1972).

Wente and Bedell. "Chronographic Method of Measuring Reverberation Time." *Journal of the Acoustical Society of America* 1, no. 3, pt. 1 (April 1930): 422–27.

Westphal, H. F. "Metal Phonograph." *Independent Educator* 25 (July 5, 1923): 25.

"What Edison Said about Music and Radio: Interview." *Musician* 36 (November 1931): 7.

White, W. C. "Electronics—Its Start from the 'Edison Effect' Sixty Years Ago." *General Electric Review* (October 1943): 527.

Wile, Raymond R. "The Background of the Entrance of the American Graphophone Company and the Columbia Phonograph Company into the Disc Record Business, 1897–1903." Unpublished manuscript, 1984.

————. *Edison Disc Recordings.* Philadelphia: Eastern National Park and Monument Association, 1978.

————. "The Fate of the Edison Phonograph Toy Manufacturing Company." Unpublished manuscript, 1984–85.

————. "The Gramophone Becomes a Success in America, 1896–1898." Unpublished manuscript, 1984.

————. "Provisional Listing of the Local Phonograph Companies, 1890–1893." *Journal of the Association for Recorded Sound Collections* 3, nos. 2–3 (Fall 1971): 13–23.

————. "The Wonder of the Age: The Invention of the Phonograph." *Phonographs and Gramophones Symposium* (July 2, 1977): 9–48.

Williams, D. "Motion Pictures that Really Talk." *Illustrated World* 26 (December 1916): 548–51.

Williams, S. T. "Recent Developments in the Recording and Reproduction of Sound." *Journal of the Franklin Institute* (October 1926).

Wilson, G. *Gramophones, Acoustic and Radio.* Edited by Compton Mackenzie and Christopher Stone. London: Gramophone, 1928.

Wilson, P., and G. W. Webb. *Modern Gramophones and Electrical Reproducers.* London, Toronto, Melbourne & Sydney: Cassell, 1929.

"A Wonderful Invention—Speech Capable of Indefinite Repetition from Automatic Records." *Scientific American* (November 17, 1877).

"The Workshop at Menlo Park." *Daily Graphic* (July 13, 1878).

Wylorn, E. J. "The Electrical Reproduction of Gramophone Records." *Gramophone* (December 1926).

INDEX